JORDAN GOODMAN's books include *The Rattlesnake: A Voyage of Discovery to the Coral Sea*. He has published extensively on the history of medicine and science, and in cultural and economic history. He is an Honorary Research Associate in the Department of Science and Technology Studies at University College London.

THE DEVIL AND MR CASEMENT

One Man's Struggle for Human Rights
in South America's Heart of Darkness

JORDAN GOODMAN

VERSO
London • New York

This paperback edition first published by Verso 2010
First published by Verso 2009
Copyright © Jordan Goodman 2010

1 3 5 7 9 10 8 6 4 2

Verso
UK: 6 Meard Street, London W1F 0EG
US: 20 Jay Street, Suite 1010, Brooklyn, NY 11201
www.versobooks.com

Verso is the imprint of New Left Books

ISBN-13: 978-1-84467-625-5

British Library Cataloguing in Publication Data
A catalogue record for this book is available from the British Library

Typeset by Hewer Text UK Ltd, Edinburgh
Printed by Scandbook AB, Sweden

For Danny and Ben

Contents

PART IV

PART V

PROLOGUE

La Selva *Comes to London*

Wednesday, 29 September 1909, was a dull and rainy day in London. In the House of Commons the questioning was about to take the members of parliament to a different and much warmer place.

Thomas Hart-Davies, the Conservative MP for the constituency of North Hackney, rose to his feet. He asked the secretary of state for foreign affairs

> whether his attention has been called to the proceedings of an English company called the Peruvian Amazon Company; whether any report as to the alleged ill-treatment of British subjects from Barbados has been made by the English Consul at Iquitos; and whether he will call for a report on the doings of this company from the local English Consul at Iquitos?

No sooner had he settled himself back on the bench than the right honourable member for Orkney and Shetland, John Cathcart Wason, a Liberal, chimed in. He asked the foreign secretary whether

> his attention has been directed to the charges made against the Peruvian Amazon Rubber Company, Salisbury House, EC; if he has been urged by the British directors of the said company or by any of the British shareholders to inquire of His Majesty's Peruvian consul with reference to the same; and if he has acceded to their request, if any?

The foreign secretary, Sir Edward Grey, was not in the House to answer these parliamentary questions, so the under-secretary of state for foreign affairs, Thomas McKinnon Wood, replied on his behalf. 'I had not heard of the existence of the company, and have no information about it. I will ask for a report.' And then followed a short exchange between McKinnon Wood and the two questioners.

> *Mr Hart-Davies*: Is the hon. Gentleman aware that the American Consul has already made a report to his Government on this company, and whether he can see his way to get hold of that report?
>
> *Mr McKinnon Wood*: I was not aware of that.
>
> *Mr Cathcart Wason*: Do I understand the hon. Gentleman to say that he has not received a request as to this company to inquire into the allegations?
>
> *Mr McKinnon Wood*: That is so.
>
> *Mr Cathcart Wason*: May I ask whether full publicity will be given in our dependencies in this part as to the proceedings of the inquiry?
>
> *Mr McKinnon Wood*: I think the first step will be to obtain the report for which I have promised to ask.

What was the Peruvian Amazon Company? Where did it operate? What were Barbadians (British subjects) doing working for it? Who was ill-treating them? Why did the Americans know more about this story than did the Foreign Office?

And why these questions now?

The Foreign Office had been caught off-guard by the parliamentary questions. There was really no excuse for their ignorance. When Hart-Davies alerted the Foreign Office that he was putting down a question for the parliamentary session of 29 September, he enclosed in his letter a copy of the previous week's issue of a magazine called *Truth*, which contained a major article about a British rubber company, the Peruvian Amazon Company, against whom allegations were being made of unthinkable cruelty to its workforce – it explained everything.

How the Foreign Office had missed the story is hard to explain. *Truth* was a popular and widely read muckraking magazine – its circulation often exceeded 20,000 copies – and it scooped this story. Now in its thirty-third year, this weekly had been founded by Henry Du Pré Labouchere, heir to a banking fortune, and long-standing radical Liberal MP for Northampton. Even though, in his later years, he handed over editorial responsibility to others, his influence remained intact: he presided over the magazine for more than thirty years, until his death in 1912. With a cover depicting a female representation of Truth holding the lamp of knowledge in her right hand and a mirror in the left, the magazine had a chatty style, providing its readers with a diet of society gossip, entertainment reviews, political commentary and exposés of financial scandal. 'People bought *Truth* with a desire to see who was "going to get it next", who or what institutions would be marked down for exposure', said Joseph Hatton, the well-known journalist and contemporary of Labouchere's. 'City men who were shaky trembled, snobs who were chary of their supposed dignity opened the paper with nervous fingers.'

Sidney Paternoster, the magazine's leading investigative journalist and assistant editor, did not disappoint his readers in the issue of 22 September, for it was not just shaky City men and anxious snobs, but the whole nation that was shocked that day. A word that had become a symbol of the evil of contemporary capitalism had returned to haunt the British public. *Truth*'s readers must have blenched when they saw Paternoster's deliberately provocative headline: 'The Devil's Paradise: A British-Owned Congo'.

Only a year had passed since the country had congratulated itself on bringing to an end one of the modern world's worst atrocities, in which brutal labour regimes had spilled the blood of millions of indigenous Congolese people in a frenzy to collect as much rubber as they could for the hungry factories in Europe and the United States. And now that dreaded word 'Congo' was back again.

In 1885, as a result of the Berlin Conference, at which the European powers negotiated their way to carving up Africa for themselves in the so-called Scramble for Africa, Leopold II, king of Belgium, had taken control of a large chunk of western equatorial Africa, about the size of western Europe, and declared it his private property. Though the wealth of the Congo Free State, as the territory was named, was at first based on ivory, by the end of the nineteenth century rubber had become the economy's main earner and contributed significantly to world output.

During the 1890s, the first unconfirmed reports started to reach England of the atrocities being perpetrated in King Leopold's Congo Free State. The rubber regime, rumours had it, was based on a quota system, and those who did not meet their targets were systematically abused, maimed and killed by a specialized terrorist militia, the Force Publique.

When these reports reached the Foreign Office, it was not prepared to do much more than monitor the situation. The alternative – to revisit the entire Berlin Act of 1885 – was politically dangerous: it would put the partition of Africa back on the political agenda, a step that was in none of the colonial powers' interest. But when these reports came to the attention of Henry Fox Bourne, the secretary of the Aborigines' Protection Society, which had been established in the 1830s in London as a pressure group to ensure the humane treatment of indigenous peoples throughout the world, he demanded that the Foreign Office should use its influence to do something to stop the atrocities.

It was an uphill struggle. The government was loath to get involved, arguing that the reports on the situation in the Congo Free State were based on unconfirmed rumours, and that to the best of its knowledge everyone there was content. Fox Bourne, however, did not accept the government's reassurance and took his concerns to the British public. It took six years of campaigning, but he managed to get a parliamentary debate on the issue, for which he and his young and very committed journalist friend Edmund Morel provided the Liberal MP Herbert Samuel with a raft of statistics and testimonies in preparation for his opening question. The ensuing debate, in May 1903, drew support from a small group of MPS who had been similarly briefed by Fox Bourne and Morel. The politicians accused Leopold's administration not only of barbarism, but of the enslavement of the indigenous people. The House was so moved by the evidence presented that a resolution was passed that day stating that the government of the Congo Free State had violated the guarantees – namely, that it treat its people with humanity and that no trading monopoly should be allowed within its boundaries – that it had made at the end of the Berlin Conference, which had brought the state into existence. The British government, the resolution concluded, should confer with the other colonial powers to force the Congo Free State to end its evil system.

But what were the facts of Leopold's system? So far, no one had actually been to the Upper Congo, the site of the alleged atrocities. The Foreign Office agreed to investigate the allegations of cruelty for itself and instructed its consul in the Congo Free State, the highly experienced thirty-nine-year-old Roger Casement, to gather impartial information.

Casement was Irish by birth, the son of a devout Catholic mother and a Protestant father. The youngest of four children, he was baptized twice: once, aged one, as a Protestant, then again, aged four, as a Catholic. Family life was typically unsettled. The father, invalided out of the army as a captain on half-pay, moved his family incessantly in search of the health that eluded him. At various times, the Casements were in France, Italy, England, and St Helier, Jersey. Then, in 1873, when Casement was nine years old, tragedy descended on the family: his mother died in childbirth, and four years later his father died, too.

Over the next few years Casement spent time near Ballymena, in what is now Northern Ireland, where his uncle owned a farm, and in Liverpool. There, in 1880, aged sixteen and after completing a standard classical education, Casement landed himself a position as a clerk in the shipping line of Elder Dempster and Company, the city's chief agents for West African shipping. Office work was not to his taste, however, and though he stuck at it for a few years he was always looking for a way out. His chance came in 1883, when he was posted as a purser on an Elder Dempster ship bound for the port of Boma, near the mouth of the Congo River.

Returning from that trip, Casement signed on again for two more voyages to Africa, and in 1884, with Africa firmly taking hold of him, he decided to remain working mostly in the Congo on various projects. In 1892 his life took a dramatic turn when he came to the attention of the Foreign Office, which offered him a clerical post in the town of Old Calabar on the Gulf of Guinea, in what is now Nigeria. Three years later, in recognition of his skills, Casement received his first diplomatic posting, as British Consul in Lourenço Marques, in Portuguese East Africa (now Moputo, the capital of Mozambique).

Casement was thirty years old, and had already spent a third of his life in Africa. He now found himself in a career that suited him well. The posting to Lourenço Marques lasted for five years. In October 1900 Casement learned that his services were now required in the Congo, on which he had become something of an expert. His new consular post, based in Léopoldville (now Kinshasa), gave him responsibility over a vast part of equatorial Africa, including the French Congo and the Congo Free State.

En route to take up his new consular post, Casement passed through Brussels, where he had an audience with King Leopold. The two met at an afternoon meal with Leopold's family, but there was little opportunity to talk business. Leopold asked Casement to return the next day, and on that occasion the two men discussed the Congo, with Leopold doing most of the talking. Conditions in the Congo were not as good as they might be, Leopold admitted, but this was down to a bad choice of personnel and to the tropical climate. The ideals of his administration remained intact, and he intended to pursue those lofty motives. Casement was not convinced.

On 4 June 1903, after more than two and a half years as consul for the Congo region, Casement received a wire from London telling him to get to the interior as soon as possible to gather 'authentic information' about the alleged atrocities. For the next three months Casement travelled more than a thousand miles on the Congo and its many tributaries, gathering information on the rubber regime. The rumours were not exaggerated. Leopold's system was brutal. In a rubber station called Bongandangu, he came face to face with the object of his investigation. 'Saw Rubber "market"', he noted in his diary; 'nothing but guns – about 20 armed men . . . most with cap guns. The people 242 men with rubber all guarded like convicts. To call this *"trade"* is the height of lying'.

Casement had single-handedly created the impartial on-the-spot investigation – what he termed a 'Criminal Investigation Department'. Determined to avoid relying on the State for assistance, Casement instead used others who knew the area well and who had access to transport: missionaries, mostly associated with the American Baptist Missionary Union, provided him with launches, contacts and translators, and with places to stay where he could interview victims of the outrages. In a letter he wrote to the American journalist Poultney Bigelow, Casement described his investigative methods.

> There are two ways of seeing the interior of the Congo State – either blindfolded or looking for the facts . . . I chose to look for the facts. I said: he who goes to a foreign country to see the people of it and form a just conclusion of their mode of life does not confine his investigations to museums, picture galleries and public buildings, or to the barracks and reviews of soldiers or State-conducted enterprises: he goes also into the

villages of the people, he speaks with the peasant and the shopkeeper and enters sometimes the dwellings of the very poor . . .

Casement's findings, documented in his constant flow of dispatches back to London, appalled and angered him. The rubber collecting system, the cornerstone of the Congo's wealth and administration, was based on coercion, violence and cruel punishment. Collection quotas were enforced by the Force Publique, the official armed force. Those not meeting targets were beaten, flogged, shot, imprisoned or mutilated – most commonly by having their hands cut off. Sentries ensured that villagers did not escape; women and children were kept as hostages to guarantee compliance from the men. And in the midst of all this, villages were being decimated, crops were going to ruin, and disease was rife. The system headed inexorably towards its own self-destruction, taking the indigenous people with it.

On 20 October, a month or so after returning from his journey into the hell of the Upper Congo, Casement received a wire from the Foreign Office ordering him to return to London and prepare his report. He left the Congo as soon as he could and arrived back in London on 1 December 1903. Ten days later a draft of his report, a large-scale analysis of the systematic abuse of human rights, was ready.

In February of the following year, the British government published Casement's damning description of Leopold's rubber system. He estimated that three million Congolese had died for rubber. This chilling report made headlines throughout the world, and resulted in demands for Leopold's regime to be brought to an end. In Britain the press played its part, as did the public meetings of the Congo Reform Association (the organization which Casement helped to found in 1904 to drum up support for action) in town halls up and down the country, to make the public aware of what was commonly referred to as King Leopold's reign of terror in the Congo Free State.

The disturbing history of Leopold's rubber regime had thus become widely known. For the next four years Leopold's Congo was seldom out of the news. *The Times* alone ran a Congo story on average every three or four days. Though readers were often spared the goriest details, they were nevertheless bombarded by graphic descriptions of one of the Force Publique's signature atrocities – the cutting off of hands and feet.

In 1908, after relentless campaigns, Leopold finally caved in to public and governmental pressure and sold his property to the Belgian state.

Casement had become an international humanitarian hero and a household name. However, within Casement at this time began the split between his loyalty to the British government that employed him, and in which he still had faith, and his identification with the victims of colonialism. The more oppression and exploitation of native people he saw in the Congo, and then in the Amazon, the greater his sense of belonging to a people – the Irish – oppressed and exploited by another – the British. Even with a sense of this inner journey, it is hard to credit how swift was his public fall from humanitarian hero in 1908 to being hanged for treason in 1916. How could this have happened? Is the Putumayo the key?

As *Truth*'s readers studied Paternoster's report of the Peruvian Amazon Company, the Congo was still fresh in their minds, and the parallels were disturbing. There was an eerie sense of déjà vu in Paternoster's exposé, but this time it was in South America, not Africa – and it was a British company that was accused.

The Company, Paternoster explained, was collecting rubber in a vast area of the Amazon basin, through which flowed its tributary, the Putumayo River. The ownership of the territory of the Company's operations was actually in dispute between Colombia and Peru, but the Peruvians were in effective control. Paternoster warned his readers that what they were about to learn of this Company's operations made for very difficult reading. 'I think it my duty', wrote Paternoster,

> to bring before the public statements which have been laid before me in regard to certain alleged atrocities in which England and Englishmen are particularly interested. They involve charges of cruelty as horrible as anything that has been reported from the Congo. They affect an English limited liability company, with English directors and English shareholders, and they have in part been made publicly without, so far as I can ascertain, any attempt at either official denial or inquiry.

The Peruvian Amazon Company, Paternoster explained, had come into existence in the previous year, registered in London and incorporated with £1,000,000 of capital. Three of its seven directors, including its chairman, were English (Paternoster did not name them). The Company's operational headquarters was in Iquitos, Peru's major Amazonian port, through which all of the rubber from the forests of the Putumayo passed before being shipped down the Amazon to Europe and the United States.

Around two dozen stations, scattered over an area exceeding 10,000 square miles, with the Putumayo River as its southern boundary, organized the collection of rubber from the surrounding forest. Each station had its own manager (*jefe* – 'chief'), usually a Peruvian, who had a staff of salaried employees (*racionales* – who were mostly Hispanic) numbering anywhere up to twenty-five men, depending on the scale of the operations. Each station operated a quota system for its collection of rubber. The collecting was carried out by the Indians, mostly Huitoto people, who had to bring their quota to the station every ten days. Once the stock of rubber in the station reached the required level, it was carried by the same Indians to either El Encanto or La Chorrera – the Company's main settlements in the region, whose staff included a general manager, a storekeeper, an accountant, and a medical officer. From there, the rubber was shipped by the Company's steam launch to Iquitos.

Behind this apparently benign organization, Paternoster pointed out, lay a brutal system in which chiefs of rubber stations were paid on commission according to the amount of rubber they obtained from the Indians. To make his point, Paternoster provided sickening descriptions of how the Indian workers were abused, terrorized, tortured, mutilated and murdered.

The agents of the company force the pacific Indians of the Putumayo to work day and night at the extraction of rubber without the slightest remuneration; that they give them nothing to eat; that they rob them of their crops, their women, and their children, to satisfy the voracity, lasciviousness, and avarice of themselves and their employees, for they live on the Indians' food, keep harems of concubines, and sell these people wholesale and retail in Iquitos; that they flog them inhumanly until their bones are laid bare; that they do not give them any medical treatment, but let them linger, eaten by maggots, till they die, to serve afterwards as food for the chief's dogs; that they mutilate them, cut off their ears, fingers, arms, and legs; that they torture them by means of fire, of water, and by tying them up, crucified head down; that they burn and destroy their houses and crops; that they cut them to pieces with machetes; that they grasp children by the feet and dash out their brains against the walls and trees; that they have the old folk killed when they can work no longer; finally, that to amuse themselves, to practise shooting, or to celebrate the *sábado de gloria* [the Saturday following Good Friday] . . . they discharge their weapons at men, women, and children, or, in preference to this, they souse them with kerosene and set fire to them, to enjoy their desperate agony.

White people had only been working in the Putumayo for about fifteen years. When they arrived, the indigenous population was estimated to be around 50,000, divided into three main groups: the Andoke, the Bora, and the Huitoto – who, with a population of 30,000, dominated the region. Paternoster was cautious about reporting how many Indians had already given their lives to the Peruvian Amazon Company, admitting that such figures were hard to come by, but he did suggest that in the past decade or so the population of the area had been reduced by 'tens of thousands'.

It is interesting that in his question to the foreign secretary, Hart-Davies referred to the alleged ill-treatment of Barbadians – British subjects – and not to the atrocities visited upon the indigenous population, which was the subject of Paternoster's article. One might wonder where Hart-Davies got his information, since the *Truth* article did not have a word in it about Barbadians.

The most likely source was Paternoster himself. Paternoster knew that there were, or had been, Barbadians present in the Putumayo. He had also tracked down and interviewed the British consul in Iquitos, David Cazes, who was on holiday leave in London. Paternoster sought to verify the information that Cazes had given him, probably through contacts at the Colonial Office in London, and concluded that the government in Barbados knew of the presence of their countrymen in the Putumayo, and also knew that allegations of ill-treatment had been levelled against the Peruvian Amazon Company.

Whatever his thoughts and feelings were about the suffering of the local population, Hart-Davies knew full well that no department of state had any right to interfere in the internal affairs of another country when it came to the plight of its own people; had he raised the issue of the Indians, the foreign secretary would simply have replied to this effect. But Barbadians were another matter. They were British subjects and had the right to appeal to Britain for protection. And it was the foreign secretary's responsibility to get to the bottom of the allegations.

Paternoster made no attempt to hide the fact that the story and all of the ghastly details had previously been printed in three newspapers: *La Felpa* and *La Sancion* in Iquitos, and *Jornal do Commercio* in Manaus. These were very obscure titles, hardly known outside the Amazon. How did Paternoster get hold of them? How did this story ever make its way out of the Amazon and to London?

For that, Paternoster could thank a brave young American engineer named Walter Hardenburg, who had only recently arrived in London from the Amazon bearing his precious cargo of documents and the memories of his own traumatic experience at the hands of the Peruvian Amazon Company's brutal employees.

Without Hardenburg, the story of the Peruvian Amazon Company's evil empire would never have left the Amazon.

PART I

1

Across the Andes

On 1 October 1907, twenty-one-year-old Walter Hardenburg, who was then working on the construction of the Colombian Pacific railway, and his fellow American workmate Walter Perkins, three years his elder, set out from the construction site at Buenaventura on the Pacific coast of Colombia for the adventure of a lifetime.

Hardenburg and Perkins had been offered better positions working on the Madeira–Mamoré railway, an ambitious project designed to bypass the unnavigable Madeira River in the western part of the Brazilian Amazon, in order to transport rubber from northern Bolivia to the Amazonian port of Manaus.

Rather than getting to the site by the normal sea-and-river route, Hardenburg and Perkins decided to make an adventure of their relocation by going overland across the Andes and into Amazonia. Those few Europeans who had made this journey before recommended that the best way to get to the Amazon from Colombia was to travel south to Quito in Ecuador, cross the Andes there and, once on the eastern slopes of the Andes, to join the Napo River and follow its course until it met the Amazon northeast of the Peruvian town of Iquitos. Hardenburg and Perkins started by following this recommendation, but at some point on their way south through Colombia, and for reasons that went unrecorded, they changed their minds and opted for the much less frequented route across the Andes in southern Colombia, and following the Putumayo River from its source high in the Colombian Andes until its confluence with the Amazon over a thousand miles to the southeast.

It was a foolhardy and dangerous decision to make. The map they had with them was large-scale, and only showed the general course of the country's main rivers; all the advice they received should have put them off their chosen route. In the southern Colombian town of Pasto, the last sizeable settlement in this part of the country, from where the pair would make their final crossing of the Andes and begin their descent into Amazonia, no one they met in their first days there could even tell them where the Putumayo was; and the one person they found who knew the river warned them not to go, for 'if by chance [they] escaped the cannibal Indians who inhabit its banks, [they] would certainly fall victims to the deadly fevers which reign there continuously'. To make matters worse, Hardenburg and Perkins also learned from General Pablo Monroy, a senior military officer who had been there himself, that about halfway down the river's course – where the Caraparaná, a major tributary, flowed into the Putumayo – they would be entering a kind of no man's land, an area whose ownership was disputed between Colombia and Peru. After more than fifty years of argument and protest, General Monroy told the pair, the two countries had recently agreed to a modus vivendi, both withdrawing their garrisons and military authorities from the region to their respective lines, while negotiations about the future of the region continued. But he did not think the Peruvians were abiding by the agreement.

But it was not all bad news, for Hardenburg and Perkins also learned from another source that they would not need to paddle all the way to the Amazon because, about 500 miles downriver, at a place called El Encanto, where the Caraparaná met the Putumayo, they would be able to catch a launch to Iquitos from where they could continue their journey to the railway construction site in Brazil. It would save them weeks of effort.

With this piece of encouragement, and despite the warnings to the contrary, the intrepid pair pressed on with their decision and spent three days in Pasto buying supplies, both for themselves and to trade, which would last them two months. It was a bewildering collection of material, from hats to knives, brightly coloured shirts, harmonicas, fishhooks and food. As Hardenburg himself put it, 'When we finally got all our purchases together, we found that we had goods enough to set up a shop and our room was so crowded with them that we had hardly space enough to turn in.'

Crossing the most easterly of the Andean peaks proved to be much more difficult than the whole journey until this point, and the 150 miles they travelled until they reached the first navigable point on the Putumayo River took them just as long as it had taken them to get from Buenaventura to Pasto. Still, they had made it so far without mishap and, on 1 December 1907, Hardenburg and Perkins – together with their provisions and now accompanied by two local boatmen, one of whom steered from the stern while the other stood watch in the bow – set off downriver in their newly purchased canoe.

The Putumayo is navigable for most of its length: from the Colombian Andes until it meets the Amazon at Santo Antônio do Içá in the western part of Brazil at about three degrees south. The river has no waterfalls or rapids. It moves along placidly, meandering in long, winding curves. As the current switches from one bank to the other, the river becomes very wide in places, and relatively shallow. This same action creates sand islands in the middle and on both sides. The forest teems with wildlife, both large and small – tapirs, peccaries (wild pigs) and capybaras (large rodents resembling guinea pigs) are especially numerous and provide excellent game – while the river is abundantly stocked with fish.

For the first few days everything went splendidly. Hardenburg and Perkins must have congratulated themselves on their decision to venture onto the Putumayo River. 'What a pleasant sensation it was', wrote Hardenburg,

> to sit calmly in the canoe, while the swift current bore us steadily onwards, and to watch the thick, tropical vegetation, which lined the banks of the stream, swiftly recede until hidden from view by a bend of the river! How different it was from the monotonous climbing and descending of the Andes that had caused us so much toil!

The banks of the river were alive with wild turkeys, ducks and monkeys; flocks of parrots flew by at great speed while the forest resounded with the squeals and howls of invisible creatures. There was no shortage of fresh provisions – wild turkeys and monkeys, in particular. The only problem was to get a good shot from the canoe, which was far from easy.

But then, no more than four days into the journey downriver, the two boatmen decided that they would go no further and ran away. Bad people, they warned, lived beyond.

Hardenburg and Perkins had no choice but to go it alone. So, on 7 December – with Perkins in the stern, perched on his high seat, and Hardenburg with eyes peeled in the bow – the two adventurers set off downriver. The next day, crossing the equator, the pair celebrated with a good stiff glass of *aguardiente*. Later the same day they stopped at a tiny settlement ('eight or ten little bamboo huts'), where the chief told them they were very brave to make the trip alone.

For the next two weeks Hardenburg and Perkins worked their way towards the Putumayo's confluence with the Caraparaná, and they experienced everything the tropics could throw at them: 'suffocating heat, and not a breath of air – our thirst was astounding'; they battled outbreaks of fever, ran out of fresh food, suffered unexpected risings and fallings of river levels, which on more than one occasion left them stranded on a sandbank with nothing to do but wait for the river to rise again; and they were attacked by gnats and mosquitoes whenever they were not attempting to shelter from bouts of torrential rain. Apart from one occasion, when they ran into a band of Indians returning from a hunt, and another when they were startled by a three-man detachment of Colombian police returning to Pasto from the Caraparaná, they never saw another human being in the jungle.

On the afternoon of 22 December they spotted a house, which turned out to belong to a Colombian rubber trader, Jesús López. López alerted them to what lay ahead and told them more about the political situation.

Hardenburg and Perkins already knew from what General Monroy had told them in Pasto—that the ownership of the area around the Caraparaná was disputed between Colombia and Peru, and that a modus vivendi was officially in place between the two countries. López warned them that the Peruvians, in clear contravention of the agreement, were harassing and violently expelling Colombian settlers. These acts, López added, were being carried out by the Peruvian military, but behind the scenes a firm calling itself the Peruvian Amazon Rubber Company was calling the shots. It was the Company's intention, maintained López, to get hold of all the Colombian concessions, by whatever means necessary.

Colombian rubber traders had been working their way down the Putumayo since the 1890s, and by the turn of the century they had reached the area bounded by the Igaraparaná River on the east and the

Caraparaná River on the west. The further they came downriver, the further they found themselves from the nearest Colombian town, while at the same time getting closer to Iquitos – the nearest Peruvian town, with vastly more resources than its Colombian counterpart. At one time there had been dozens of Colombian rubber stations in this area, but by the time Hardenburg and Perkins were on the Putumayo only three remained, the rest having been taken over by the Peruvian Amazon Rubber Company.

López told them not to take the launch from El Encanto to Iquitos, suggesting a safer alternative route. He recommended that they should aim for Remolino, five days further down the river and the site of another Colombian post. From there they could travel overland to the Napo River further to the south, which would take them to a point where it flowed into the Amazon just above Iquitos. There was regular traffic on the Amazon where the Napo joined it, and they would find it easy to get to Iquitos this way, which would also avoid the trouble between the Peruvian and Colombian factions on the Caraparaná.

Hardenburg and Perkins saw the sense in López's advice; besides which, the combination of incessant rain and persistent attacks by gnats had brought to an end their initial romance with the Putumayo. At Remolino they would be able to sell their canoe, which, López promised, would be easy – Antonio Ordoñez, a Colombian who collected rubber at a place called La Unión on the Caraparaná, and who used Remolino as his shipping post for Iquitos, would certainly buy it.

On 30 December Hardenburg and Perkins reached Remolino, intending to bid the Putumayo farewell and reach Iquitos shortly. Ordoñez was not in Remolino, however, but away on a rubber-collecting excursion. Hardenburg left Perkins to wait with the canoe and travelled alone to La Unión, hoping to find Ordoñez there. But when he got to La Unión he could not locate Ordoñez, and instead pressed on to another rubber station, a place called La Reserva, where, he was told, there was another rubber trader who could help him out. This time Hardenburg was more fortunate. At La Reserva a Colombian, David Serrano, a 'short, middle-aged, coffee-coloured gentleman', agreed to help Hardenburg and Perkins by buying their canoe and any other goods they were willing to sell. Serrano sent three local guides to find Perkins and bring him and the sale goods back to La Reserva. Serrano instructed the guides to tell Perkins to make his way first to a place called Josa, Serrano's landing stage on the Putumayo near the mouth of the Caraparaná River, where he could leave the canoe and their personal baggage. The idea was a good one, since the onward route, overland to the Napo River and thence Iquitos, would pass by Josa. Luckily, Serrano needed to go to Iquitos, and he agreed to accompany the Americans to their destination. Things could not have worked out better.

While the guides were away fetching Perkins, Serrano showed Hardenburg around, and told him a harrowing story about his treatment at the hands of the Peruvian Amazon Rubber Company that had recently become so powerful. About a month ago, he told Hardenburg, a number of the Company's employees had turned up at his place. They chained him to a tree and, before his appalled eyes, raped his wife, whom they had dragged from the house. These men then helped themselves to his stock of goods and, their business done, returned to their launch carrying away Serrano's wife and their small son. He had not seen either since, though he had learned that his wife had been forced to become a concubine of Miguel Loayza, the manager of the Peruvian Amazon Rubber Company's station at El Encanto; his son had been made Loayza's personal servant.

This outrage against Serrano had come to the attention of the Colombian authorities, and one of them, Jesus Orjuela, the newly appointed police inspector for the region, was expected any day. Indeed, no sooner had Serrano's local guides set off to fetch Perkins than Orjuela, accompanied by another Colombian, arrived at Serrano's place. Orjuela expressed confidence that he could come to some agreement with the Peruvian Amazon Rubber Company, and with Miguel Loayza in particular, to make an accommodation with the Colombians in the spirit of the modus vivendi supposedly operating between the two nations.

On 4 January Perkins and the guides, carrying the sale goods, arrived at Serrano's. While Perkins dealt with the terms of the sale, Hardenburg decided to accompany Orjuela to El Dorado, another Colombian rubber station downriver, to which Loayza was to be invited for a conference concerning the future relationship between the Peruvians and the Colombians in the region.

A day later the negotiating party set off downriver for El Dorado. While Hardenburg was away, Serrano surprised Perkins by offering to sell him a 'half-interest in his establishment at a very low figure – because of his fear of the Peruvians'. 'I accepted that offer, thinking I would be able to become friends with the authorities and that no objection could be raised. It was my intention', he recalled a few months later, 'to settle this matter with Serrano when we reached Iquitos. His business was in gathering wild rubber for which purpose he had about forty Indians.' That business concluded, Perkins settled back to wait for Hardenburg's return.

But the peace was soon shattered. On 12 January a Peruvian gunboat, the *Iquitos*, in company with the *Liberal*, one of the Peruvian Amazon Rubber Company's steam launches, docked at La Reserva. There were hundreds of soldiers aboard the boats. A party of them landed. They were looking for Serrano, but he had fled into the forest, obviously (and understandably) terrified. They ransacked the place and took away the goods in the storehouse and almost 2,000 kilos of rubber. In spite of Perkins's protests, the soldiers imprisoned him aboard the *Liberal*.

It transpired that Serrano's station, La Reserva, was in fact the second stop for the military operation. Previously they had stopped at La Unión, where the Peruvians had totally overwhelmed the Colombians, killing many of them. All the rubber was stolen, and La Unión itself was burnt to the ground.

The gunboat and the *Liberal* continued downriver to El Encanto. Later that day, at Argelia, between La Reserva and El Dorado, the two boats intercepted the canoe carrying Orjuela and Hardenburg, who were returning to Serrano's place after a futile attempt at making peace with the Peruvians: despite several attempts to make contact with him, Loayza never turned up for the appointment in El Dorado. Orjuela and Hardenburg were promptly seized and thrown aboard the *Liberal*.

Hardenburg was astonished to find Perkins already imprisoned on the boat. Perkins explained what had happened. Hardenburg now understood why Loayza had ignored invitations to talk. From Argelia, the *Liberal* and the *Iquitos* continued downriver, but not before stopping at El Dorado, which was promptly destroyed.

At dusk, on 13 January, the *Liberal* and the *Iquitos* docked at the wharf in El Encanto. Hardenburg and Perkins were forced to spend the night on the floor of a small, unlit room. The next day Loayza told them that they would be going to Iquitos once the *Liberal* was ready to sail. As for their baggage, still at Josa, Loayza promised to collect it and have it shipped to Iquitos.

Pretending that they were working for a large American syndicate and that any harm to them would reverberate right back to Washington, Hardenburg and Perkins managed to wrangle a concession out of Loayza. Hardenburg, it was decided, would go to Iquitos as Loayza insisted, while Perkins would remain to make sure that Loayza kept his word as far as the baggage was concerned.

On 17 January 1908 the *Liberal* was ready to go, and Orjuela and Hardenburg were escorted to the boat. Earlier that day Hardenburg learned that Gabriel Martínez, the Colombian *corregidor* (magistrate) for the Putumayo, had been kidnapped on 20 December further up the Putumayo, and had been a prisoner in El Encanto since then. He, too, would be going to Iquitos.

For the next fortnight the *Liberal* steamed its way towards Iquitos. After leaving El Encanto, the boat reached the mouth of the Igaraparaná, where the Peruvian Amazon Rubber Company had a number of important rubber stations, including its major settlement, La Chorrera. The boat went a short distance upriver to the shipping port of Santa Julia. There it took on firewood, turned around and continued downriver until it met the Putumayo.

After what Hardenburg described as a tedious journey, the *Liberal* finally arrived in Iquitos on 1 February. That same day *El Oriente*, one of Iquitos's chief papers, hailed the Peruvian victory in La Unión, framing it as a fight between invading Colombians and patriotic Peruvians, with headlines such as 'Defeat and Cowardly Flight of the Colombians' and 'Courage and Dash of our Officers and Soldiers'. The paper also carried a list of the boat's passengers, reserving a special paragraph for an American civil engineer, W.E. Hardenburg, who, according to the paper, 'had been sent by the Colombian government to undertake studies of the area on behalf of an American syndicate'.

The great adventure had turned into a harrowing experience. Hardenburg was alive, but very angry. 'I hate these people and in case of a war I will return to Colombia and offer my services to you', he later wrote to Dr Gonzalo Miranda, a Colombian official whom he and Perkins had met in Pasto. His experiences at the hands of the Peruvians preyed on his mind. Though Hardenburg himself had not witnessed any specific acts of violence against the Indians while on the Putumayo, he had seen the tell-tale signs of beatings and whippings, in the shape of scars on their backs – the so-called Mark of Arana.

While in the Putumayo, Hardenburg had learned that a wealthy merchant in Iquitos named Julio César Arana owned the Peruvian Amazon Rubber Company that had terrorized the Colombians and destroyed their settlements. Stumbling out of the *Liberal*'s hold and into the tropical sunshine, Hardenburg found himself in a bustling, cosmopolitan Amazonian town whose lifeblood was fed by the rubber trees that grew in the vast surrounding jungle. Soon he would be facing Arana himself.

2

Iquitos and Rubber

Iquitos was Peru's major Amazonian settlement, but was isolated, apart from a telegraphic link, from Lima, the capital, and from the rest of the country. When asked what he knew about the town, Lucien Jerome, the British chargé d'affaires in Lima, simply stated: '[It] is in another world and [London] is nearer by mail than we are. Letters take three months and some to get to Lima from Iquitos!' Travel between Lima and Iquitos was done by ship, down the Amazon to its mouth on the Atlantic at Pará, and then either catching a ship around the bottom of South America and up its western coast, or across the Caribbean to the isthmus of Panama, crossing it by train and then proceeding down the western coast of South America by ship. It took months. The land route, which involved crossing the Andes, was ferociously difficult: at least as difficult as Hardenburg and Perkins's own experience in Colombia. Only the foolhardy went that way.

Isolated from Lima and the majority of the Peruvian population, who mostly lived to the west of the Andes, Iquitos had a decidedly eastward orientation, looking down the Amazon to Pará, 1,900 miles away, and then beyond, to Europe and the eastern United States. There was not much evidence of Peru in Iquitos. Almost everything was brought in via the Amazon River. Most of the town's important buildings, both private and public, were built from material imported from Europe – the stone, the iron and steel and, especially, the vibrantly coloured Portuguese tiles that adorned many private homes. In 1890 a prefabricated iron house, built and designed by Gustave Eiffel, arrived in Iquitos from Paris.

Iquitos did not have a promising start as a commercial centre. Jesuit missionaries had been spreading the word of God and converting the locals from their base in Quito, Ecuador, since the seventeenth century.

By the mid-eighteenth century they had reached the Amazon, and near the site of the future town of Iquitos they founded a mission village. The process of converting the local people was difficult at first: there was resistance to conversion, and many of the missionaries died from disease. But no sooner had they begun to make a success of the mission than the Spanish king, Charles III, ordered all Jesuits, who he thought too inclined to create their own state within the state, to leave Spanish America (and Spain). The mission village was abandoned, the population shrank, and the rest of the world forgot the area for the next century.

But, around the middle of the nineteenth century, Iquitos, with a population of not more than 200 people, almost all of them Indians, found itself with a new and unexpected importance. In 1851, Peru and Brazil agreed in an international treaty (grandly named the Special Convention of Commerce, Navigation and Limits) to liberalize navigation on the Amazon River. The treaty also provided for agreed borders between the two countries, and thereby guaranteed Peru's eastern frontier. Very soon thereafter, steamships began to ply the Amazon from Brazil to Peru.

Iquitos began to expand. Foreign shipping and capital, primarily British, were invited into the little port. There were new dockyards, ironworks, brick-making facilities, sawmills, and all the paraphernalia of an industrial infrastructure. By 1862 the population of Iquitos had increased fourfold to over 800 – a quarter of whom were foreigners, mostly British. In 1864 a naval station was established with four new boats, all built in England. The population continued to grow and diversify, while foreign commercial houses set up business and river traffic increased. Iquitos became the region's main port, from which Panama hats and sarsaparilla, the region's chief exports, made their way to European markets. In return, Iquitos imported textiles, footwear, food and liquor. By 1870 the value of the town's trade had increased a thousand-fold since the Peruvian–Brazilian agreement of almost twenty years earlier.

But this was nothing compared to what was to come. Iquitos was about to become a boomtown, all because of a single revolutionary material: rubber.

It is hard to imagine a world without rubber, but such a world existed until about 150 years ago. Rubber had been known in Mexico, Central

America and the Amazon for centuries, and used to make balls, religious figurines and torches; people in the Amazon region mostly used it to make waterproof boots.

When, in 1736, the French astronomer and explorer Charles-Marie de La Condamine sent a sample of rubber to Paris from Quito, it made very little impression. It was no more than a curiosity: a material that was indeed unique – it bounced, and it could be stretched to many times its own length and then snap right back – but without any obvious use. A friend of La Condamine's and a fellow scientist, François Fresneau, had spent some time in French Guiana, where he saw local people making waterproof footwear using fresh latex, the sticky sap that flowed in a number of wild tree species and which they had managed to extract by incising the bark. When Fresneau returned to France in 1748, he began working on the problem of how to make rubber practicable – in other words, how to make it into a liquid rather than a solid, so that its waterproofing properties could be employed in the same way as in Guiana. Fifteen years later, in what may have been the first scientific paper on rubber, Fresneau reported that turpentine, when used as a solvent, turned rubber into a liquid which could then be applied to fabric to make it waterproof.

Unfortunately, when the problem of applicability had been solved, another more serious problem was encountered. The rubber solution turned out to be chemically unstable. Its texture changed with temperature: hard and brittle in the cold, and soft and sticky in the heat. Within a short time after being applied to textiles for waterproofing, the rubber would begin to flake off: rubber boots had a short life before they started to crack and fall apart.

The solution to rubber's chemical instability came in 1839, when Charles Goodyear – in his Woburn, Massachusetts, factory – successfully stabilized rubber by mixing it together with sulphur and heating the mixture: the process came to be known as vulcanization. Rubber production soared dramatically: between 1830 and 1850, the world's annual rubber output increased almost tenfold to 3.3 million pounds.

And with the huge increase in production, the uses to which rubber were put multiplied enormously: as well as waterproofing, rubber was employed where elasticity, rather than rigidity, was required – gaskets, hoses, belts and buffers; gloves, syringes and elastic bands; telegraph cables and electrical insulation; flooring; undergarments, condoms, diaphragms and cervical caps.

But the biggest change in the use of rubber was still to come. Since the Roman period, carts and carriages had had an iron band fitted to their wooden wheels. Once vulcanization had solved the problem of rubber's instability, it was possible to make the rolling surface from solid rubber rather than iron. Though solid rubber tyres first appeared in the late 1840s, rubber's high price – combined with low demand from cart and carriage makers – constrained the market, and their use remained limited.

Then in the 1860s a new device appeared that would in time take rubber into a new era. The first examples of the new technology, the ordinary bicycle, or penny-farthing (so-called because its front and rear wheels were of different sizes), proved to be largely impractical and attracted only a small following, who saw them as expensive toys. The machines were difficult to mount and dismount; they required an immense physical effort to operate, since the wheel turned only once for each turn of the pedals; they were unreliable and uncomfortable on long journeys; and even when rubber tyres were fitted to the wheels, the ride was still rough, since the rubber absorbed only a small proportion of the shock: no wonder they were called boneshakers.

Bicycle technology advanced very quickly, however, and by the mid-1880s a new design had emerged that solved most of the disadvantages of the previous generation of machines. The new model, called a safety bicycle, incorporated wheels of equal size and a chain-drive to the rear wheel, leaving the front wheel free for direct steering. A few years later the transformation of the bicycle from an impractical curiosity to a truly effective method of transport was completed when John Boyd Dunlop, a Scottish veterinarian, successfully introduced the pneumatic, or inflatable, tyre. The pneumatic tyre, filled with air rather than solid rubber, absorbed the shocks of the road perfectly and, for the first time, gave a smooth ride. The sales of bicycles rocketed and the first consumer craze was underway, with the result that rubber production more than doubled between 1890 and 1900, exceeding 100 million pounds per annum.

By the turn of the century, all of the world's largest and best-known tyre companies – Michelin in France, Pirelli in Italy, Dunlop in Britain, and B.F. Goodrich, Goodyear and Firestone in the United States, the leading firms of the so-called second industrial revolution, when science and technology were applied to industrial production – were in business and were making bicycle tyres. Their fortunes were about to undergo another, even more dramatic change, particularly in the United States. The late nineteenth century saw the first automobiles being made. Early automobile manufacturers, primarily Benz in Germany and Peugeot in France, owed many of their ideas and much of their experience to the bicycle. The world's total production of automobiles stood at only 280 in 1895, all of them made in Germany and France; five years later, output had risen dramatically, to 10,000 vehicles. By this time the automotive pneumatic tyre, perfected by André Michelin in France, was fitted to every car. It was in the United States, however, that the car really came into its own, as Americans abandoned the two-wheeled bicycle for the four-wheeled motorized device. By 1907, world output had risen to 90,000 units, the United States accounting for almost 60 per cent of the total. And then, a year later, out of his factory in Detroit came the first of Henry Ford's affordable cars, the Model T – and the United States never looked back. By 1908, automobile production in the United States had doubled to 125,000 units. So enormous was the change caused by the adoption of the pneumatic tyre that by 1910 about 70 per cent of all the rubber produced in the world went into the automotive sector – cars, trucks and buses. By then the world's output of rubber stood at 160 million pounds per annum, or fifty times what it had been in the middle of the nineteenth century.

Rubber production first began on the islands around Pará, at the mouth of the Amazon, but by the time of the 1890s bicycle craze it had spread westward along the Amazon River into the Acre district of Brazil, the Beni district of Bolivia, southeastern Peru and, most recently, the Putumayo region. The Amazon region is rich in latex-producing trees. It is the natural habitat of *Hevea brasiliensis*, the principal source of most of the world's rubber. Several species of *Hevea* grew in the Putumayo, but it was not the first tree that Europeans harvested. There was also another latex tree growing, called *Castilloa*. It is a massive tree, often reaching more than a hundred feet in height. It contains a lot of latex, but little of it can be reached by slashing the bark without damaging the tree. The most effective way of getting the *Castilloa*'s latex was to chop it down and then cut deeply into its trunk, thereby releasing all of the latex in one go. This highly wasteful method often yielded 200 pounds of latex from a single tree. It was this tree that first attracted itinerant Colombian rubber traders – *caucheros*, as they were called – to the region in the latter part of the nineteenth century. *Caucheros* moved around the forest identifying stands of *Castilloa*, harvesting them, moving on, and then repeating the process. In only twenty years, the *caucheros* had destroyed most of the *Castilloa* stands.

They then turned their attention to *Hevea*, which, while being less productive than *Castilloa*, providing just a few pounds of latex annually, did not have to be destroyed to obtain its precious yield: it could be tapped. Shallow incisions were cut in the bark and the latex would ooze out drop by drop. Tapping saved the tree, but it required a different kind of labour force: one that knew the forests intimately and how to find the individual trees; one that knew how to tap the trees properly (where to put the incisions, and how frequently to collect the latex); one that was available throughout the tapping season, sometimes all year round – in other words, the indigenous people of the area.

The rubber trade in the Putumayo region was now based mostly on *Hevea*. *Hevea* grew in a dispersed pattern; about fifty trees, on average, grew in a square mile, and each Indian worker tended about a hundred trees – fifty in the process of being tapped and fifty in their resting phase. Those who organized the workforce were still called *caucheros*, though they no longer did the work of collecting rubber. The Indians of the Putumayo who did do the work – mostly Huitotos and Boras – had their own particular way of tapping the trees and preparing the rubber. Incisions were made in the bark, and the latex was allowed to run down the trunk of the tree, where it coagulated naturally into strips of rubber. (This was in contrast to the prevailing method in most of the Amazon basin, where the latex was collected in cups attached to the trunk). The strips were then taken to a stream, where they were washed and prepared for shipping.

South American rubber accounted for the bulk of the world's production, averaging about 70 per cent during the first decade of the century. Though Peruvian production was small in comparison to that of Brazil, the largest producer in Amazonia, at about 10 per cent of the total it was not insignificant, especially in Iquitos and Peru in general.

Thanks to rubber, Iquitos became a boomtown, growing much faster than all of the other settlements jurisdictionally controlled by the vast Department of Loreto. It became increasingly clear to the Loretano politicians that keeping the regional capital in Moyobamba, a small Andean town famed for its Panama hats, made no sense in this age of the Amazon rubber boom. And so, in 1898, the capital of the department was officially moved to Iquitos.

Now, ten years later, with a population of 15,000, Iquitos was not just a regional capital but a major Amazonian town, of vital importance to the nation. During the first decade of the century, Iquitos handled about 12 per cent of total Peruvian foreign trade, and provided Lima with 16 per cent of its customs revenues. Militarily, too, Iquitos was crucial, since it was from this port town that the Peruvian navy plied the waters of the Amazon and the Putumayo, guaranteeing Peruvian interests in the region: the Colombians, by contrast, had no ships on the Putumayo. As well as being both nationally and regionally important, Iquitos was a very diverse town, probably more cosmopolitan than anywhere else in Peru. Consulates from the United States and several European countries, including Great Britain, were there to represent their expatriate population and to provide the commercial and legal support to expedite the export of rubber. Great Britain was the town's chief economic partner, its importance marked by the presence of several British banks and trading firms – about half of the town's rubber exports were destined for Liverpool. Following not far behind Britain in economic importance were Germany, France and the United States. The Booth Steamship Company of Liverpool provided Iquitos with its connections to the rest of the world: there were regular sailings to Manaus and Pará, and from there to Barbados (and onwards to New York), Liverpool, Le Havre, Lisbon, and Hamburg. The pound sterling was the town's unofficial currency.

3

Arana's World

Back in Iquitos, February and March 1908 passed, and still there was no sign of Perkins. While waiting for him, Hardenburg had been kicking his heels and, thanks to the high prices in town, getting into debt.

April arrived, and, worryingly, there was still no word from Perkins. Hardenburg's luck, however, had taken a turn for the better. He had got himself two jobs: as a draughtsman, working in the local college; and as a teacher of English to a well-heeled clientele. Making savings would be difficult in such an expensive town, but even so, he hoped to clear his debts shortly.

Then Hardenburg heard the best news yet. Perkins was alive and well, and expected in Iquitos in a few weeks. On 22 April the Peruvian launch from El Encanto tied up at the wharf in Iquitos. Perkins walked off in the same clothes he had worn when Hardenburg last saw him. He was penniless, just as Hardenburg had been.

Perkins related how, after Hardenburg's departure, he had been kept a virtual house-prisoner in El Encanto. On 20 March Miguel Loayza had forced him to sign an affidavit saying that he was in El Encanto under Peruvian protection because his life would be in danger were he to remain with the Colombians, and that he was being well-treated by Loayza and his subordinates. Though the document also stated that his baggage would be recovered, Perkins was never allowed to return upriver to the spot where he had hidden it, and no one from the Company was sent to retrieve it. The bags were stuffed with personal belongings, engineering books and instruments, all the artefacts and geological specimens they had collected on their way downriver, technical papers, and personal diaries and journals.

Aside from one diary that Hardenburg had kept with him, everything was lost.

Perkins gave more details of what had happened during his detention. The Peruvians had finally caught up with David Serrano. They

> returned to Serrano's and burned his buildings, murdered him and twenty-eight other Colombians who were quartered there. They took these twenty-eight poor men, who had gathered here for mutual protection, tied their hands behind them and shot them to death. They not only shot them to death, but horribly mutilated their bodies with their machetes and threw them into the river.

While they were both in Iquitos, Hardenburg and Perkins decided to seek compensation for their losses. They blamed both Arana's company and the Peruvian military for what had happened to them. To get the compensation process underway, Hardenburg and Perkins complained directly to Guy King, the American vice-consul in Iquitos and a practising dentist, about how they had been mistreated and what they had lost. But, as Perkins later told the officials at the State Department, the interview was far from satisfactory. Basically, King told them not to bother. Iquitos was a lawless place, and interested parties would do whatever they could to discredit their case. As they all knew, King's livelihood was dependent on these same people, and he did not want his lucrative business to suffer through unprovable accusations and complaints.

Disappointed with King's response, the only logical step seemed to be to take their complaint directly to Arana.

By a stroke of luck, Arana happened to be in Iquitos when Hardenburg and Perkins went to lodge their complaint at his door. He had just returned from London, where he had intended to float a new concern – the Peruvian Amazon Rubber Company – with vast capital reserves. But poor trading conditions had forced him to postpone the flotation, and he was now back in Iquitos waiting for things to improve.

The rise of Julio César Arana's fortune and power was very rapid, and entirely the result of the Amazonian rubber boom and Iquitos's position in it. Arana was born on 12 April 1864 in the town of Rioja, in northern

Peru, situated between the cordillera rising high behind it and the lush valleys of the Amazonian forests below. The Arana line hailed from the town of Cajamarca, in the Andean highlands to the southwest of Rioja, and from there the men of the family had spread out in all directions, seeking their fortunes and finding different fates. Martín Arana, Julio César's father, ended up in the respectable straw-hat trade in Rioja.

Julio César entered his father's business aged nine, and over the next few years he hawked his father's goods over an increasingly large area. When Julio was fifteen, Martín Arana, rather than see his son enlist in the war against Chile, sent him to Cajamarca, where he learned bookkeeping and general business administration.

Two years later, Arana knew enough about business to begin to take advantage of the new economic opportunities that the rubber boom was bringing to the Peruvian Amazon. Instead of working out of Rioja and the Andean hinterland, Arana decided upon the town of Yurimaguas on the Huallaga River, a tributary of the Amazon, as the base of his operations. He would now be able to sell his father's Panama hats throughout the Amazon basin, venturing into Brazil and Colombia as well as northeastern Peru.

Soon, however, Arana realized that much more money could be made out of rubber than out of Panama hats. But he needed more cash to invest, and it came by way of a very convenient marriage. At the age of twenty-three, after a six-year courtship, Julio César Arana married his childhood sweetheart, Eleanora Zumaeta, who was from a well-heeled Rioja family. He could now put the pieces in place for a profitable commercial venture. In 1888, the year after his marriage, Arana invited his new brother-in-law, Pablo Zumaeta, to join him in business. Together, the partners opened a trading post in the nearby town of Tarapoto, in a rich rubber-growing district. The following year they moved deeper into the trade by buying a part of a rubber forest near Yurimaguas. Arana and Zumaeta then set off for the Ceará, the northeastern Brazilian dustbowl, to hire cheap labour, possibly some of the cheapest in the world. The Ceará had recently experienced a devastating drought in which half a million people had lost their lives; those who had survived were desperate for work. Arana and Zumaeta found twenty men who would sell themselves for practically nothing to escape their hell.

Debt peonage, whereby an individual bound him- or herself to a creditor, and worked for him until the debt was cleared, was a fundamental part of the Peruvian labour system. The debt could be incurred in a number of ways, such as the creditor paying the cost of getting the person to the workplace, or for provisions, or simply an advance on wages. Slavery had been abolished in Peru in 1854 but debt peonage, which was perfectly legal, was widely regarded as a way of keeping wages down and making Peruvian primary products, such as minerals, sugar and rubber, competitive on the international market.

And so, with their Brazilian peons working the rubber trees, Arana invited another brother-in-law to join him and Pablo in the rubber trade. In 1889, the three men set up business in the boomtown that was Iquitos.

Arana rose rapidly to a position of great importance and power through his involvement in the rubber trade. In 1902 his was one of a handful of small and medium rubber exporting firms in Iquitos: it accounted for about 8 per cent of Iquitos's rubber exports and about 5 per cent of its total imports. But he was well on his way to leaving the competition behind, and it was the Putumayo that proved the key to his eventual dominance of the trade. He was already doing enough business in the Putumayo with the Colombian traders to ensure that most of them were on his books: the Colombians had to sell their rubber in Iquitos, and it was there that they also purchased their supplies and negotiated credit, because their own supply lines were so distant and difficult to access. Arana arranged everything for them.

However, being a mere provider and facilitator was not enough for Arana. He wanted greater involvement in the rubber trade than this, and decided that his best strategy would be to enter into partnership with the leading Colombian traders in the Putumayo. The decision could not have been wiser. His first partner, Benjamin Larrañaga – one of the pioneers of the Putumayo rubber business – sold out to Arana in 1903; later that same year another Colombian, Gregorio Calderón, did the same. Arana had become a rubber trader, and set up his new company, J.C. Arana y Hermanos, with its headquarters in Iquitos. As partners he took on his two brothers-in-law, Pablo Zumaeta and Abel Alarco, and his own brother Lizardo. Very soon after its creation, Arana opened a branch office of the Company in Manaus, where Lizardo directed operations.

Arana was now in a powerful position. He was cash-rich and could easily have extended trade credit and mortgages to the remaining Colombian rubber traders in the Putumayo area. Instead he decided he wanted their concerns for himself, and offered them partnerships in the way he had to Larrañaga and Calderón. Arana's financial reserves were substantial. From 1904 onwards Arana annexed valuable rubber properties on both the Caraparaná and Igaraparaná rivers, amounting to over forty settlements.

At this point Arana recruited Barbadians to work for him. Besides being on the regular steamer route from Manaus to Europe and the United States, Barbados had become a source of cheap labour, and the island's government strongly encouraged emigration to solve its economic problems. The island's sugar-based economy was in serious trouble, and a significant proportion of Barbadian men had no employment. A large number had already left to work on the Panama Canal project. Arana sent his brother-in-law Abel Alarco to take advantage of the economic crisis to recruit a cheap labour force. Over nine months, some 200 Barbadian men became indentured, initially for a period of two years, to Arana's company. The Barbadians expected to be employed as labourers, but Arana had other plans for them. By using foreigners with no ties to the locality or the people, he was able to initiate a more ruthless regime. It was extremely difficult for the Barbadians to disobey orders; as foreigners, they could hardly melt away into the surroundings even if they wanted to escape. In this remote part of the Amazon basin, there was really no one and nowhere to turn to for help.

By 1907, Arana was the only Peruvian rubber trader in the Putumayo region: his steam launches alone visited the area. The Colombians had mostly disappeared, and the small handful who refused to sell out to him were at his mercy, deep in the remote jungle.

While Arana was turning the Putumayo region into his personal fiefdom, he was also entrenching his position as a rubber trader: his exports soared from 35,000 pounds in 1900 to 1.4 million pounds in 1906, by which time he had become Iquitos's leading rubber exporter, shipping about one-third of the town's rubber downriver and thence to the bustling ports of Liverpool, Le Havre, Hamburg and New York. He had also become politically powerful in Iquitos, in Loreto, and across the Andes in Lima. His presence in the Putumayo gave Peru important leverage in its boundary dispute with Colombia. At the same time, having Arana in the area also meant that he could provide Lima with intelligence about any encroachments by Colombians. It was a very cosy and mutually reinforcing relationship. Arana, the powerful merchant and staunch patriot, had forged a formidable economic and political foundation for himself.

Arana's ascendancy was not yet complete. Rubber was an international commodity, and Arana's sights went far beyond the Amazon and his business premises in Iquitos and Manaus. Europe, after all, was within easier reach than Lima. In contrast to the other merchants in town, many of whom flaunted their wealth and position by having their dwellings decorated in the most beautiful and lavish imported tiles, Arana's house was modest. He did not really see himself as a resident of Iquitos: he wanted to make his mark as a man of the world. By 1906 he knew Paris, Bordeaux and Biarritz as well as he did the Amazonian towns. In 1907 he moved his family to Biarritz, and the middle of that year found him shuttling between Biarritz and Paris.

But it was the City of London – the financial centre of the world – that was uppermost in Arana's mind. His plan was quite simple. Having become the main supplier of rubber from the Peruvian Amazon, he was coming to London to incorporate his enterprise. On 6 September 1907 Arana created a company called the Peruvian Rubber Company, which purchased the business and properties of J.C. Arana y Hermanos. Later that month the Company's name was changed, and it began trading as the Peruvian Amazon Rubber Company. Its flotation, with nominal capital of £1 million, was ready.

But despite the publicity and the tastefully produced prospectus, the flotation ran into problems as the world rubber price collapsed. Late 1907 witnessed a bank panic in the United States, followed by a stock-market crash: the ripples were felt throughout the world as prices and output fell sharply. Arana was advised to hold back until conditions improved, and he returned to Iquitos.

Now, in May 1908, listening to Hardenburg and Perkins make a case for their losses in the Putumayo, Arana was polite but unhelpful. As Perkins later recounted:

We laid the matter before J.C. Arana who was in Iquitos at the time
of my arrival there. We did this, simply stating what our luggage was
composed of, and that we thought we should be paid for it. He promised
'to see about it'.

But they heard no more from Arana. His silence, together with Dr
King's reluctance to do anything, forced Perkins and Hardenburg to
change their tactics.

Meanwhile, economic conditions began to improve and rubber prices
began to rise. It was time for Arana to return to London and resume the
flotation of his great Company.

Before doing so, he made two significant changes. The word 'rubber'
was dropped from the firm's name, and it was restyled the Peruvian
Amazon Company. It had also assembled an impressive board of British
directors. The first was Henry Manuel Read, an old South American
hand, having been, at various times, manager of the London Bank of
Mexico and South America; a director of the Peruvian Corporation,
a sprawling company based in London, with controlling interests in
Peruvian railways, steamers, mines and guano deposits; and a director
of Lima Light Power and Tramways Company. Read had twenty years'
experience in Peru, but had never ventured beyond the coast. The others
were John Russell Gubbins, a businessman with forty years' experience
in Peru, and Sir John Lister-Kaye, an impeccably reared aristocrat with
royal connections – formerly Lieutenant Royal Horse Guards and
Groom-in-Waiting to Edward VII. Lister-Kaye was easily the most
distinguished member of the board, and one of its most socially respected.
He and his wife were highly sought-after society figures on both sides
of the Atlantic, moving easily between London and the country, and
between New York and Newport. The British board gave the Company
the kind of stature and importance that would win it respect in the City
of London, and from all those whose financial dealings took them there.

The Peruvian Amazon Company was successfully floated on 8
December 1908. The public was offered 300,000 shares at £1 each, while
the remaining 700,000 ordinary shares stayed within the Arana family,
giving them control over the new Company. The board of directors
and the registered headquarters of the new Company were in London.

Organizing the day-to-day activities of the Company were two offices: one in Iquitos, where Pablo Zumaeta was the general manager with direct responsibility for operations in the Putumayo; and the other in Manaus, where Lizardo Arana was in charge of commercial transactions in this hub of the Amazonian rubber trade.

Arana was on top of the world. He was in complete control of a vast rubber-producing territory – at more than 10,000 square miles, the largest of its kind in South America – into which no one could venture without his knowledge and permission.

4

Saldaña Rocca's World

Desperate to air their grievances and to make a successful claim for compensation from the Peruvian government, Hardenburg and Perkins decided Iquitos was a dead end. A more promising route, they thought, would be to seek compensation by pressing their claim in the United States through the State Department. As Perkins came from a family with political connections, he decided to take their case to Washington, while Hardenburg remained in Iquitos.

By the end of May 1908, Perkins was on his way by steamer to Manaus. By a strange irony, aboard at the same time, and also bound for Manaus, was Julio César Arana. Stranger still, he made Perkins a business offer.

> During the voyage we conversed about the rubber industry and when we reached Manaos [*sic*], where he has an office, he had a letter written, making me a business proposition intended for Hardenburg and myself jointly. Nothing had been said about why he should do this, more than that he said the Peruvian employees he had on those lands offered to us, were very inefficient. I have no reason to think that he made us this liberal proposition to deter us from making a claim for damages. It was a plain business proposition, open for our acceptance or rejection.

Once Perkins was back safely in the United States, he immediately started pestering the State Department about their losses and seeking compensation. The State Department reacted by dragging its feet for months, most of the time ignoring Perkins; when it did contact Perkins, it was to announce that the department was only willing to consider a claim for $5,000, as opposed to $20,000. And then things got worse. It turned out that the State Department had informally approached the Peruvian government, which had agreed, as a special favour, to compensate their losses to the tune of $2,500 – an eighth of what Hardenburg and Perkins had originally demanded. This was a severe blow. They had both hoped for much more. Perkins lost interest in the matter, and turned his attention to making a new life for himself in his home country. He and Hardenburg would never see each other again.

Ever since he had been a boy growing up on his parents' farm – first in Galena, Illinois, and then in Youngsville, New York, near the Catskill Mountains – Hardenburg had dreamt of seeing the Amazon. But working in Iquitos was probably not how he had imagined he would be spending his time on that great river.

And then, one day in June 1908, about four months into his stay in the town, Hardenburg's life took a dramatic turn. A young lad had appeared at the door of the building on Iquitos's main street where Hardenburg had borrowed office space for his English lessons. Hardenburg had never seen the lad before, and was therefore surprised when he said he had come especially to speak to him – but not about taking classes.

The boy's name was Miguel Galvez. He explained that he was the son of Benjamin Saldaña Rocca, a maverick newspaper owner who had recently been forced out of town, and was now working in Lima. The forty-three-year-old Saldaña Rocca had distinguished himself as a soldier, but had decided some time ago to settle in Iquitos. In a foretaste of things to come, on 9 August 1907, while Arana was in Europe, Saldaña Rocca petitioned the judge of the criminal court in Iquitos to proceed with charges against eighteen employees of J.C. Arana y Hermanos. The petition provided brief details of horrible acts of violence and barbarism against the Indians who collected rubber for the Company in the Putumayo region. One incident, perpetrated at the Ultimo Retiro section (a Company station to which rubber was brought), involved two Barbadians. Saldaña Rocca described the sickening scene:

> The sub-manager, Argaluza, ordered the death of an Indian woman called Simona, because he thought she had relations with a young man whose name was also Simon. The death of this unhappy woman was most terrible. Argaluza ordered the Barbadian negroes Stanley Lewis and Ernesto Siobers, known by the nickname Frailecito ['little monk'],

to administer 155 stripes to the woman, and when her thighs were cut to pieces he locked her up in a room and left her until she was worm eaten; then the brave Argaluza ordered one of his employees to kill her. The latter refusing to kill Simona, Argaluza took his rifle and said: 'If you don't kill her, I will kill you', thus forcing the ignorant employee to become an unwilling criminal.

Saldaña Rocca urged the judge to move quickly,

> as the bones of thousands of Indians who have been murdered lie scattered round the houses of the sections such as Matanzas, Ultimo Retiro, Sabana, Santa Catalina, San Victor and all the other dependencies of El Encanto and La Chorrera . . . a visit of inspection [should] be undertaken as soon as possible, before the bones of the victims can be made to disappear.

But all Saldaña Rocca got from the court was silence.

Two weeks later he tried a different and more daring approach – he made public his attack on Arana in the first issue of his own newspaper, *La Sancion*. The title, best translated as 'The Castigation', gave a clue that this was no ordinary newspaper.

Saldaña Rocca, editor and proprietor, was on a crusade. He was going to tell the truth about what was really going on in Iquitos behind the veneer of prosperity and progress. Iquitos was a dangerous place, especially for those on the wrong side, he told his readers. 'Enough of mysteries and cover-ups', he declared,

> enough of derision, abuse, prevarication, thefts, assassinations, embezzlements and fraud. In such a noble and worthwhile task nothing nor anyone can stop me: I will fight undaunted and without respite, scorning the switchblade of the assassin and the pistol of the thug.'

The paper contained a variety of articles and notices covering local news, court reports, port movements, poems and small literary pieces; hard-hitting swipes at his competition, the newspaper *El Oriente*, which did not share Saldaña Rocca's view of the Iquitos establishment; snippets of news from Lima and overseas papers; and, as he promised, the uncovering and hounding of those committing crimes against the people.

The main architect of this wave of criminality, Saldaña Rocca maintained, was Julio César Arana. In almost every issue of the paper, Saldaña Rocca published damning revelations about his prime target. These took various forms – sometimes just an editorial comment; sometimes a lengthy attack, as when, over a three-week period, he published the content of his unsuccessful criminal petition; and from the start, the printing of eyewitness accounts, by past employees of Arana's company, of how Arana was running his operations in the Putumayo as a coercive and violent system and about the torture, maiming and murder of the indigenous people.

The first issue of *La Sancion* set the tone for the paper. It contained a letter from Julio Muriedas, who had worked for Arana in La Chorrera, one of the regional headquarters of the Company in the Putumayo, for three months. Muriedas described what he had witnessed in the Matanzas section, whose chief, Armando Normand (of whom a great deal more would be learned over the coming years), operated a reign of terror. 'The chief,' Muriedas wrote,

> Armando Normand, applies 200 or more lashes, which are given with
> rough scourges of crude leather, to the unhappy Indians, when they –
> to their misfortune – do not deliver punctually the number of rolls of
> rubber of the weight desired; other times, when the Indian, fearful of
> not being able to deliver the required amount of rubber, flees, they take
> his children, suspend them by their hands and feet, and, in this position,
> apply fire, so that with the cruel pains produced by this torture, they will
> tell where their fathers are hidden.

La Sancion, with its motto 'To defend the interests of the people', seems to have been popular. Though originally planned to appear twice a week, within a few months of its first appearance *La Sancion* became a daily. By then it had been joined by another Saldaña Rocca title, *La Felpa*, which was launched on 31 August. *La Felpa* ('The Scolding') was quite different from its sister paper. It was shorter in length, at only four pages, appeared fortnightly, and used various features to make its point, including a political cartoon as the paper's centre spread.

In case Saldaña Rocca's readers had any doubts about what was going on in Arana's empire, the very first issue of *La Felpa* carried a series of four graphic tableaux entitled 'The Crimes of the Putumayo': FLAGELLATIONS, MUTILATIONS, TORTURES, and TARGET PRACTICE. These showed how the Indian workers were being horribly maltreated.

Over the coming months, Arana's Putumayo operations would continue to make *La Felpa*'s centre spread; and sometimes so did Arana himself, always appearing perfectly turned-out as a proper Edwardian gentleman – a sharp, neatly trimmed beard and a smart, well-fitting suit adding to his distinction – but never as a man with clean hands. On more than one occasion, Saldaña Rocca had him portrayed as a devil; Arana and his men were usually surrounded by skulls.

The last issue of Benjamin Saldaña Rocca's newspaper came out on 22 February 1908, three weeks after Hardenburg's arrival in Iquitos.

Galvez told Hardenburg that his father had been tipped off that the police were on their way to escort him out of Iquitos. It was no coincidence that Arana had just returned from London. Before he fled, Saldaña Rocca had had just enough time to gather all his documents, which he left with Galvez's mother, who kept a boarding house on the waterfront. Galvez heard from his father in Lima, who urged him to pass the package of documents on to someone who would make good use of them in his continuing crusade against Arana. Hardenburg was the person he chose, though we do not know why. Perhaps it was because he was an American, an outsider in Iquitos.

At any rate, Hardenburg accepted the package. The material, most of which has survived, contained the revealing letters written to Saldaña Rocca, many of which had already been printed in *La Sancion*, together with back issues of both of Saldaña Rocca's titles. Reading the graphic testimonies that Galvez handed him, Hardenburg finally understood what lay behind the scars – the Mark of Arana – that he had seen on Indian bodies in the Putumayo: the abusive violence, the maimings and killings, that were part and parcel of collecting rubber in Arana's Putumayo.

Saldaña Rocca's material galvanized Hardenburg's desire to expose Arana, and over the next twelve months he collected his own evidence. While on Arana's company launch travelling to Iquitos, Hardenburg had met two Colombians, and he now called upon their personal contacts in Iquitos, sympathetic Colombians and Peruvians similarly disaffected with Arana, to testify in writing to what they had witnessed or experienced in the Putumayo. In his search for corroborating evidence, Hardenburg received unsolicited letters, as well as responses to detailed questions he sent out to specific individuals. Hardenburg was highly organized, and asked very pertinent questions: Who extracts the latex from the trees? How are these people paid? How does the Company treat its workers? Is it true that the bosses treat the Indians barbarously, that they beat and maim them? Is it true that they cut off their arms, legs and heads? Is it true that they shoot them for fun? He received answers in long testimonials, all of them sworn in front of a notary in Iquitos. They made disturbing reading.

Hardenburg had managed to collect testimonials from twenty people willing to recount their experiences of Arana's empire. The evidence he had collected was clear: the abuses were unimaginable. At the same time, Hardenburg became increasingly aware that it was unsafe for him to stay in Iquitos – though, in his account of his time there, he did not say whether he had actually received threats. He suspected, however, that his extracurricular activities were known. He told his English students some weeks before his departure that he would be suspending the classes. By then he had already decided to use the material he had collected and his own experiences in the Putumayo to write a book exposing the atrocities committed by Arana and his men.

At the beginning of June, Hardenburg bundled together his book manuscript, the depositions made to him, and those he had inherited from Saldaña Rocca, and made his way to the Booth Steamship Company wharf, where he boarded a ship bound for Pará, and eventually Liverpool.

PART II

5

Over to the Foreign Office

Hardenburg was on a mission. From Liverpool he made his way to London, where he found lodgings near St Pancras train station. Early in August, he visited the offices of the Anti-Slavery and Aborigines' Protection Society in Vauxhall, South London.

The Society had a fearsome – and well-deserved – reputation for rooting out and then pursuing perpetrators of what we would now call human rights abuses. The Society was in fact of quite recent origin, having been formed in June of that year as an amalgamation of two older societies – the British and Foreign Anti-Slavery Society and the Aborigines Protection Society. Both had originally been formed in the 1830s to ensure that the Emancipation Act of 1833, which outlawed slavery in Britain and its possessions, would function as an inducement and an example for other nations to abolish slavery in their respective countries and possessions. The newly amalgamated Anti-Slavery and Aborigines' Protection Society had a broad agenda to protect the welfare of indigenous people everywhere. It had large worldwide networks of correspondents who reported on local cases of abuse; they lobbied members of parliament and the Colonial and Foreign Office; and they kept their members up to date with the progress of campaigns through their magazines.

Hardenburg had a meeting with John Harris, the Society's organizing secretary. Explaining who he was and what he had come about, Hardenburg presented Harris with the material he had brought out of the Amazon. Harris later recalled how moved he had been by the testimonials – especially since he was then helping to organize the work of the Congo Reform Association. He had no doubt that the testimonials were telling the truth; the echoes of the Congo were unmissable. Harris immediately prepared letters of introduction to various prominent members of the Society but insisted, when Hardenburg returned two days later, that he should not delay in taking the story to Sidney Paternoster at *Truth*. From his own experiences with the Congo campaign, Harris had learned how important it was to garner public sympathy as soon as possible. *Truth* was the most effective way of achieving quick results.

Paternoster certainly stirred it up. On 27 September, the week after publishing 'The Devil's Paradise: A British-owned Congo', Robert Bennett, *Truth*'s editor, received a letter from the Peruvian Amazon Company's headquarters in London Wall, in the City of London, dated just a couple of days earlier. It was fairly short and to the point.

> The Directors have no reason to believe that the atrocities referred to have in fact taken place, and indeed have grounds for considering that they have been purposely mis-stated for indirect objects. Whatever the facts, however, may be, the Board of this Company are *under no responsibility for them, as they were not in office at the times of the alleged occurrences* [my emphasis].

The letter was printed in the following week's issue of the magazine (29 September 1909), in which Paternoster continued to provide the reading public with further eyewitness accounts of conditions in the Putumayo. This time Paternoster raised the temperature further. He startlingly revealed, through a testimonial by an ex-employee of Arana's named Celestino Lopez, that at the rubber station of Santa Julia it was a 'negro' who had 'flogged most barbarously' three Indian women. Later in the same article, Paternoster provided further evidence – in the shape of a testimonial from a Colombian trader that had appeared originally in the *Jornal do Commercio* of 14 September 1907 – that some Barbadians in Arana's employ were as much the perpetrators as the victims of abuses.

Paternoster ended his commentary on the criminal acts of the Company by repeating his challenge:

> I trust that the directors of the Peruvian and Amazon Company [*sic*] will be the first to admit that the case as it stands demands their earnest attention, and that they will, after fully investigating all the circumstances,

take effectual steps to remove all ground for unfavourable criticism of their business in future.

Paternoster had not only ruffled the Peruvian Amazon Company's feathers: the Peruvian government had also taken offence at what he had reported in the 22 September issue of *Truth*. In a letter to *Truth*'s editor, Eduardo Lembcke, the chargé d'affaires at the Peruvian legation in London, expressed deep concern at the allegations levelled at the Peruvian Amazon Company. Lembcke began by categorically denying the allegations. It would be impossible, he remarked, for his government not to have known about any such acts on the Putumayo, since the area was well served by state officials and had a strong military garrison. The Putumayo was not, he added, 'a sort of no-man's land'; it is 'in direct communication by steamer and other rapid routes with Iquitos'; and Iquitos 'is connected by telegraphic and wireless installations with Lima and the whole of the Republic'. In short, 'it is impossible to admit that acts of the nature described could have been committed without the guilty parties being promptly and severely punished by the authorities'. As for *La Felpa* and *La Sancion*, they

> should not be given the least credit, as both these papers were started by the same editor for dishonest purposes, and for that reason were so shortlived. The said papers published fantastic crimes alleged to have been committed by the employees of the firm of J.C. Arana and Hnos., and when the employees of this old and well-known house commenced proceedings for libel against the said editor, he disappeared in order to evade the grave responsibility he had incurred.

Lembcke ended this robust letter by upholding the honour of the Peruvian military.

> I must therefore repudiate in the most deliberate manner the accusation contained in the said article and based on the malicious information supplied to you, and I protest most emphatically against references therein made that soldiers of the Peruvian Army could be capable of committing the acts of inhumanity described by Mr Hardenburg.

Sidney Paternoster did not, of course, let Eduardo Lembcke have the last word. Refuting the chargé d'affaires' claims, he again used Hardenburg's first-hand knowledge, emphasizing that Saldaña Rocca had never been prosecuted, and that after leaving Iquitos he was openly working for a newspaper in Lima; that it was Saldaña Rocca who had denounced the Company and not the other way around; that the Peruvian government had agreed to compensate Hardenburg and Perkins. In a clear reference to the Congo, he also pointed out that soldiers or civilians in out-of-the-way parts of the world were quite capable of acts of cruelty and oppression towards indigenous people.

From this point events snowballed. Allegations and counter-allegations peppered the pages of the British press. But ultimately *Truth* could only expose and embarrass the British-listed Peruvian Amazon Company. Only the British government could take the matter further. It was up to the Foreign Office, at whose door the problem was laid by the parliamentary questions, to get at the truth.

The attention of the Foreign Office, and that of its secretary of state, Sir Edward Grey, was mostly focused on continental European affairs – particularly Germany's naval build-up, which in a decade had seen the size of the country's navy increase until it was second only to that of Britain. Grey had been in the post since 1905 and was considered a success: he had already scored a significant diplomatic achievement with the Anglo-Russian accord of 1907, which led directly to the Triple Entente between Russia, France and Britain.

But, although the Amazon was a world away from Great Power politics, the Foreign Office could hardly pretend that it had had nothing to do with the Putumayo: after all, British subjects were living and working there, and it had a responsibility to protect their welfare. To help the Foreign Office get to the bottom of the story, Hart-Davies mentioned that David Cazes, the British consul in Iquitos, happened at this time to be in London. The Foreign Office should lose no time in contacting him.

On 1 October Francis Campbell, the assistant under-secretary of state at the Foreign Office, wrote to Cazes at his London address asking him to provide Sir Edward Grey with a response to the allegations contained in the 22 September issue of *Truth* and the subsequent parliamentary questions. Cazes responded promptly, saying that the allegations were, on the whole, unfounded. The two Iquitos papers that were used by *Truth* had 'little standing or reliance'; the Barbadians – most of whom had gone home, he said – had complained in the past to him of being ill-treated, but many of the complaints were unjustified; from what he had seen of the Putumayo Indians, they were well-treated; and, as for Arana, he and his Company were, Cazes insisted, 'very attentive to the complaints'.

Cazes's letter did not, however, find much favour back in the Foreign Office. He was an unpaid servant (as were many consular officials), and the Foreign Office suspected that he was involved in the rubber trade. Moreover, as one clerk acutely pointed out, the 'Cazes letter is not really to the point. The question is are the atrocities alleged by *Truth* to be perpetrated in the name of a British Co., or on its behalf, true or not.' Cazes's response appeared ambiguous at best. The one conclusion that could be drawn from Cazes, however, was that there were probably no Barbadians left in the Putumayo; and even if there were, as one clerk put it with the full weight of the racism and prejudice of the time behind him, 'their evidence would be worth little all West Indians being liars'.

Several days after his letter had arrived at the Foreign Office, Cazes appeared in person to clarify and correct some of his written statements. The Barbadians had first been imported four years before, he said, but they could not adapt to the climate. Most had left, and the few who did remain were free to come and go as they pleased. Cazes was sure that the reports of cruelty to the Indians were exaggerated, and that the stories had originated with the Colombian government, who had much to gain from embarrassing the Peruvians. He also thought that the American consul in Iquitos had visited the Putumayo and submitted a report to Washington, though he did not know the substance of it.

Meanwhile, the Foreign Office had also contacted Charles des Graz, the resident British minister at the Lima legation, and Victor Huckin, the British consul in Bogotá, for any information they had. Graz wrote back that he had little to comment, as the Putumayo was so far from Iquitos, and Iquitos was even further from Lima. Huckin confirmed that he had heard that Colombians had been harassed by the Peruvians in the Putumayo, but he had no further details at hand.

As for the report on conditions in the Putumayo prepared by

the American consul in Iquitos, and referred to in Hart-Davies's parliamentary question, the Foreign Office contacted James Bryce, the British ambassador in Washington, who passed on the request to the State Department. The acting secretary of state, Huntington Wilson, wrote back to Bryce a fortnight later that his department had no such report, contradicting what Cazes had said in his interview at the Foreign Office.

But the State Department was wrong. Two reports had in fact been received. Had they simply been mislaid? Or did the State Department have some reason to withhold the reports at this time?

An American consulate had been opened in Iquitos in 1906, reflecting the growing importance of Peruvian Amazon trade to the United States. Once Kansas-born Charles Eberhardt had settled into his new post, he began sending dispatches giving his State Department superiors, and potential American investors, a picture of Iquitos and its surrounding region.

During 1907 Eberhardt met and befriended Georg von Hassel, a German civil engineer and explorer who had spent the better part of fifteen years in South America, mostly working for the Peruvian government on land surveys. Hassel's 1903 map of the Peruvian Amazon was, according to Eberhardt, 'the most reliable and authentic one, and, though published some four years ago . . . still, in the main, accurate'. Eberhardt was convinced, as were many American and European anthropologists, that indigenous cultures were on the brink of extinction. Even in the short time since the publication of von Hassel's map, Eberhardt was certain that 'some of the smaller tribes may have ceased to exist'. Eberhardt was in a unique position to shed some light on the little that was known of the culture of these people. He submitted his ethnographic information to the State Department in a report of 30 November 1907.

The report was typical of ethnographic accounts of the time, with sections on customs, religion, material existence, and cannibalism, and a few photographs used to illustrate particular points. It was towards the end of the report, however, that Eberhardt stepped onto more controversial terrain, in a small section on slavery.

It was clear that Eberhardt had been deeply disturbed by what he had witnessed on his trip. He likened the prevailing labour system of debt peonage to slavery – Peruvians, he commented, would resent him saying so. It was not peonage that worried him so much as instances of the sale of Indian slaves, normally to households in Iquitos, who would use loopholes in the law to camouflage their purchases. Eberhardt described the process, but felt it should not be made public – at least not with his name attached.

Apart from the enslavement of Indians in Iquitos households, Eberhardt observed another, disturbing, practice. 'That there is considerable maltreatment of the Indians of certain districts', he wrote,

> there can be little doubt. In fact, they are often most cruelly treated and tortured, in a manner similar to the reports we read from the Congo, and I myself have seen some very inhuman acts regarding which I shall deal more fully in a separate, confidential report later on, touching general conditions in the territory in dispute between Peru and Colombia.

That promised report was written on 3 December 1907. Its innocuous-sounding title, 'General Conditions in the Putumayo River District of Peru', gave little hint of the allegations it contained. Eberhardt had spent six weeks in the Putumayo River area with Hassel and on its two main tributaries, the Igaraparaná and the Caraparaná. Though he excused himself for having not spent enough time to acquire a thorough knowledge of what was going on in the area, Eberhardt felt that he had seen enough of the conditions 'which a promoting company would probably not make public, and which the department, at least, might be interested in knowing'.

Eberhardt told of a tract of rubber land of approximately 12,000 square miles, bounded by the Caquetá, Igaraparaná and Putumayo rivers, where the indigenous people were experiencing the most horrible conditions. Eberhardt estimated that 10,000 Indians were involved, their lives totally controlled for the purposes of collecting rubber by a group of foremen and their assistants, all armed, numbering about 200. 'In the vicinity of La Chorrera', he wrote,

> considerable land has been cleared . . . and it is a sad sight to see these Indians – once the owners of this vast region – men, women, and children alike, filing along in the distance over this clearing, heavily

laden with rubber from their rubber forests, which they lay at the feet of their conquerors.

Eberhardt recounted stories of brutality, violence, murder and terror inflicted on the Indians as they were forced to collect rubber, for which the foremen received a percentage. They drove the Indians to the point of death – many of them, including children, being mutilated and brutally beaten as a lesson to the others. Those who tried to escape were rounded up at gunpoint.

> When the Indians flee to the forests, expeditions headed by armed whites and made up of Indians of neighboring tribes toward whom the runaways have always been hostile go in pursuit, and so, hunted by the whites and surrounded on all sides by hostiles of their own race, they are eventually killed or brought back captives to work as slaves of the whites . . .

Eberhardt remarked that, in the past two years, Barbadians had been recruited as armed overseers. He had learned quite a lot about what was going on in the area from them.

Eberhardt's report betrayed his frustration at being unable to bring any pressure to bear on the Peruvian government. He was, as he put it, 'consul of another Government'. And he added, tellingly:

> Nor as a plain American citizen could I have had anything to say on the subject, when I remembered our own treatment of the North American Indian, whom we killed because he would not stand by submissively while we took away his lands'.

His superiors in Washington were not pleased with that comment.

What was going on in the Putumayo, Eberhardt explained, could only be likened to what had been exposed in the Congo several years earlier. The criminal acts Eberhardt witnessed and heard of were being committed, he told the department, by employees of a private company based in Iquitos: J.C. Arana y Hermanos.

Eberhardt's report reached Washington early in February 1908, but he wanted his authorship to be concealed. If, he wrote, the conditions he described should be exposed,

I should prefer that it come from some other sources, for I was treated with the utmost kindness and consideration by the representatives of the company during the entire trip, as will be the case with anybody visiting that district from Iquitos, from the fact that they must depend entirely upon the company for transportation and accommodations in general.

Not long after, Eberhardt left Iquitos, and went home on leave. He quit the Iquitos consulate early in 1908, and moved on to the less politically sensitive posting of Barranquilla, Colombia.

Eberhardt's observations were extremely insightful, and would have been very useful to the Foreign Office; but their existence was denied and, for now, the Foreign Office was left with Cazes. It had to look elsewhere to confirm or deny the allegations.

Fortunately, when Charles des Graz telegraphed to say that he could not be of much help, he added that a Captain Whiffen had made a lengthy visit to the Putumayo in the previous year, and that he was now back in England. Graz was certain he would be of use.

The Whiffen lead was a godsend because, until this point, the Foreign Office had had to rely on Hardenburg's evidence alone. True, he did provide documentation to support his allegations against the Peruvian Amazon Company, but there was no independent way of assessing his 'facts'. Moreover, he was not a British subject. What the Foreign Office really needed was corroborating evidence from a source that they could assess to their own satisfaction. Who better than an officer in His Majesty's army?

6

An Officer and a Gentleman

Captain Thomas William Whiffen would prove to be a key figure in investigating the conditions in the Putumayo. He had visited the area and met with Julio César Arana. He was also involved in one of the Amazon's most enduring and controversial mysteries – the disappearance in the forests of the Putumayo of the French explorer Eugène Robuchon.

Though no one at the Foreign Office seemed to remember, Captain Thomas Whiffen had in fact come to the department's attention a few months earlier. In early July 1909 it had received a letter from the British consul in Pará stating that, a month before, Whiffen had walked into the consulate, long after his reported murder 'by uncivilised Indian tribes in the Caquetá region of the Amazon whilst prosecuting a journey of exploration from Iquitos to Manaõs [*sic*]'. Ambrose Pogson, the British consul, thought that, for a man who had been missing for almost half a year, he was 'in comparatively good health'.

Whiffen was thirty years old at the time. He came from a wealthy family. His grandfather Thomas Whiffen had founded the pharmaceutical firm that bore the family name, and his father, Thomas Joseph Whiffen, carried on the business. But chemical formulae, figures and stocks were of little interest to Thomas William. Instead, he was attracted to military life and travel. Serving in the Boer War with the Royal Inniskilling Fusiliers, he was wounded in December 1899 in the Battle of Colenso. For several years he appears to have drifted inside the military, alternately fit and unfit for active service. He was promoted to captain in 1904, and in 1905 he joined the 14th Hussars. About a year later he went onto half-pay, with no duties in the service. He was free to travel, and the Amazon beckoned.

Whiffen wanted to solve the mystery of the French explorer Eugène

Robuchon, who had disappeared late in 1905 in the Putumayo region while under contract to the Peruvian government to survey Arana's territory. Robuchon's disappearance had shocked European and American geographical and anthropological societies, which had become complacent about the dangers that awaited European explorers in the wild.

Eugène Robuchon had arrived in Iquitos in July 1903, from where he had planned to get to an area of northeastern Bolivia, which he wished to explore in depth. He had brought his wife and his dog along. Robuchon hoped to make important ethnographic, zoological and botanical collections, and to produce a travel narrative replete with photographs and phonographic recordings.

Robuchon was a professional explorer. Since his youth in the Vendée region of France, spent helping his father, Jules, who was a professional photographer, he had been fascinated by South America, especially its geography and natural history.

This was his second trip there. On the previous one he had met a young Indian woman, whom he baptized and named Hortensia. They were married on their return to France. He and his wife were returning to visit her family in northeastern Bolivia, and Robuchon wanted to take the opportunity while there to make a thorough exploration of this relatively unknown area.

While the couple were in Iquitos, outfitting for their journey further up the Amazon towards Bolivia, they met Julio César Arana. Robuchon's credentials and his zeal for exploration impressed Arana so much that he invited the couple to visit the Putumayo. Robuchon remarked to his father that Arana had 'shown great kindness' to them. Towards the end of September, Robuchon, Hortensia and Othelo (his Great Dane), after boarding one of Arana's steamers in Iquitos, found themselves in La Chorrera, rather than northeastern Bolivia.

For the next two weeks, Robuchon and a party of guides and carriers from La Chorrera went exploring, and traversed a significant part of Arana's territory. During this period Robuchon tried to see and experience as much as he could of the indigenous people, and seems to have been satisfied with the results. He collected many artefacts, including a few skulls; witnessed a strange tobacco rite and a cannibalistic

feast; took many photographs and captured the dialects he heard on
wax cylinders. He was energized by the jungle, despite being lost for
several days on end. He found the Huitoto and the Bora people cordial
to him, though the fear of being eaten by them preyed on his mind. He
appreciated having his dog and his guns with him while he stayed with
them.

Meanwhile, Robuchon's activities had come to the attention of the
Peruvian government. Hoping to legitimize its claims to the Putumayo
region, it instructed Arana to ask Robuchon to make a complete survey
of his property. A contract to that effect was drawn up and signed in
September 1904.

Robuchon was given very precise instructions on the route he was
to follow, taking in the entire region bounded by the Igaraparaná,
Caraparaná and Putumayo Rivers. He was also to record the area's
natural history and ethnography, and to produce a photographic
record of his explorations, paying especial attention to landscape, the
indigenous people and the rubber stations.

In August 1905 Robuchon sent Hortensia back to his family in France,
and embarked on his trip. A few months later, on 14 November, he was
in the small rubber post of Urania, on a tributary of the Igaraparaná near
the northern extremity of Arana's territory. Here he took the chance of
writing to his father again. This would be his last opportunity, as his
work would take him to parts of the region from where communication
with the outside world would be impossible. Robuchon was embarking
on a sweeping exploration along the boundary of Arana's land, starting
with a long overland track to the Caquetá River. Once there he planned
to journey by canoe until he reached the Cahuinari, and from there back
to the Igaraparaná. He knew that this part of the trip was 'excessively
dangerous', but he was confident that, should anything happen to him,
'his friend Monsieur Arana would not forget Hortensia'.

Nothing more was seen of Robuchon. He had just turned thirty-three.

Arana wrote to Hortensia – who was living in Poitiers with her in-
laws since her return to France – on several occasions during 1906,
hoping that one day he might be able to send her news that her husband
had returned from the forest. Such things did happen, he assured her.
But, in the summer of 1907, Arana wrote saying that they had given up
all hope that her husband was still alive. Arana said that what he was able

to find out for sure was that Robuchon had last gone into the forest with two Indian guides at the end of December 1905, and that he had not been heard of again. The guides had vanished as well. The best guess was that he had disappeared in the environs of the rubber station of El Retiro by the banks of the Putumayo. A part of his baggage had been retrieved, and a 'few written lines indicating the direction he was going to take but which, because of the action of the humidity, were now illegible'.

Despite the fact that Arana had promised Robuchon that, if anything happened to him, he would look after Hortensia, she never heard from Arana again.

In April 1908 Whiffen set off from London for the northwest Amazon. The standard account of Robuchon's fate, which had first been given by representatives of Arana's company, was that he had been killed by local people – and possibly eaten. Whiffen, on the other hand, had heard a story that Robuchon was alive but was being held as a prisoner by a band of Indians.

Whiffen arrived in Iquitos via Manaus in the second week of June. While there, he met and subsequently hired a Montserratian named John Brown, who had been working in the Putumayo for Arana's company for several years. Brown had good knowledge of the Putumayo and of Huitoto, one of the dominant language groups of the region. Cazes arranged for Whiffen to get a passage on one of the Peruvian Amazon Rubber Company's launches going to El Encanto, which he reached in mid-August. Several days later, Whiffen, Brown and more than twenty Indians, many of them armed, headed out into the jungle in the direction of the Igaraparaná, their destination being the rubber station of La Chorrera.

On 22 August, the party reached La Chorrera, and from there Whiffen's route took them cross-country towards the Cahuinari and Caquetá rivers, which they reached almost one month later. This was the area where Robuchon had last been seen alive.

By the end of October 1908, Whiffen and his party had reached the point where the Cahuinari meets the Caquetá. In the clearing they found evidence of a deserted shelter, which Brown confirmed was Robuchon's last camp; and soon thereafter Whiffen unearthed 'eight broken photograph plates in a packet, and the eye-piece of a sextant'.

And that was about it. Nothing more of interest came to light, though various paths from the clearing were carefully examined. Believing that Robuchon would have chosen to escape from his predicament by working his way further down the Caquetá, Whiffen decided to follow his hunch all the way downriver, until a point not far short of where the Caquetá meets the Apaporis River. When nothing turned up, Whiffen reversed his course to explore the other side of the river. There he came across the wreck of a raft, which Brown confirmed was Robuchon's. But it held no clues.

For the next two months Whiffen and his party headed northward through the jungle towards the Apaporis River, hoping that the Indians living in this area would have some information; but nothing came of his enquiries.

Whiffen and his party made it back to La Chorrera on 22 February 1909. He had seen a fair bit of the land beyond the Putumayo. He had not, however, solved the mystery of Robuchon's disappearance. Whiffen's best guess was that Robuchon had been 'located by a band of visiting Indians, captured, and either murdered or carried away in captivity to their haunts in the north bank of the Caquetá'. According to Whiffen, Robuchon probably died in March or April 1906.

Back in Iquitos, rumours abounded that Robuchon had been disposed of by Arana's men, as he had taken incriminating photographs of the horrible crimes they had committed. These rumours were illustrated by Saldaña Rocca who, in *La Felpa*, printed two cartoons on the topic – one showing Robuchon's death on Arana's conscience, and the other a sketch of an Indian being flogged, based on a photograph of Robuchon's (the original of which survives). Both Hardenburg and a visiting Colombian poet, Cornelio Hispano, claimed to have seen prints of Robuchon's photographs of atrocities circulating in Iquitos.

It did not take long for the Foreign Office to track Whiffen down to a hotel in Harrogate, where he was recuperating after his gruelling Amazonian experiences. On 18 October 1909, Whiffen telegrammed to say that he was happy to help with a report; three days later his report arrived in Whitehall. Detailed and running to thirteen pages, it took the form of a set of responses to particular statements made in the issues of *Truth* for 22 and 29 September, and 6 and 13 October.

It was fortunate for the Foreign Office that Whiffen was not off adventuring somewhere, for he turned out to be as helpful as Cazes had been unhelpful. Whiffen explained that he had passed through the Putumayo region on two occasions in the past year or so. Though he had not personally seen any evidence of atrocities, he was absolutely certain that they were taking place. When Whiffen was in the Putumayo area, on his first visit, his movements were known in advance, and he guessed that Company representatives had carefully removed any evidence of abuses: 'prisoners were liberated, flogging ceased, and outwardly affairs assumed a peaceful and a humane aspect'. On his second visit, however, he had discovered, hidden in the forest beyond the houses, stocks and whipping posts. It was then that the stories he had picked up in Iquitos began to make sense. He had heard some horrifying accounts which were very similar to the ones that Hardenburg had collected.

In his Foreign Office report, Whiffen produced evidence from John Brown, his guide in the Putumayo and, according to Whiffen, a reliable witness. Brown's account was at least as appalling as the ones reproduced in *Truth*. He related to Whiffen how

> in 1906 or 1907, [two section chiefs] had in custody the Chief of a tribe from the vicinity of Morelia, who was accused of conspiracy against them. After a drunken orgy the man was tied to a tree in the compound. The two section heads proceeded to have a shooting match; the man who excised the Indian's penis by means of a bullet to be declared the winner. The native was afterwards despatched according to the ordinary method.

Whiffen spoke about the system of collecting rubber as 'absolutely that of forced labour with its necessary and attendant evils'. He was particularly struck by the demoralization that he found prevalent among the Hispanic chiefs of the rubber stations, a characteristic 'inseparable from the placing of practically absolute power in the hands of such men'. Whiffen then went on to relate a conversation he had had with Abelardo Agüero, the chief of the Abisinia rubber station.

> Agüero confided to me one day that he did not treat his Indians in the same brutal fashion as was customary amongst other Chiefs of Sections.

If a man refused to work or failed to bring in his quota of rubber, he gave him three chances: the first time he warned him, the second he beat him, and as to the third – well, he took care that the man did not have a fourth chance.

These chilling descriptions fully supported what had appeared in *Truth*. But Whiffen also provided vital information on the standing of the Putumayo with respect to Peruvian interests in the region. He was absolutely certain that the

> territory, some hundreds of square miles in extent, is administered by the Company itself, there being no effective administration or occupation by the Peruvian Government. The Commissario of the Central Government at Lima makes an occasional voyage to the district, returning to Iquitos in the same launch after a few days stay . . . he, together with the few soldiers in the territory, is a secretly paid servant of the Company.

Another piece of information Whiffen provided was that many of the instances of atrocity were actually performed by Indians on Indians, under command of employees of the Company. He explained that the Company would take on (and arm) young Indian men of a tribe hostile to that being dealt with, 'thus putting them perhaps at the mercy of their hereditary enemies', who were also in fear of losing their own lives if they failed to carry out their instructions. Finally, Whiffen told the foreign secretary that he had met Arana in Manaus in June and confronted him with what he had learned in the Putumayo. 'Explaining the situation', Whiffen wrote,

> I received promises from him that the Chief of the Putumayo district, Macedo, should be immediately recalled, and that searching reforms should be inaugurated, together with a complete change of personnel. I have no means of knowing whether these promises have been kept.

Whiffen's report dealt squarely with the allegations of atrocities committed by the Peruvian Amazon Company. It thoroughly supported Hardenburg's assertions. The Foreign Office was able to accept Whiffen's report as true not only because he was an officer and a gentleman – the War Office, too, was prepared to attest to his character. 'He was', they said, 'a sensible kind of fellow . . . what he says is to be credited'. Just the guarantee they could understand and accept.

Full and truthful as Whiffen's report was, it had been about a month since Hart-Davies's parliamentary question, and still the Foreign Office had learned nothing more about the Barbadians – their main concern at this point. Just a few days after the parliamentary questions were asked, the Colonial Office told the Foreign Office that they had no information on the subject from the government of Barbados. This was untrue, as Paternoster himself had discovered, and as Cazes's letter to the Foreign Office made clear. The Foreign Office kept pestering the Colonial Office about what they knew. At the end of October the Earl of Crewe, secretary of state for the colonies, gave in to pressure and telegraphed Governor Carter in Bridgetown asking him straight out 'whether negroes were ill-treated, [and] whether they still work for the Company.'

A day later the Colonial Office had its answer. 'On several occasions', Carter answered in a telegram,

> Barbadians have complained of ill-treatment whilst employed [in] Peru in the service of Arana Hermanos. British Consul Iquitos obtained dismissal of Ramon Sanchez Commercial Agent Putumayo in consequence of complaints received from Barbadians against him. No Barbadians working for Company now, emigrants to Peru have ceased for 3 or 4 years.

If this was true, then the Foreign Office had nothing further to do. The complaints were well in the past. 'It seems that we have at present no grounds of complaint against the Co. a propos of Barbadians so the enquiry is perhaps scarcely necessary', wrote an official.

But then, everything changed. Louis Mallet, an assistant under-secretary of state at the Foreign Office, with over twenty years' experience at the department, conducted an interview with Captain Whiffen on 10 November. Silent about the Barbadians in his written report, Whiffen now presented new facts. First of all, he said, there had been 200 or 300 Barbadians and other British West Indians in the service of the Company when he was in the area, just a year ago. And then he added the most serious charge: 'Some of them', he said,

> are practically slaves as they are in debt to the Company and have to work out their debt in service – others are well paid. They and Peruvian half castes are the slave drivers of the Indians and are used to inflict the punishments described in *Truth*.

This was totally at odds with the information that came from the Colonial Office and from Cazes. The Foreign Office pressed the Colonial Office for more information. They wanted a report from the Governor of Barbados responding to Whiffen's very serious revelations. To move things along, the Foreign Office repeated two other facts it had learned from Whiffen: one, that John Brown, his guide in the Putumayo, could now be contacted in Montserrat; and two, that Whiffen had already written to the governor of Barbados telling him what he knew of the Barbadians and their circumstances.

Despite the urgency, the machinery of colonial government moved sluggishly, and the answers, when they came, were insubstantial. By the end of November, a full month after the interview with Whiffen, all that the Foreign Office had heard from Barbados was what they already knew. The key questions – Were there Barbadians still in the Putumayo? And what were their circumstances? – had still not been answered from within government circles.

Amid the silence, however, the Colonial Office did make the suggestion that 'it is worth considering whether a consular officer should be sent to make inquiries on the spot and that if Sir E. Grey decides to send an officer, it might be well if he could be accompanied by some Barbadian official'. The Colonial Office's suggestion fell on deaf ears at the Foreign Office. Louis Mallet responded in a cool, logical and ultimately dismissive manner: 'It would be useless, *if it were possible*, to send a Consul. He would be allowed to see nothing – the country is almost impassable, and without the goodwill of the Company, it is not possible to live in the Putumayo.' 'Captain Whiffen,' Mallet added, 'laughed at the idea when I suggested it.'

Truth, meanwhile, continued its own campaign against the Peruvian Amazon Company and continued to publish on the subject throughout October and the first half of November.

The main thrust of Paternoster's attack on the Company now was that it was ducking out of the allegations by repeating that it had no responsibility for what might or might not have happened in the past. Paternoster insisted, however, that, at the very least, it had a responsibility for finding out whether the allegations were true. The public, he claimed, demanded it.

There is no evidence to suggest that *Truth* had heard anything from the directors of the Company. While there was silence from the London board, its supporters in Peru weighed in with counter-accusations. One set of these appeared in a letter first printed in the Lima newspaper *El Comercio*, a copy of which came into Paternoster's possession from a shareholder of the Peruvian Amazon Company. Juan Tizon, who identified himself as being closely associated with the Peruvian Amazon Company and having recently been prefect of Loreto, wrote the letter from Iquitos. Hardenburg, he said, was a blackmailer. The truth about Hardenburg, Tizon said, was the following. Along with other engineers, Hardenburg had been working for the Colombian government on a railway project not far from the Putumayo, but had fallen out with his superiors. He had decided to try his luck in Peru, but had got no further than La Unión where, unfortunately, he had become caught up in an attack by Colombians on the launch *Liberal*, with the intent of taking its valuable cargo of rubber. The Peruvian naval vessel *Iquitos*, which happened to be in the area, came to the assistance of the *Liberal* and successfully repulsed the Colombian attack, but in the ensuing confusion Hardenburg became separated from his baggage. Hardenburg had been offered, and had accepted, passage on the *Liberal* on its return trip to Iquitos. Tizon explained that Hardenburg's baggage had most likely been stolen from him during the skirmish by Indians; but Hardenburg, when he got to Iquitos, insisted that Arana's company was responsible for its loss, and demanded compensation to the tune of £7,000. Hardenburg threatened that if he did not receive this money he would

publish a book in which he would depict the imaginary horrors, which, according to him, were being committed in Putumayo. When

I left Iquitos Hardenburg was still there earning a living as a teacher of English, but . . . he has recently left for Europe where he has carried his threat into effect.

In the 27 October 1909 issue of *Truth*, Paternoster repudiated every single statement of Tizon's letter; but engaging in accusation and counter-accusation was not going to help the cause. The directors of the Peruvian Amazon Company had to act – but who could make them?

Meanwhile, Arana had entered the picture. Cazes let Sir Charles Hardinge, the permanent secretary at the Foreign Office, know that Arana had written to him at his private London address, asking him what he had said about how the Barbadians had been treated in the Putumayo. The Foreign Office forbad Cazes to answer him.

Arana's writing to Cazes at his private address suggested an improperly close relationship between them; but that Cazes consulted the Foreign Office about it implied he might be willing to switch sides.

The time had come to review the situation. Near the end of November, Louis Mallet, who had interviewed Whiffen and knew more about the state of affairs in the Putumayo than anyone else in government, undertook to write a memo summarizing what was known about what he was now calling the 'Peruvian Amazon Atrocities'. Because of its high profile, Mallet's memo would direct what the Foreign Office should do next.

The memo captured the dilemma facing the Foreign Office. Mallet felt that the allegations that the Peruvian Amazon Company had horribly abused its Indian labour were essentially true, but he could not see what the British government could do about it. As he put it,

Even if the Company, if gently approached, promised to make reforms, how could we see them carried out? If we were aggressive the Company would register itself in another country. We could not send an expedition to Peru, to this remote and savage spot. We could not ask the Consul at Iquitos to go there – and it would be useless if he did for all trace of cruelty would disappear as he advanced.

'Arana', Mallet continued,

> promised reforms, asked to see Captain Whiffen in Paris a few months ago, and told him that the reforms were progressing and again confirmed this in London a few weeks ago. But Captain Whiffen is convinced that nothing is being done at all and there can be no proof if anything is done.

Mallet also did not doubt Hardenburg's integrity. He had learned from James Bryce, the British ambassador in Washington, that the US government knew about Hardenburg and Perkins's misadventures and their witnessing of the murder and other outrages committed on the Colombians, and had no reason to doubt that the pair were telling the truth. The Peruvian government, he added, had more or less accepted their claims by agreeing to compensate the two men for their losses.

On the basis of everything before him, Mallet recommended that the time had come for the Foreign Office to initiate a more direct approach. He advised that it should take the unprecedented step of writing directly to the Peruvian Amazon Company at its headquarters in the City of London.

'Proceed accordingly', Grey noted in his characteristic bright red ink at the end of Mallet's memo. 'It is a most horrible story.'

7

Our Man in the Putumayo

On 24 November 1909 a letter went to the Secretary of the Peruvian Amazon Company at Salisbury House, London Wall, the Company's registered address in the City of London. The letter began by saying that Sir Edward Grey, after studying independent reports, was fully convinced of the truth of the state of affairs in the Putumayo, as stated in several issues of *Truth*.

There followed a point-by-point indictment of the Company's procedures, including the following facts as they were understood by the Foreign Office: that the Peruvian government's representative and the soldiers in the area were in the Company's pay; that the Indians were compelled to work under a system of forced labour; that the Company employees who directed the Indians were paid by result, not salary; that 'organised tyranny accompanied by gross abuses must almost necessarily ensue when such a system is introduced'; that the instances of 'ill-treatment, rape, mutilation and murder' were true; that the Colombians had been massacred and Serrano brutally murdered; and that Julio César Arana, the owner and one of the directors of the Company, had known what was going on, and was therefore complicit in the atrocities.

The letter ended with a request for assurances from the Company's directors that they had already taken, or were now prepared to take, measures to reform the Company's procedures and administration, including changing its personnel, for, as the letter continued, 'it is clearly highly discreditable, as your Board will doubtless admit, that a British Company should be in any way responsible for the present disgraceful state of affairs, the existence of which there is unfortunately no reason to doubt'.

Two days later, on 26 November 1909, the Peruvian Amazon Company acknowledged the receipt of the Foreign Office's letter, but it would be over a month before they responded in full.

The Foreign Office was now inextricably involved in the Putumayo. It had taken a bold step in writing directly to the Peruvian Amazon Company: this was not something the Foreign Office did lightly. While it waited for an answer, there were some loose ends to tie up.

One of these concerned the United States. On the same day it received the acknowledgement from the Peruvian Amazon Company, it dispatched a letter to James Bryce, the British ambassador in Washington, bringing him up to date on all the events surrounding the Putumayo issue. Included with the letter were copies of several issues of *Truth*, a copy of Whiffen's report, and a copy of the letter to the Peruvian Amazon Company. These inserts were for Bryce's attention, but Bryce was to take one further step – a step that had to be taken very carefully, and whose outcome was by no means a foregone conclusion. Grey wanted Bryce to share these with the State Department, 'to enquire whether the United States Government would in the circumstances be prepared to join with His Majesty's Government in calling the attention of the Peruvian Government to the matter.'

Bryce had been made British ambassador in 1907, during President Theodore Roosevelt's second term, and knew and liked the United States: Charles Hardinge, the permanent under-secretary under Grey, remarked that Bryce knew more about American history and the country's constitution than did most Americans.

At the core of US–Latin American relations lay the Monroe Doctrine, first articulated by the US Congress in 1823. This rationale came directly out of the Latin American wars of independence during the first two decades of the nineteenth century. The United States, itself born of revolution, was the first country to extend diplomatic relations to the newly formed South American republics. As administrations came and went, the interpretation of the Monroe Doctrine changed, but its basic tenets remained the same as far as American policymakers were concerned: to exclude European influence from the continent, and to expand US trade and investment and foster peace and stability in order to do so.

For most of the nineteenth century, the chief concern of the United States was its own continental development, and the Monroe Doctrine remained largely in the background. But as the century drew to a close, the United States, now one of the world's major economies, began to involve itself in the imperial struggle with the great European powers and Japan; at the same time, it embarked on a more aggressive policy towards its Hispanic neighbours.

In December 1904, President Roosevelt articulated an important reassessment of the Monroe Doctrine when he spelled out to Congress what came to be called the Roosevelt Corollary: namely, to add to the authority of the Monroe Doctrine the right of the United States to intervene in Latin America, especially to ward off any growing European interests, and to be able to coerce the republics in case they went astray, in American eyes.

While President William Howard Taft, who had been elected president in 1908 following Roosevelt's two terms in office, adhered to the principle that the United States had a right to intervene in Latin America, he advocated using dollars, in the form of substantial loans to Latin American regimes, rather than bullets, to bring about closer ties. In its ideal form, Taft's dollar diplomacy was an economic rather than a military policy; in practice, US troops were prepared – and sometimes deployed – to shore up tottering regimes.

This, then, was the background to the relationship between Britain and the United States when it came to Latin American affairs. In practice, it meant that Britain would defer to America's overwhelming interest in the region and not do anything to antagonize the country's leaders. As the foreign secretary, Sir Edward Grey, commented on the accommodation between the two countries with regard to the Central American republics: '[they] must succumb to some greater and better influence and it can only be that of the USA'. That same comment could be taken to apply to all of Latin America.

Now, in late 1909, Bryce was being asked by Sir Edward Grey to get the Americans involved in the Peruvian Amazon Company affair. Bryce accordingly wrote to Philander Knox, the secretary of state, on 11 December 1909. The request for the assistance of the American government was gingerly placed within the body of the letter, suggesting that representations to the Peruvian government 'will come with greater force if made jointly by the two Powers whose citizens have been witnesses'. All Bryce could do now was wait for a reply.

Meanwhile, John Cathcart Wason, the Liberal MP who had asked one of the first parliamentary questions about the Putumayo back in late September, now returned to questioning the Foreign Office. He wanted to know what claims were being made against the Peruvian Amazon Company with regard to their ill-treatment of the Barbadian workers.

Mallet confirmed that complaints of Barbadians being ill-treated had reached the Colonial Office in the past; but no current claims, to his knowledge, were being made against the Company. Mallet also had more information about the scale of the Barbadian presence in the Putumayo. Between September 1904 and June 1905, over 200 Barbadian men had been recruited to work in the Putumayo on two-year contracts, and a certain Abel Alarco, an agent of Arana's company, had seen to all of the arrangements. As to the present situation, Mallet could add nothing. The Colonial Office had still not established whether any Barbadians remained in the area working for Arana.

At about this time, the Foreign Office was told by Travers Buxton, the secretary of the Anti-Slavery and Aborigines' Protection Society, that his organization had been disturbed by the articles in *Truth* narrating 'the systematically cruel treatment of native Indians employed by the Peruvian Amazon Company', and that they had been writing to the Company since early October asking for the directors to receive a small delegation from the society, which wished to discuss the allegations and ask for a full investigation of them. So far, the Company had not agreed to a meeting.

The Foreign Office viewed the Society's involvement as problematic. 'It is very tiresome', Mallet wrote to his colleagues, 'that this society should interfere and we must be careful not to be dragged into another Congo affair and not to be forced into a hostile attitude to Peru.' By this Mallet meant that, when it came to Latin America, the British government had to move cautiously and always with the full support of the American government. He warned his colleagues that the Foreign Office must not let itself be pressured by the Anti-Slavery and Aborigines' Protection Society to act impulsively.

While the Foreign Office's deliberations on whom to contact for corroborative information were kept firmly within the department's four walls, the Anti-Slavery and Aborigines' Protection Society had been keeping the issue in the public eye by informing leading British newspapers such as *The Times* and the *Manchester Guardian* of their own dealings with the Peruvian Amazon Company.

The Peruvian Amazon Company replied to the Foreign Office by letter on 30 December 1909. The directors of the Company, it said, had known nothing of the allegations until they read them in *Truth*; if such atrocities had taken place, they happened before the board was constituted, and the directors could not be held responsible for past events; Hardenburg and Whiffen were, in any event, blackmailers, and their statements were consequently worthless. The letter denied all the other allegations that were printed, including the crucial one that the Indians were made to work under a system of forced labour.

Included in the Company's letter was a printed circular addressed to its shareholders and signed by Julio César Arana. He categorically denied that any atrocities had occurred, and turned the burden of proof onto *Truth*, which had described, in his words, 'deeds so vile that it seems incredible that such an important newspaper should have given them prominence without a fuller inquiry'. In support of this, Arana made the following pledge:

> I absolutely deny that lawlessness has of late existed in the Putumayo Region, for neither the Peruvian Authorities, who efficiently fulfil their duties of maintaining order and administering justice, nor I myself would have allowed such a state of things to exist.

Arana then launched into an attack on Hardenburg, accusing him of blackmail, citing in evidence a telegram from Arana's lawyer in Iquitos, which spoke of Hardenburg demanding £7,000 to stop him from publishing in London a 'defamatory book against the firm in the Putumayo'. Arana continued this line of argument by informing his shareholders that Captain Whiffen, too, had sought to blackmail him. He described how, in early October, after returning home from his travels in the Putumayo, he had met Captain Whiffen in Paris, where Whiffen had told him that he had been contacted by *Truth* for a statement about the allegations, which he knew to be false, and would be saying so. Knowing that Arana was on his way to London, Whiffen told him to meet him there, at his club. After dining at the Café Royal, the pair went on to the Alhambra music hall in Leicester Square, before adjourning to the Royal Automobile Club in Pall Mall. There, recounted Arana, Whiffen demanded the sum of £1,000 to tell *Truth* what Arana wanted told. Arana said that he took the offer to the board, which promptly refused to accede to Whiffen's proposal. The following day Whiffen called on Arana at his hotel, hoping for money. When it was not forthcoming, Whiffen prepared that 'most untruthful report' for the Foreign Office.

The rest of the circular lauded the Company's achievements, assuring its shareholders that everything had been and was being done to ensure that the agents and employees of the Company behaved properly. It ended on a very upbeat note:

> I can only assure the Shareholders that . . . every care will be taken so that [the management] may be conducted . . . in such a manner that they will be proud to be connected with this great enterprise, which is at present passing through initial difficulties, but for which a most satisfactory and brilliant future can safely be predicted.

Once the Company's letter and Arana's circular had been passed around the department for comment, Mallet again took charge of how the Foreign Office should handle its response. There was no point, he argued, in going over the same ground as before, because the Company would simply answer with counter-accusations, including charges of blackmail against Hardenburg and Whiffen. Both *Truth* and, through its members, the Anti-Slavery and Aborigines' Protection Society, had ensured that the public wanted answers, not counter-accusations. What was needed, Mallet urged, was to insist that the board find out what was going on in the Putumayo, to

> satisfy public opinion in this country by instituting a thorough and impartial investigation into the state of affairs . . . with the object of devising a system of reforms in the administration which will put a stop to the present abuses and prevent their recurrence in the future.

He recommended that the Foreign Office suggest to the Company that they should dispatch an impartial commission, which would carry out the required investigation.

Sir Edward Grey agreed to this approach. Mallet was now also thinking of attaching a British consular official to the proposed commission but, according to him, the time was not yet ripe to suggest that to the Company. On 8 February 1910, the Foreign Office wrote to the Peruvian Amazon Company suggesting the way forward. If the Company was still 'obdurate', as the Foreign Office put it, then it would call in Sir John Lister-Kaye, one of the Company's directors, for a chat.

The rest of February passed with only silence from the Company. Little, indeed, was progressing in the Putumayo story in London, apart from a further communication from the Colonial Office, which finally came up with an exact figure – 196 – for the number of Barbadians who had emigrated to Peru to work for Arana. This was a useful piece of information, but the more important question of whether any Barbadians were still in the Putumayo remained unanswered.

And then, on 8 March 1910, that issue was put smartly aside when a letter arrived at the Foreign Office from the Peruvian Amazon Company. The Company had a new secretary, Henry Gielgud, who had previously worked for the accounting firm of Deloitte, Plender, Griffiths & Co. He had spent late May, June and July 1909 in the Putumayo auditing the Company's books and visiting rubber stations around La Chorrera and El Encanto. When he returned to England, he made a report to the board on 24 November 1909 of his visit to its Putumayo properties, which, according to the Company's then secretary, was highly complimentary. Conditions there were described as excellent. From the Company's point of view, therefore, he was an excellent choice for secretary: he had been to the Putumayo and would toe the Company line.

Orme Garton Sargent, one of the Foreign Office's junior clerks, was the first to react to the letter:

> The tone of the letter is somewhat truculent and does not hold out much prospect of the Co. being ready to listen to reason. They bring forward no new facts but merely deny once more in toto the allegations basing themselves on Arana's statement enclosed in their previous letter and on the Peruvian Chargé d'Affaires' letter to *Truth*.

He advised that nothing could now be gained by going over the same ground again, and that the Foreign Office should answer the letter by repeating that the Company should undertake an investigation on the spot to find out who was right – Hardenburg and Whiffen, or Arana.

Louis Mallet agreed wholeheartedly with Sargent's analysis, but felt that a more psychological approach at this point might be better. The response should simply say that the Company's letter made it perfectly clear that they had no intention of investigating the allegations, and leave it at that. Mallet, as usual, got his way, and with approval from Grey, a letter conveying this short, abrupt point was sent on 31 March to the Company's headquarters.

A fortnight earlier, an unexpected letter had arrived at the Foreign Office by way of the Colonial Office. It was from Montserrat, and it contained a statement by John Brown, Captain Whiffen's guide during his visit to the Putumayo.

Brown's statement went straight to the point: 'I will tell you everything I know about the ill-treatment of the English subjects who live in Peru.' He continued:

> They beat us with swords, they put us in guns [hands tied across knees with guns underneath knees], and did us all manner of wickedness. We cried for help but there was none. We tried to escape, but there was no means of doing so – only one small steamer which belonged to the same company and they would not take us away. They still continued beating and ill-treating us English subjects, and they treated the Indians in the same way. The cruelties practised in that place are shameful. They [the Spaniards] would take a man, tie his hands together behind his back with chains and hang him up, and then beat him with sticks or swords.'

Brown recounted that he had arrived in the Putumayo in April 1905 in a party of fifty West Indians, most of them from Barbados. Though their contracts ran for only two years, they found it impossible to leave after their time had expired. The West Indians were hired, he said, to go into the forest to look for Indians and kill them. If they refused, they were beaten.

Brown had managed to escape from the Putumayo in June 1908 by the Company launch, on the grounds that he wanted to remit money home from Iquitos. It was then that he had met Captain Whiffen and told him all that he had seen in the Putumayo. He then accepted Whiffen's invitation to join him on the expedition to the Putumayo to search for Robuchon. Brown also said that he had told Cazes about the cases of ill-treatment, but nothing had come of it. Indeed, Brown was convinced that Cazes 'seemed to me to be in league with the Peruvians'. The statement ended with a plea: 'The other British subjects cannot get out, they are slaves. They are in need of help and there is no help they can get.'

The Foreign Office now had its first real confirmation that Barbadians had still been working for the Company in the Putumayo in 1908. Yet prejudices at the Foreign Office almost dismissed Brown's testimony, when Sir Charles Hardinge, the permanent under-secretary, cast doubt on the reliability of the evidence, arguing that the writer would have needed a diary of events in order to recall dates and names so precisely – the implication being that black people kept no such records.

Armed with John Brown's supporting statement, the Foreign Office was more certain than ever that Barbadians were still working for Arana, and that the abuses were continuing. The presence of the Barbadians in the Putumayo was the Foreign Office's only entry point into a matter which, politically, was predominantly a Peruvian one. Only a British consul and an official of the Barbadian government, who could talk directly to the Barbadians, could assess once and for all whether the abusive system persisted. At the same time, the Foreign Office wanted to involve the Peruvian government, but needed American support to do so – on that it was still waiting to hear from the American administration whether it was willing to make a joint representation with the British.

On 11 April 1910, in Washington, James Bryce indicated that the United States would probably not be going along with Britain, certainly not at this time. Though he had still not heard officially from the secretary of state, Bryce had learned that the American government was trying to broker a deal between Ecuador and Peru concerning their border disputes, and that pursuing the Peruvian Amazon Company case would endanger these talks.

Bryce was right. After having argued over their borders since independence more than eighty years earlier, Ecuador and Peru had finally agreed to let the king of Spain arbitrate their cases. The king's decision was due in June 1909, but when the Ecuadorians learned by way of a leak that it was not going to be favourable to them, they withdrew completely from the negotiations and put their country on a war footing. The Peruvians responded in like manner. In both countries, nationalistic demonstrations were held and hostile public opinion was stoked. By April 1910, with thousands of troops amassed on both sides, war seemed inevitable. The US secretary of state, Philander Knox, who had previously proposed US arbitration between the two countries, sought the help of Brazil and Argentina to get Peru and Ecuador to the negotiating table.

According to Bryce, Knox's hands were tied: the moment was far too sensitive for him to approach the Peruvians on any matter other than their dispute with the Ecuadorians; even answering Bryce's letter might be construed as implicit agreement with the British position. Although it had no official confirmation of this from Knox, the Foreign Office was not hopeful.

Away from Whitehall, the Anti-Slavery and Aborigines' Protection Society was upping the pressure on both the government and the Company. The Foreign Office received a string of letters from the Society pushing it for an answer from the Company, and insisting that the Company send a commission to the Putumayo with a British consul attached. The Society also reminded the Foreign Office that

> in many of its features the system of enforced rubber collection closely resembles that of the Congo State; moreover, [we do] not hesitate to say that nothing reported from the Congo has equalled in horror some of the acts alleged in detail against this rubber Syndicate. The nature of the evidence is indeed too revolting to permit of full publicity . . .

As if this were not enough, the Society also (and to the annoyance of the Foreign Office) coordinated a petition among its affiliated, mostly Christian, organizations demanding of the Foreign Office that 'British representatives should be appointed on such a commission, and that in any enquiry which may be held a British Official should be present during the proceedings to watch British interests'. The Society also passed to the press its correspondence with the Foreign Office, and reprinted these letters in its own magazine, the *Anti-Slavery Reporter and Aborigines' Friend*. The Society also sent a stream of letters to the Peruvian Amazon Company itself, reminding it of the serious allegations of cruelty and worse in the Putumayo.

There was further pressure on the government in parliament, where questions continued to be asked about the Peruvian Amazon Company. British MPs kept the Putumayo issue in the public eye while pressing the government for action.

It was to be a combination of the Society's efforts and a groundswell of public opinion through parliament, more than the Foreign Office, that forced the Peruvian Amazon Company to bow to an investigation. On 8 June 1910, the Company wrote to the Foreign Office informing it that the Company was arranging for a commission of investigation to go to the Putumayo 'to report on the possibilities of commercial development of the properties of the Company and also to enquire into the present relations between the native employees and the Agents of the Company'. Henry Gielgud, the Company secretary, would be one of its members, as would Colonel Reginald Bertie of the Royal Welsh Fusiliers. Bertie was known to the Foreign Office as the younger brother of Sir Francis Bertie, the British ambassador in Paris. The Foreign Office hoped that Colonel Bertie would be impartial, but they were not sure that he had no connection with the Company. Other members had yet to be appointed.

Junior Clerk Orme Sargent welcomed the Company's positive attitude. 'They have I suppose at length realised that they had better take some action with a view to vindicating themselves in the eye of the British public.' We can only imagine what conversations took place around the board table as they discussed the Foreign Office's recommendations. The directors probably decided that holding out against public opinion could hurt the Company more than giving in. Making a stand against the Foreign Office might antagonize the Company's shareholders, who would dislike the publicity. At least one of the directors, Sir John Lister-Kaye – whose identity had so far not been made public – would not have wanted to draw attention to himself, as his several directorships in the City depended on his good name.

The Company agreed to send a commission. It was a big step forward, and the moment had come to persuade the Company to allow government officials to accompany the Commission. Parliamentary questions and letters from the Anti-Slavery and Aborigines' Protection Society to the Foreign Office ensured that the pressure was not relaxed. In mid-June, Sir Edward Grey announced to the House of Commons that he was going to suggest to the Company that a consul and a Barbadian official should accompany the Commission.

A week later, though, came the disappointing confirmation from Washington that Knox and the State Department were indeed too involved in the border dispute between Peru and Ecuador to make a case of the serious allegations made against the Peruvian Amazon Company. The State Department was happy to let the British government proceed with its own investigation, since the Company was British.

This was a setback, for sure, but better news was on its way. On 13 July 1910, the Peruvian Amazon Company stated that it had no objection to Grey's suggestion of attaching government officials to the Commission – so long as the Peruvian government agreed to the idea. The Commission's composition, the Company announced, was now set. Gielgud and Bertie would be going as planned, and they would be joined by three others: Walter Fox, a botanist with a special interest in rubber trees, and one-time superintendent of the botanic gardens in Penang, British Malaya; Louis Barnes, a former tropical farmer with experience in sugar plantations in South America and Africa; and Seymour Bell, a merchant. The Commission, the Company reiterated, would be looking only into current conditions, and would not enquire into past relations between the Indians and the agents of the Company. Arana repeated this in a letter he wrote to Cazes on 25 July. The Commission had only a commercial purpose; investigating 'crimes said to have been committed in the past years' was the business of the Peruvian government alone. It was Sir Edward Grey, Arana noted, who was calling it a 'Commission of Investigation' only to satisfy those MPS who continued to ask questions in the House of Commons. Colonel Bertie confirmed the specific, limited nature of the Company's Commission in an interview with the Foreign Office.

A few days later came word from Lima that the Peruvian government had no objection to a British consul visiting the Putumayo. The Company, though, had the upper hand. The Putumayo properties were closed to the outside world – access was only possible on Company launches; and the Company's agents would be able to stage-manage the investigation and expose only the benign side of the operations to outside eyes. Whiffen had experienced this. As to having a consul attached, the directors were probably hoping for someone in the Cazes mould, who would be vulnerable to the Company's influence.

Several names of likely consular candidates had already been suggested in the Foreign Office. One was Lucien Jerome, the British chargé d'affaires in Callao, Lima's port city, who was then temporarily running the consulate in La Paz, Bolivia. A preferred alternative was the permanent British consul in La Paz, Cecil Gosling, who was on leave in England at the time. While these names were being discussed, however, full diplomatic relations between Bolivia and Britain, which had been suspended fifty years earlier, were restored. Gosling returned to La Paz and Jerome to Callao. David Cazes had already ruled himself out because of his close ties with Arana. No other names seem to have surfaced. The idea of sending a Barbadian official was dropped because the Barbadian legislature was unwilling to cover the costs.

Behind the scenes, however, the Anti-Slavery and Aborigines' Protection Society continued to influence events, and worked strenuously to ensure that their candidate for impartial observer was chosen. After several meetings with Sir Edward Grey, beginning in early June, they got their way. The Society's preferred candidate was none other than Roger Casement, whose report on conditions in the rubber-growing area of the Congo Free State had been instrumental in bringing Leopold's evil regime to an end.

If the Peruvian Amazon Company thought it would be able to hoodwink the Foreign Office's appointment to the Commission, they could not have been more mistaken. This was no David Cazes. Roger Casement was the most experienced and most widely lauded investigator of human rights abuses of his day. He was an absolutely committed humanitarian, and would stop at nothing to get to the truth.

8

Eyes of Another Race

In late June 1905, Roger Casement was awarded the Companion of Saint Michael and Saint George for his work in the Congo – an order reserved for those who had distinguished themselves in Britain's foreign service. On two occasions, however, Casement avoided presenting himself at Buckingham Palace, on the grounds of ill-health. He wanted to turn the award down, but his friends convinced him that it would be unwise to burn his bridges at this point. Reluctantly, he accepted their advice. He was torn between being an Irish nationalist and a servant of the British state. He feared that his award would be frowned upon in Ireland. In a sign of things to come, Casement explained in a letter to Edward Clarke, an assistant clerk at the Foreign Office: 'You know I am a confirmed Home Ruler . . . and I shall now be regarded askance in every respectable quarter of Ireland.'

Wherever he went and whomever he met, Roger Casement rarely failed to make a deep, lasting and highly favourable impression. Edmund Morel, who spearheaded the Congo Reform Association and became a very close friend, described Casement, then aged thirty-nine, at their first encounter in late 1903 only days after arriving in London from the Congo:

> It was one of those rare incidents in life which leave behind them an imperishable impression. I saw before me a man, my own height, very lithe and sinewy, chest thrown out, head held high – black hair and beard covering cheeks hollowed by the tropical sun. Strongly marked features. A dark blue penetrating eye sunken in the socket. A long lean, swarthy Vandyke type of face, graven with power and withal of great gentleness. An extraordinarily handsome and arresting face.

The politician and writer Stephen Gwynn, who was Casement's exact contemporary, provided a very similar picture of the man when they were both attending a Gaelic festival in County Antrim (now in Northern Ireland), in June 1904. 'Knight errant he was; clear-sighted, cool-headed, knowing as well as any that ever lived how to strengthen his case by temperate statement, yet always charged with passion.' Behind those fine, unforgettable looks was also a rare speaking voice: 'Casement doesn't talk to you – He purrs at you', said a consular colleague.

Despite the praise he had received from the government and the public, Casement had become uncertain whether he was really cut out for the consular service. His relationship with the Foreign Office had become strained over his Congo report. Though it had been published promptly, the decision was taken that the report would omit all personal names and even place-names, substituting instead letters and symbols, arguing that it was the system and not individuals that was on trial. Casement was furious, but his protests fell on deaf ears. He even thought of resigning from the consular service in protest. He went on leave without pay instead.

By mid-1905, Casement was in financial trouble. Whatever he felt about his superiors in the Foreign Office, he had to get paid work in the consular service. He began to search for a position in September of that year, by writing directly to the foreign secretary, Lord Lansdowne.

For many months Casement received no reply. He was getting desperate. 'My plans are not of my own making', he wrote in March 1906 to his cousin Gertrude, 'and my movements do not altogether depend on my own wishes'. And so it dragged on until, finally, at the end of July, Casement heard that he was about to be offered a post. Bilbao was indicated initially, but when the offer came it had been changed to the Brazilian town of Santos, São Paulo's port.

Casement arrived in Santos on 9 October 1906. He hated it as soon as he landed. By late June 1907 he was back in London and once more considering leaving the service for good, turning down a posting in East Africa. Continuing to vacillate over his Foreign Office career, Casement learned that a vacancy had opened in Haiti and that the job was his from the end of December. He was interested, but when he visited the Foreign Office in November the offer had mysteriously metamorphosed into another Brazilian posting, this time at the Amazonian port of Pará (present-day Belem).

Casement hemmed and hawed, but the Foreign Office was firm: it was Pará or nothing. And so, once again, Casement packed his bags to cross the Atlantic to Brazil. While he knew little of Santos before he got there, Pará was another matter: the previous consul, William Algernon Churchill, had stayed for almost ten years, and had already briefed him on what he should expect. The city was large, with a population exceeding 120,000 people; the rainy season, lasting from January to June, was very disagreeable; and the cost of living was very high. On the other hand, there was little to do – only writing and sending trade reports back to London.

Casement left England on 18 January 1908, and travelled to Paris to visit friends. He then headed north to Le Havre, where he boarded the Booth steamer RMS *Anselm* for Madeira, and then spent a couple weeks on the island before boarding SS *Clement*, another Booth steamer, bound for Pará.

By coincidence, travelling to Pará on the same steamer was Julio César Arana, who was returning to Iquitos following the temporary suspension of his company's flotation in London. Exchanging pleasantries at the captain's table as they crossed the Atlantic, the Peruvian and the Irishman, each in his own way highly distinguished looking, had no inkling that in eighteen months time one would be exposing the atrocities perpetrated by the other.

Disembarking at Pará on 21 February, Casement took formal charge of the consulate on 1 March. No sooner had he done so than he started complaining to Lord Dufferin, a clerk at the Foreign Office, about the state of his office – especially the cavalier treatment of its confidential archives, the fact that prostitutes were using the building to solicit business, and the extortionate cost of living. Not for the first time, he threatened to resign.

Casement could not shake off his dislike of Pará. In late April and early May, he left the city to travel up the Amazon to Manaus as a guest of the Booths, who owned and ran most of the steamships on the river, including those to Iquitos; from Manaus he went to the building site that was the Madeira–Mamoré railway. In July he fell ill and went to Barbados to recuperate, but it afforded him only a temporary respite. In early November he wrote to the British chargé d'affaires in Brazil that he had had enough: 'The Doctor', he wrote,

> says I must get away or I shall break down . . . I presume F.O. will permit me to go away – or I fear a complete breakdown here. The place is not fit for a dog – & to be losing a great deal of money as well as one's strength and health is not good enough . . . It is a loathsome place – and people.

On 4 December he was in Liverpool, just off the boat from Pará and on his way to Dublin: 'I am much better for getting away', he commented with relief to Morel.

He may have hated Brazil, but he could not escape for long. Shortly after arriving back in England he learned that he had a new posting and a promotion. He had been selected to be the British consul-general in Rio de Janeiro. He accepted immediately: it was the most senior post he had ever been offered and, for the moment at least, his misgivings and criticisms of the Foreign Office were put aside.

Casement extended his leave of absence as long as he could, but by early March he was on his way to Rio, officially taking charge of the consulate on 22 March 1909. Predictably enough, he hated Rio too, as he kept telling Morel on every occasion that offered itself. After five months' residence, it was already a 'long nightmare'. His reaction to Rio was the same as it had been to Pará. The only saving grace about Rio was that he was in a senior position, and that he spent a great deal of time in Petropolis, forty miles directly north of Rio – originally the summer residence of the Brazilian emperors, but now the home of the foreign diplomatic corps.

Casement's lively correspondence with Edmund Morel gives us a rare glimpse into his unfolding political consciousness – something that he naturally withheld from his superiors at the Foreign Office; indeed, the Foreign Office – and in particular the foreign secretary, Sir Edward Grey – was a particular target of Casement's invective. Casement was robust in his criticism. As far as he was concerned, Grey was a failure. He was duplicitous, saying one thing and doing another; he was weak and without policy; and he was mistaken in his choice of friends and foes, particularly in siding with the French over the Germans. Casement cited Grey's treatment of Ireland; his inaction over the Congo; his part in the Denshawai massacre in Egypt of 1906; and his abandonment of Dinuzulu, the Zulu chief who was tried for treason in 1908 (he protested his innocence, and was released after two years in prison to live out the rest of his life on a farm in the Transvaal). Although Grey was the specific target of his ire, Casement was contemptuous of the Foreign Office in general, saying on one occasion: 'If the F.O. were to blow up tomorrow, save for the loss of historic records, it would be a great blessing for the country to be left for six months without such an institution'.

Casement also had contempt for Americans, and particularly for Teddy Roosevelt, whom he also thought duplicitous. When Roosevelt told the British, in his famous Guildhall speech of May, either to rule Egypt or get out, Casement had had enough. 'It is impudent in the extreme for this man to go round Europe haranguing people on their duties to civilization when his own country presents one of the most lawless aspects of modern life the whole world affords.' When Morel tried to tell Casement that England and the United States were the two 'great humanitarian powers', Casement responded by saying, 'England more than America perhaps – but both are materialistic first and humanitarian only a century after.'

Not surprisingly, given that these letters were written to Morel, the Congo was still the main topic under discussion. In a revealing passage, Casement seemed to accept African colonialism as a fait accompli, but for Africans, he argued, it had come with a terrible price. 'What has civilization itself been to them?' he asked Morel rhetorically, 'A thing of horror – of smoking rifles and pillaged homes – of murdered fathers, violated mothers and enslaved children.' The solution to the continent's troubles could only come by the European powers including Africans as partners in a humane political process – 'the stream of gentler humanity', as he put it.

Though most of their correspondence concerned the Congo, Casement began to talk increasingly about Ireland and his own sense of Irishness. In April 1907 Casement had revealed to his friend and colleague, the political activist and intellectual Alice Stopford Green, that it was during the time he was investigating Leopold's evil-doing that he had first confronted his own sense of being Irish. 'When up in those lonely Congo forests where I found Leopold – I found also myself – the incorrigible Irishman', he wrote. It was then that he had understood clearly that he was not only witnessing gross abuses of humanity, but also seeing the plight of the Congolese through the eyes of a people, the Irish, who had suffered similarly under British rule. 'I realized then', he explained,

> that I was looking at this tragedy with the eyes of another race – of a people once hunted themselves, whose hearts were based on affection as the root principle of contact with their fellow men and whose estimate of life was not of something eternally to be appraised at its market 'price'.

He admitted that, before seeing conditions in the Congo, he had convinced himself that imperialism was good:

> British rule was to be extended at all costs, because it was the best for everyone under the sun, and those who opposed that extension ought rightly to be 'smashed'. I was on the high road to being a regular Imperialist jingo.

He was now over that phase of his life. He ended the letter to Alice Stopford Green with the following prophetic words: 'And I said to myself then, far up the Lulanga river, that I would do my part as an Irishman, wherever it might lead me personally.'

Now, at the end of June 1909, writing to Morel from Brazil, his attitude to British rule in Ireland had hardened further.

> It is not British honour appeals to me so much as Congo men and women. British honour, so far as I am concerned, disappeared from our horizon in Ireland more than a century ago – and I am chiefly concerned in endeavouring to recover our own Irish honour.

Casement gave whatever money he could spare to Irish causes, such as the Irish Language Colleges in Cork, and promised financial support for several publications. Ireland consumed his mind as it did his bank balance. He knew, however, that power was not in the hands of the politicians who held public office. Whether he was beginning to think about a militant form of Irish nationalism is not clear, but he knew that any struggle would be hard. The world was not as it seemed. 'Our

rulers', he reminded Morel, 'are not necessarily a few cabinet ministers
– but the great financial, territorial, commercial and a host of other
interests . . . great, greedy strongholds of worldwide power'.

After almost a year in Rio, Casement requested and was granted
leave of absence. On 1 March 1910 he left Rio and headed to Buenos
Aires. Three weeks later he was in Bahia, from where he crossed the
Atlantic back to Europe, eventually landing in Liverpool on 1 May. As it
turned out, while he would never return to Rio, he was still not entirely
done with Brazil.

The first half of May he spent in London, before leaving for Dublin
and Belfast. He then headed towards the Casement family seat of
Magherintemple, Ballycastle, in County Antrim. For two weeks,
Casement busied himself with family social occasions. But on 17 June
a letter arrived for him that brought the festivities to a halt. Casement's
life was about to take a new turn.

The letter was from Reverend John Harris at the Anti-Slavery and
Aborigines' Protection Society in London. Harris had been speaking
to the Foreign Office for a few weeks about whom to send to the
Putumayo, and Harris's letter to Casement told him unofficially that Sir
Edward Grey had agreed that he should be the choice. Harris wanted
to see him at the Society's offices in London, and he also wanted him
to meet several MPs who were eager to talk to him about the Putumayo.
At once Casement wired back to say that he would be in London in a
week's time.

On 23 June he met both Harris and Travers Buxton, the secretary,
at the offices of the Society. After they had shared their Putumayo
material with him, Casement went to the House of Commons, where he
met several MPs, including Sir Charles Dilke, the veteran of the Congo
episode; and Noel Buxton and Josiah Wedgwood, both of whom had
long anti-slavery associations.

The next three weeks were taken up with meetings and social events
in London, and Casement saw Edmund Morel, Arthur Conan Doyle
– whom he had met a few years earlier – and Alice Stopford Green,
among others. On 13 July, the day that the Foreign Office learned
that the Peruvian Amazon Company had agreed to a consular official
accompanying the Commission, Casement called on William Tyrrell,

Sir Edward Grey's private secretary, who told him that he would be going to the Putumayo. Casement was then sent to Grey's office for a private meeting.

During their meeting that day, Casement and Grey spoke about the difficulties that lay ahead. They both agreed that arriving 'at a wholly independent opinion of the facts connected with the recent charges against the Company's officials' would not be easy, but Grey was not dictating how Casement should go about his work. Casement's official brief was to look at allegations of ill-treatment of British subjects by a British company – a legitimate issue for a British official to investigate on foreign soil. And that is what was publicly said about Casement's functions. Privately, though, Grey told Casement that he should find out 'the facts connected with the general rubber regime in the country visited', but that he should do so as discreetly as possible. Other than that, Casement was given carte blanche, including freedom of travel to the Putumayo by some other means than with the Commission, should the opportunity present itself.

The departure of the Peruvian Amazon Company Commission was imminent. Casement spent the preceding week in a frenzy of activity: two days at the Foreign Office poring over documents; dinners with family members and friends; a quick trip to Ireland; another day at the Foreign Office; meetings at the House of Commons. On Saturday, 23 July, he boarded a train for Southampton. The sailing of the *Edinburgh Castle* for Madeira was scheduled for later that day.

What was going through Casement's mind as he boarded the *Edinburgh Castle*? When Harris contacted him in Ballycastle, Casement jumped at the chance. It was as though he had been waiting for this moment; as he once put it to Morel concerning Leopold, he was a 'tiger who knew . . . where to sniff his prey'. He clearly relished the possibility of repeating his Congo success: he had already tackled one of the greatest rivers in the world to reveal horrendous atrocities; now he had the chance to travel up another of the world's great rivers to expose more horrors. Even before Harris's letter, Casement knew something of what had been going on in the Putumayo. He had read the early issues of *Truth* when in Rio de Janeiro. He had, moreover, alerted the Foreign Office to trouble in the Putumayo between Peruvians and Colombians in June 1908, just a few months after he had taken charge of the Pará consulate. On that occasion, an article had appeared in *A Provincia do Pará*, the city's leading daily, with the headline 'Bloody Violent Crime: Horrible Atrocities'. The article accused the Peruvian Amazon Rubber Company of the attack on the Colombians (and Serrano's horrible murder) at La Unión and La Reserva. At about the same time, Casement received a visit from Captain R.G. Williamson of the *Clement*, which had brought him and Arana to Pará a few months earlier. Williamson told Casement then that he, too, had heard about trouble in the Upper Amazon, and in particular in the Putumayo, the property of Julio César Arana. Casement later recalled that he had no authority to investigate and report on the trouble, since it was not in his consular jurisdiction.

For diplomatic reasons, Casement was confined to investigating the condition of the Barbadians he hoped to meet in the Putumayo. The Indians – the real witnesses and victims – were probably beyond his reach, but Casement must have been wondering how he might get closer to them. As he made his way to Madeira on the first leg of his voyage, Casement had plenty of time to reflect on these past events and on how he was going to get to the bottom of the allegations. His Congo experience would come in very handy. Casement and the Commission members arrived in Madeira on 27 July. Four days later they were all aboard SS *Hilary*, of the Booth Steamship Lines, heading across the Atlantic for Pará.

Casement knew that he had been given a tough assignment. He was surrounded by a group of men who had a very different agenda to his. They were going to make an assessment of the current commercial situation in the Putumayo and make recommendations for further improvement – theirs was an economic and financial mission.

Casement was obliged to travel as a guest of the Commission ('From start to finish I shall be doing everything "by your leave"') not only because those were the terms of his engagement, but also because it was impossible to reach Arana's territory without using one of the Company's launches. It was a closed shop. Worse still, he was not convinced that much would come of the investigation. 'We shall be fairly well hood-winked', he confided to Morel.

Casement had learned that the Commission members knew little of the charges that had been made in London against the Company.

Casement did all he could to inform them of these issues. Before he left England, Casement was shown all the material that both the Foreign Office and the Anti-Slavery and Aborigines' Protection Society had amassed. Among it was Hardenburg's book manuscript, which included the affidavits he had collected in Iquitos testifying to Arana's violent regime. Casement took a typed copy of this document with him. Four other books – Henry Bates's *The Naturalist on the River Amazon*, Alfred Wallace's *Narrative of Travels on the Amazon and Rio Negro*, William Herndon and Lardner Gibbon's *Exploration of the Valley of the Amazon* and Reginald Enock's *The Andes and the Amazon* – would provide him with rich descriptions of the region. But most important of all was his copy of Eugène Robuchon's posthumously published travel account, *En el Putumayo y sus afluentes*, edited and translated by Arana's close friend and the Peruvian consul in Manaus, Carlos Rey de Castro, and hurriedly published in Lima in 1907, with the words 'Edición Oficial' ('Official Publication') emblazoned on the cover page, in time for the planned flotation in London of the Peruvian Amazon Rubber Company. Under his careful (and selective) editing of Robuchon's journal, Rey de Castro succeeded in portraying the Company as a civilizing force, changing the Indians from their 'wild and cannibalistic primitive state to useful commercial subjects'. Because Arana intended to use Robuchon's account as the Company's prospectus, the book contained information that appeared nowhere else: it contained a detailed description, including many photographs and a map, of the area he was going to visit, and a full list of the rubber stations and the names of their managers.

Casement showed the Commission members both Hardenburg's manuscript and Robuchon's book, so that they would have some context for understanding the testimonials he was hoping to collect, and that they were going to hear.

They arrived in Pará on 8 August. Casement found the city unchanged, and could not wait to leave. But the *Hilary* remained in the port for four days, during which Casement spent time with both the British and American consuls. On 13 August the ship was ready to depart for its next and final port of call – Manaus.

A day before they were due to dock, Casement learned that Colonel Bertie, the Commission's leader, had been advised by the ship's doctor that proceeding any further up the Amazon would be detrimental to his health, and that he should return home. Though Casement was aware in Pará that Bertie had not been feeling well, it came as a blow that he would be abandoning the trip. Bertie, Casement believed, would have provided the kind of objective, impartial leadership that the Commission needed; when the Foreign Office learned of Bertie's return, they, too, shared Casement's dismay. The new leader would be Louis Barnes, the Commission's expert on tropical agriculture and the member with the most extensive experience of working in primary production.

On arrival in Manaus on 16 August, the Commission and Casement went their separate ways upriver to Iquitos. The Commission boarded the *Urimaguas*, a Peruvian Amazon Company launch, and Casement, wishing to rely as little as possible on the Company's hospitality (following the strategy he had adopted in the Congo), continued his journey aboard the *Huayna*, a smaller ship belonging to the Booth line. Casement hated Manaus, and the intense heat certainly didn't help. As for his floating home for the next several days, it was, he wrote irritably, a 'beastly ship'.

Leaving Manaus on 17 August, the *Huayna* passed the mouth of the Putumayo River six days later, and the mosquito-infested waters became shallower and murkier. The going was tough and erratic, with lots of time at anchor. He expected the *Urimaguas* to have caught up with his boat by now, but there was no sign of it. Later, after what seemed agonizingly slow progress, the *Huayna* reached the Brazilian–Peruvian border, completing formalities first in Tabatinga and then in Leticia, the first Peruvian settlement on the Amazon (it is now in Colombia). Restless at the little ship's lack of progress, Casement found some comfort in conversation with the captain who, on one occasion, confirmed somewhat matter-of-factly that Indians were the victims of forced labour, and that their children were sold into slavery in Iquitos and elsewhere further up the Amazon.

Fortunately, on 29 August the *Urimaguas* caught up with the *Huayna*, and Casement took his chance to change to the faster ship. He was now back with the Commission members, playing bridge with his hosts. The next day they passed the mouth of the Napo River, and twenty-four hours later reached Iquitos, their final destination, docking at eight o'clock in the morning.

Now the real work would begin.

PART III

9

The Uttermost Parts of the Earth

'Caoutchouc was first called "india rubber"', Casement jotted down in the notes he was making while in Leticia, four days before disembarking in Iquitos, 'because it came from the Indies, and the earliest European use of it was to rub out or erase. It is now called India rubber because it rubs out or erases the Indians.'

Casement was disappointed by Iquitos, as he had been by every city he had been posted to in Brazil. It was, he thought, well situated – that is, it had a broad expanse of river on its doorstep – but it was far too hot and had too many mosquitoes for Casement's liking. As for the look of the town itself, Casement had only critical things to say: ' . . . horribly neglected & dirty. The "streets" atrocious, the homes poor. Hundreds of soldiers in blue dungarees . . .' But as Casement would discover, Iquitos, like the Amazon itself, was full of news, rumour and general deceptiveness: gossip was very hard to avoid, but truth was hard to find.

Casement's first day there gave him a good taste of what was to come. After being whisked off to Cazes's home, where he had been invited to stay while in Iquitos, Casement met with the prefect of Loreto, Dr Alayza Paz Saldan, with Cazes present as interpreter. Casement found Soldan, who had only recently taken over as prefect, to be straightforward and honest – unlike the previous incumbent, who, according to Hardenburg, had been in the pay of the Peruvian Amazon Company. But Soldan seemed unaware of what was going on in the Putumayo, saying only that Arana's company was contributing immensely to the prestige of Peru. When, towards the end of their two-hour talk, Casement asked Soldan to whom he should refer his concerns should he find the condition of the British subjects wanting, Soldan suggested any one of three Company agents. When pressed for the name of a Peruvian government official, Soldan suggested the *comisario*, Señor Amadeo Burga – the brother-in-law of Pablo Zumaeta, Arana's brother-in-law. Casement now had a pretty good idea of what he was getting himself into. Arana had stretched an impenetrable web of influence over the Peruvian Amazon, and there was no way of entirely avoiding his family, associates, and friends.

The next day, 1 September, was Casement's forty-sixth birthday. His first job was to find an interpreter – someone who knew the local Indian languages plus Spanish, or ideally English. Casement understood very well that an interpreter would be key to the Commission's work. While aboard the *Edinburgh Castle*, about midway between Southampton and Madeira, Casement had written to Gerald Spicer at the Foreign Office to try to get John Brown, Whiffen's Putumayo guide, to meet him in Iquitos. Brown was married to a Huitoto woman and knew the language of her people: there could not have been a better choice. But when Casement arrived in Manaus, he learned from the Foreign Office that Brown was ill in Montserrat.

This was a major setback, and it was looking as though the Commission would have to rely on interpreters provided by the Company at the individual rubber stations. Such interpreters were bound to be loyal agents of Arana; they would doubtless report everything that happened back to their boss.

Few in Iquitos seemed to know the Huitoto and Bora languages, used by the two major linguistic groups in Arana's territory. But then a ray of hope appeared, when Casement heard of an Indian who was able to speak Spanish as well as seven other Indian languages. This man was then working on the Napo River, about 200 miles from Iquitos, and Casement wasted no time in chartering a launch to bring him to the town. In five or six days, Casement estimated, he would have the perfect interpreter.

Meanwhile, Casement still did not know for certain whether there were any Barbadians left working for the Company (he only had the Foreign Office's best assessment that some were probably still there) and, if there were, where they might be found. The question tormented him because he had no right, as a foreign official, to question anyone other than British subjects; if all the Barbadians had left, the trip – the whole enterprise – would have been in vain.

Cazes in London had told the Foreign Office very little of what he must have known about the situation in the Putumayo – probably in the hope that if there were no Barbadians in the picture there would be no inquiry. But once the investigation was underway, Cazes, as British consul, had to appear cooperative at least. He had Casement to stay, and helped him make the necessary contacts. He even informed Carlton Morris, the unofficial voice of the Barbadian community in Iquitos and known jokingly as the Barbadian consul, that Casement was on his way. Morris was in the confidence of many of the Barbadians, and was eager to meet and talk with Casement.

Casement was about to strike gold. For the first time since the revelations had appeared in *Truth*, there would be a positive answer to the big question: Were there still Barbadians working for Arana? In the afternoon, two Barbadians came to see Casement at Cazes's residence. They had arrived from the Putumayo on the Peruvian Amazon Company launch *Liberal* a few days before, and Carlton Morris had seen to it that they visited Casement as soon as possible.

The first man Casement interviewed was twenty-nine-year-old Frederick Bishop. He had been contracted in Barbados for work in the Putumayo in March 1905, and travelled to Peru with a batch of men that included John Brown. Not long after he arrived at the Putumayo, he had been assigned to Eugène Robuchon as a guard on his second and fatal journey into the forest. When Robuchon knew he was in trouble, he had sent Bishop and a number of Indians back to Morelia, the closest rubber station, to get help. Bishop almost died getting back to Morelia, but managed to arrange a relief party to return to Robuchon. But when, after some time, the relief party found Robuchon's last camp, he had vanished.

Bishop had worked for Arana for more than five years in the area around La Chorrera, the Peruvian Amazon Company's main settlement on the Igaraparaná River. During this time he had learned the Huitoto language, and knew many of the agents employed by Arana. He answered questions put to him by Casement – and occasionally by Louis Barnes, the Commission's leader, who was also present – and his answers confirmed what Whiffen and Brown had said in their separate statements about the abuses committed. His job was to go into the forests, armed, to round up Indians who had failed to collect the requisite amount of rubber. The recalcitrant Indians were rounded up at the point of a gun and marched to the rubber station, where they were flogged on their bare buttocks; the bleeding cuts were washed with vinegar or salt, and then they were sent back to the forest for the next collection cycle. Punishments meted out for not delivering rubber in sufficient quantities included being put into chains or into the stocks.

In Casement's words, Bishop

> declared that Indians were entirely enslaved, that they were hunted, flogged, chained and murdered, and that he himself had been up to the very date of his departure, actively employed in flogging and otherwise coercing the Indians, to compel them to work rubber or supply the other wants of the Company's agents. He made categoric statements as to murders of Indians occurring within his knowledge, of gross and constant immorality indulged in by many of the principal agents, and of a system of robbery and oppression of the Indians quite as black as anything alleged by Hardenburg.

Horrors aside, Bishop provided other information, which amplified certain points made by Hardenburg and Robuchon. For example, the Indians received no regular payment for the rubber. Sometimes, if they brought in even more rubber than they were supposed to, they were given items such as gowns, knives and axes. They received no food to take with them into the forest for the next collection – though they were fed, to an extent, in the stations themselves. They were 'half-starved'; their own vegetable and fruit plots were neglected, because they had no time to tend them, so great was the pressure to bring in rubber. The Indians grew weaker, and the weaker they became the less rubber they could collect, and so the more they were punished.

The rubber collections were run with the help of the Barbadians, and an armed force of Indians and half-castes called the *muchachos de confianza*, and those Indian chiefs who made their people work for the Company. 'The system was not trade at all; it was a lie to call it so – the Indians were slaves, and had to do what they were ordered', declared Bishop. Bishop had a lot more to say, and Casement recognized that he was invaluable: he could speak Huitoto, knew the Putumayo and its evil system right up to the present time, and was prepared to talk. Promising him protection, Casement asked him to work as his personal servant and interpreter on the trip to the Putumayo. Bishop accepted.

Over the next few days, Bishop elaborated on many of the points he had made during his first interview, naming names and citing many instances of brutality on the part of the Company's agents. He also emphasized that, when Gielgud and Whiffen had separately visited Arana's territory, everything was cleaned up and evidence of evil-doing hidden: the recalcitrant Indians were marched into the forest and held there until the visitors had departed. It was only because of the presence of John Brown that Whiffen had learned anything about what was going on.

The next Barbadian whom Casement interviewed was a man named Nellice Walker, aged twenty-seven, who had been recruited a little before Bishop. Unlike Bishop, Walker ended up in El Encanto, the Company's station headquarters on the Caraparaná. His account was utterly different from Bishop's. He had not himself witnessed any ill-treatment towards either fellow Barbadians or Indians, and had heard of none. It seemed to him that this sort of abuse happened at La Chorrera rather than at El Encanto, which was under the authority of Miguel Loayza, who seemed to be a decent person.

But, while Walker offered no new information about abuse, he did give Casement what he wanted more than anything else. The Foreign Office's hunch was right: Walker confirmed without doubt that there were still a number of Barbadians working up in La Chorrera – perhaps nine or more – but only one other at El Encanto. Casement now had the informers he would need to make a proper investigation of conditions. Would he find them? And, more important, would they talk?

The weather in Iquitos then took a turn for the worse – it rained heavily for several days. During this time, Casement hosted a dinner for the Commission members, David Cazes and his wife, and two others – Pablo Zumaeta, a senior official of the Peruvian Amazon Company and Arana's brother-in-law; and Lizardo Arana, Arana's brother and business partner. Lizardo knew the Commission and Casement quite well, since they had all travelled together to Iquitos from Southampton.

Casement was keeping his enemies close. He confided in William Tyrrell, Sir Edward Grey's private secretary, that inviting 'two of the principal criminals' was a wise move. 'We are all of us acting with great caution', Casement wrote,

> and secrecy even (as if we were the criminals) for it is clear the rascals are very suspicious – especially of me. I . . . drank their health in Iquitos champagne and said nice things! The dinner cost me £12 – but I fancy the toast will cost me dearer some day . . . Putumayo is a 'sealed book' even in Iquitos – it is amazing how everyone nearly is either afraid or 'in the swim.'

On 9 September Casement received four more Barbadians. The first three men proved to have little to say. They had worked on the Company's launches in different positions – one a fireman, one a mechanic, and the third a steward. None had done any shore work, and so they knew nothing about conditions in the rubber stations. But the fourth man had quite a story to tell.

Joseph Labadie, who was not entirely sure how old he was but guessed he was twenty-two, had been in the area for the past five and a half years. His first assignment was in the Iquitos area, working as a steward on one of the boats used by the Iquitos Trading Company, in which Cazes had a stake. After a few months, he obtained work as a cook on one of Arana's Company launches, and soon ended up in El Encanto in the same role. He then moved over to La Chorrera, where he was given a gun and told to 'work with the Indians' at the rubber station called Sur, a few hours walk to the southwest of La Chorrera. It was at Sur that Labadie witnessed a dreadful murder.

He recounted that one day, about two years before, Carlos Miranda, the chief of the station, ordered one of his *muchachos de confianza* to go into the forest and bring back a woman with him. Soon thereafter, the 'boy' returned with the woman, who was chained around the neck. Miranda then ordered another 'boy' to take her into the bushes and shoot her. She got two shots, said Labadie, who witnessed the gruesome episode. He continued: 'They cut off her head, after shooting her, and it was brought in to them all and shown to the Indians, and they were told if they "did bad" they would be treated the same way.' Then they burned the body. Labadie had never seen the woman before this day, nor did he know what she had done wrong.

Labadie had left the Company's employ about a year previously. He concluded the interview by repeating that 'in the sections [rubber stations] the men in charge did just as they pleased; they flogged Indians, and killed them and burnt them, without anyone stopping them.'

Casement retired to bed early, comforted by a good dose of quinine. In the night the rains lashed Iquitos with thunder and lightning.

Having intervewed Labadie, Casement thought he had seen all the Barbadians in Iquitos who were willing to talk to him.

As the scheduled day of departure for the Putumayo approached, Casement's plans hit a setback. The launch that he had sent up the Napo returned to Iquitos without the interpreter. The Indian man, it was reported, had gone further up the Napo, and was probably in Ecuador by now. It was not worth the expense, Casement thought, of sending a launch that far upriver to find him. But in the meantime, while the launch was away, Marius Vatan, a French trader and one-time French consular agent in Iquitos, had recommended a trustworthy Peruvian named Viacara, who knew the Huitoto and Bora languages and whom Arana had at one time employed. Viacara had left the Company after refusing to shoot two Indian chiefs. This alone made him a potentially more reliable interpreter than any the Company would supply. This, together with Bishop's presence (and his knowledge of Huitoto), reassured Casement that they would get by.

The launch that would take the Commission and Casement to its first major stop, La Chorrera, was the *Liberal*, which had arrived from the Putumayo on 10 September, the day after Casement had spoken to Labadie and the others. Casement learned from them that four Barbadians were on the launch; but when he asked to meet them, they refused. One in particular provoked Casement's interest: Stanley Lewis had appeared in Hardenburg's account on more than one occasion.

The time had come to wind things up in Iquitos. Casement was in a hurry to send his first letter to Gerald Spicer at the Foreign Office, together with the depositions he had taken from the Barbadians. He wanted this early draft report to get to the Foreign Office before he left for the Putumayo; he feared that anything might happen to him up there. La Chorrera was more than a thousand miles from Iquitos. As Casement put it in his covering letter,

It is only sent to you in case I might get lost or disappear or something up there, or die of fever, and my papers might be overhauled long before they reached Iquitos, or they would be at the mercy of the people, who are in dread of our visit. I am viewed with grave suspicion already, I think, but as I have got the commission with me we are all right.

The first ship to depart Iquitos was the *Urimaguas*, the launch that had brought the Commission members to Iquitos from Manaus; but Casement, suspicious of Arana and his agents, would not entrust his material to it. Casement had learned that Arana was actually travelling to Manaus on it. Instead, he entrusted the package to the *Huayna*, which was leaving Iquitos the same day as were he and the Commission.

As Casement was busily preparing the material for the Foreign Office, he received a visit from Adolfus Gibbs, one of the four Barbadians who had arrived in Iquitos on the *Liberal* the day before. They had initially refused to talk, but evidently one of their number had since changed his mind. The twenty-four-year-old Gibbs said he had been contracted in April 1905 along with ninety fellow Barbadians. After working in and around Iquitos, he ended up at La Chorrera, and from there transferred to the rubber station of Abisinia – a five-day hike southeast through the forest. He often went out on commissions to round up Indians. On one occasion, while operating out of Morelia, a station under the jurisdiction of Abisinia, Gibbs witnessed the decapitation of a sick and emaciated Indian, who, when released from the stocks, had tried to run away while still wearing his chains. The murder was carried out by one of the *muchachos*, a man of eighteen. He chased the man, dragged him back to the station, and then chopped his head off with a machete. A few minutes later, this same *muchacho* decapitated another young man, also because he had tried to escape.

Gibbs told this story to Casement in the presence of Louis Barnes, the head of the Commission. He was willing to tell more, but since he was working as a fireman on the *Liberal* the rest of his deposition could wait. As evening drew in, Casement strolled over to the offices of Booth Steamships and entrusted his bulky letter to their safekeeping for delivery.

Clearly, as the members of the Commission realized, these Barbadians were confirming everything that Hardenburg and Whiffen had alleged

– except for one point that Whiffen had stressed: the Barbadians, he had contended, were often used to mete out punishments, while, so far, except for Bishop all of the men Casement had interviewed had denied any part in the violence and murders. They were witnesses only, they maintained. Stanley Lewis's reluctance to talk to Casement was possibly because he was not so innocent.

On 14 September, the *Liberal* was ready to depart for the Putumayo. Casement, Frederick Bishop, Viacara – the Peruvian interpreter – and the Commission members all joined the ship. Casement expected Gibbs to be on board, and intended to interview him again, but was disappointed to hear that he had deserted. On the other hand, Stanley Lewis was working on the ship as a steward, and would be trapped on board for a week or more with his would-be interrogator.

10

La Chorrera

Casement found it hard to get comfortable aboard the *Liberal*. During the day it was blisteringly hot, and at night it was cold. The mosquitoes, 'like drops of fiery poison', continued their assault even on the broad expanse of the Amazon River. For three days the *Liberal* steamed downriver, at one point almost capsizing because of a violent hurricane, and narrowly avoiding a tornado in midstream, until, just before midnight on 16 September, the ship turned in at the mouth of the Putumayo River for its long ascent towards La Chorrera.

During the voyage Casement slept feverishly. His demeanour eventually improved, when he realized that the vicious mosquitoes had departed and that the sandflies, which he had been warned were worse, were actually not so bad. A day later, the *Liberal* passed through the Brazilian military post and customs, and entered the disputed territories claimed by both Peru and Colombia. Herons, small green parrots and several species of palm were a welcome sight.

It was now 18 September, and still Stanley Lewis had not approached Casement, even though the Captain told him that his presence was required. Then, two mornings later, when the ship was about ten hours from the mouth of the Igaraparaná, Lewis appeared and submitted himself to Casement's scrutiny. Like the other Barbadians, Lewis had come to the Peruvian Amazon in 1905 – though, aged fifteen at the time, he was considerably younger than most of his countrymen and fellow workers. Lewis could not remember everything that had happened since his arrival in the Amazon, but he did recall that he had worked in several places under the overall control of La Chorrera, including La Sabana and Santa Catalina to the east, and Ultimo Retiro to the north. Although he had moved around a little, his responsibilities were always the same: to round up Indians to bring their rubber to the station. As in the other cases Casement had heard about, the chief of the section or his underlings gave orders to flog those Indians who had not done what was required of them.

At this point in the questioning, Casement surprised Lewis by asking him about the incident when he had allegedly flogged an Indian woman. Lewis admitted that he had done this, along with another man known as El Frailecito ('the little monk'), whose name was Ernest Seales. The station's subordinate chief had ordered the two Barbadians to flog a woman named Simona. After the flogging, Simona was taken out into the forest and shot by a man. This man, who would not identify himself other than by the initials M.G., had written about this incident in a letter dated 16 July 1907 to Saldaña Rocca, which formed a part of Hardenburg's depositions.

Lewis said that he had never punished any more Indians after that time, and was tortured for his intransigence by José Fonseca, the chief of the Ultimo Retiro station. Lewis was lucky, he admitted, that he had got away from Ultimo Retiro (and Fonseca), and found work on the Company launches.

The details, Casement wrote, were 'revolting' but convincing. The ship stopped at Pescaria, a small fishing village belonging to the Company, and Casement saw several Huitoto women who, he concluded, were in sexual servitude. The next day, 21 September, the *Liberal* was making good time up the Igaraparaná. It was no more than a hundred yards wide. A deep, slow-moving river, clearer than it looked – 'more like pea soup or lentil broth' – it wound its way northwest through overhanging bush: the 'canal in the woods', as Casement romantically termed it. In the morning, the *Liberal* docked at another Company post. It was called Indostan (Hindustan), one of the many somewhat absurd names given to these remote places. Consisting of little but a single dwelling house and a large clearing, Indostan existed to provide cassava, rice, sugar and other foodstuffs for the personnel at La Chorrera, further up the Igaraparaná. According to Casement, some fifteen to twenty Indian boys and girls worked on this plantation, all showing signs of malnutrition, or worse. 'Several of them were sick with fever and three little girls, quite children, were in a half-starved condition, and yet busily employed. The only well-fed persons were the white man Zumaran [the manager] and

his Indian mistress.' Casement would see a lot more situations like this
in the weeks to come. At Indostan, Casement also saw his first example
of the appalling punishment handed out to Indians. 'Found prisoner
[in] heavy chain ('Bolivar', a Boras boy), crime trying to escape. It was
round him from the neck to the waist and then padlocked to one of his
ankles.' Casement did not believe Zumaran that Bolivar had tried to
escape. The Commission members agreed, and had Bolivar released to
be taken with them to La Chorrera.

Casement had now seen for himself, in just one Company outpost
– and not even a rubber station at that – all the tell-tale signs that
everything he had read had prepared him for: malnutrition and disease,
slavery, and abusive and illegal punishment.

As the *Liberal* worked its way up the Igaraparaná, the land became
higher and the air clearer. Casement spoke again to Lewis, who provided
more gruesome details of José Fonseca's regime at Ultimo Retiro:
'murders of girls beheadings of Indians and shooting of them after they
had rotted from flogging' – 'disgraceful statements', Casement recorded.

About twenty hours after leaving Indostan, the *Liberal* reached La
Chorrera.

La Chorrera – literally 'spout' or 'gully' – was sited just below a steep
cataract of the Igaraparaná. The settlement had been built high up on
the banks of the river. As soon as the *Liberal* tied up, four Peruvian
Amazon Company dignitaries boarded and welcomed their guests. The
delegation's head was Juan Tizon, who had been with the Company for
only a few months, having previously been a bureaucrat in Iquitos and, for
a short time, acting prefect of Loreto. His name would have been familiar
to Casement, because Sidney Paternoster had reprinted a letter of Tizon's,
refuting all charges made against the Company, in *Truth* on 27 October of
the previous year. A surviving photograph of him shows a kindly-looking
man, and this is precisely how he struck Casement: the acceptable face
of the Company's operations. Here in La Chorrera, Tizon represented
the administration of the Company, and was overseeing the work of the
managers of El Encanto and La Chorrera. He would be with Casement
most of the time. Next below Tizon in the Company hierarchy was Victor
Macedo, the manager of La Chorrera, followed by Dr José Rodriguez, the
medical officer, and the accountant, Francisco Ponce.

With sweeping views, fast-running water and relatively fresh air, La Chorrera certainly had its physical charms. The human scene, however, replicated the wretchedness Casement had seen earlier, at Indostan. One of the first sights to greet Casement as he stepped off the launch was three Boras Indians showing 'broad scars on their bare buttocks – some of them 1½" or 2" broad. Weals for life. This is their wealfare, their daily wealfare. All slaves.'

Casement wasted no time in getting down to business. The next day, 23 September, he asked Tizon and Macedo to bring to him five Barbadians he had caught sight of the previous day. As he waited for the men, Casement brooded on his situation and the likely outcome of his investigations. Sir Edward Grey, it is true, had given him a free hand, but his instructions were disturbingly vague in their purpose. Here he was, a representative of the British government in a foreign country, asking British subjects how they had been and were being treated by servants of a Company that was registered in London, and was at the same time Peruvian. He was here as a guest of the Company and with the permission of the Peruvian government. But where would the investigation lead him? What was its greater purpose? Should he content himself with 'a perfunctory enquiry, as to whether they are happy, well treated or in distress etc.'?

Casement faced a real dilemma. He wanted to know the truth, and only the Barbadians could give him the facts he sought. To get them to talk – possibly to incriminate themselves – he needed to offer them protection, effectively to take them out of the Putumayo with him. He had to make sure, at the same time, that Tizon, upon hearing the Barbadians' evidence, did not take it upon himself to alert the authorities in Iquitos.

Casement feared that, once the Peruvian authorities in Iquitos had got their hands on the Barbadians they would be made scapegoats, and that the real criminals would get away scot-free: 'The Barbadians will be nobbled and terrorized into denying everything', he remarked. Casement, in the Putumayo, felt himself in the middle of a criminal net, and he could not imagine that it would be any different in Iquitos. He was being hosted by a murderer and waited on by his henchmen. How could he feel safe anywhere? Casement's best hope was that Tizon would be so convinced by the Barbadians' evidence that he would take the matter straight to the Company's management in Iquitos, to insist on far-reaching reforms. That, after all, was the real purpose of the investigation. Involving the judicial authorities in Iquitos would only bring the investigation to a halt. It was a risky strategy, but there was really nothing else he could do.

So Casement decided he would actively engage Tizon and make sure that he attended the interviews, with Louis Barnes, the head of the Commission, present as well. The interviews began in the early evening. Victor Macedo was clearly anxious about the proceedings. He planted himself near the door that opened onto the building's veranda, nervously awaiting the Barbadians. Casement did not invite him in. After all the anticipation, this first meeting did not begin well. Casement was certain that Donald Francis, the first man to be interviewed, was lying (he later admitted it to Casement); the next two men, who were employed in La Chorrera, knew nothing about life outside the settlement. But the fourth man, James Chase, was ready to talk. Chase was twenty-three years old and had been in the Company's employ since 1904. For a few years he had worked in La Chorrera and Ultimo Retiro, but he had been to Iquitos for medical treatment. When, in April 1908, he returned to the Putumayo, he was sent to Abisinia, the rubber station run by Abelardo Agüero, a man who had first been mentioned in Whiffen's Foreign Office report of the previous year. Chase's job, like that of so many of the other Barbadians, was to go out on the so-called commissions, to round up the Indians and their rubber. He had witnessed floggings and killings until quite recently. Chase was not comfortable talking. He gave his evidence 'under a sense of fear; his agitation was plainly marked, and he was greatly disconcerted'. Tizon interrupted Chase's accounts on several occasions, trying to assure Casement that the killings were exceptional and that the floggings were a thing of the past; but Chase kept to his story. 'This man's interrogation', Casement remarked, 'constituted for him a trying ordeal.'

Tizon was on the defensive, and this was not good for Casement's plan. The next witness, however, was completely convincing. Stanley Sealy was twenty-one years old when he had first arrived in La Chorrera. Between 1905, when he was recruited in Barbados, and May 1908, when he went up to the Putumayo, he had worked in various jobs, mostly in Iquitos. The promise of a decent salary attracted him to the Putumayo.

In the little time he had been in Arana's territory, he had witnessed some horrible scenes and had, he admitted, participated in others. Casement was moved by his testimony. 'Sealy', he wrote,

> spoke like a man throughout and my heart warmed to the ugly black face, shifting from side to side, his fingers clasping and unclasping but the grim truth coming out of his lips. Says he had flogged Indians himself – many times – very many times.

Sealy spoke of flogging men, women and children. The chief of the station ordered the floggings, specifying the number of lashes (sometimes as many as twenty-five), depending on how short they were of the quota of rubber. The Indians just lay down and took it, he said.

Tizon reacted at last, saying that only sweeping reforms would do.

As they were winding up this first day's business, Frederick Bishop, Casement's guide and interpreter, told him that another Barbadian had just shown up. He wanted to speak to Casement, and he had come especially for this purpose from his job on the Company's launches that plied the upper part of the Igaraparaná, above the falls.

Early the next morning, 24 September, Joshua Dyall appeared. Casement did not warm to Dyall – 'the man is a brute', he concluded, 'but has been employed by greater brutes'. Dyall, who had been brought over from Barbados at about the same time as the others, spoke about the early days in Arana's employ, and mentioned by name a long list of Barbadians he knew. Many had left, but a few still remained. This was excellent information, because until now Casement had not known precisely which rubber stations he needed to visit. Ultimo Retiro, Matanzas, Abisinia, and La Sabana (sometimes referred to as Savana), he now learned, would be worth visiting. Dyall thought that there were no more than ten Barbadians out there.

During the course of his testimony, Dyall confessed to the murder of five Indians: two he had shot, two he had beaten to death, and one he had flogged to death. He did not do this, he said, of his own volition, but under orders from the station chiefs for whom he was working. These names Casement knew well from Hardenburg's manuscript and Robuchon's book: José Fonseca, now at La Sabana, Alfredo Montt at Ultimo Retiro, and Armando Normand at Matanzas.

Sealy's and Dyall's chilling and compelling evidence had convincingly won Tizon over to Casement's argument that the Barbadian evidence could stand just as it was, and that Tizon could and should act on it alone. He confided in Casement that he now understood the system to be one of slavery, that it had to change, and that the station chiefs were criminals who were capable of anything. What he feared most was that if these allegations led to the Company being shut down, a far worse system might take its place, in which the individual station chiefs, with their armed gangs and local power, might inflict even greater harm on the Indian population. Casement fully agreed. 'If the Company were to disappear', Casement remarked, 'the fate of these unhappy Indians would be far worse.'

After a five-day stay, during which they interviewed six Barbadians, Casement, the Commission and Tizon left La Chorrera on 27 September to go upriver to the rubber station of Ultimo Retiro. With them were several Barbadians: Frederick Bishop, plus Sealy and Chase, who had been recruited to act as servants, guides and interpreters to the Commission members.

The next morning they arrived at the small rubber station of Occidente. There were no Barbadians here, but the Commission had chosen to stop because it was their first opportunity to observe how the Indians drew the latex from the trees – one of the objectives of their commercial investigation. Occidente was typical of many rubber stations. About every fortnight, the Indians who lived in the surrounding forest were required to bring their quota of rubber, called a *puesta*, to the station. Weighing up to fifty pounds, each *puesta* consisted of slabs of rubber in the shape of sausages – called *chorizos* – about one yard long. The *chorizo* was made by first coagulating the latex tapped from the rubber trees, and then successively washing the resulting mass with cold and hot water, and finally beating it into shape with wooden pestles. Once each Indian had delivered four or five *puesta*s to the station, the collection cycle was complete, and the shipment – the *fabrico* – was ready to be moved by the Indians to La Chorrera.

The station consisted of two buildings. One, a large house, provided accommodation for the staff and acted as a storehouse for the *fabrico* until it was ready to be moved. On the veranda stood the instrument that played the key part in the system of terror – the *cepo*, or stocks. It was there to punish Indians who failed to deliver their quota of rubber. Casement described it as consisting of

two long and very heavy blocks of wood, hinged together at one end
and opening at the other, with a padlock to close upon a staple. Leg-
blocks so small as just fit the ankle of an Indian are cut in the wood.
The top beam is lifted on the hinge, the legs of the victim are inserted in
two of these holes, and is then closed down and padlocked at the other
end. Thus imprisoned by the ankles, which are often stretched several
feet apart, the victim, lying upon his back, or possibly being turned face
downwards, remains sometimes for hours, sometimes for days, often for
weeks, and sometimes for months in this painful confinement.

The *cepo* at Occidente was over 13 feet long and 7 feet high. The diameter
of the leg-holes, of which there were two dozen, was a mere 3.25 inches.

The other building on site was the *maloca*, a communal house, covered
with a thatch of palm leaves. The *maloca* was the Indian community's
ancestral and sacred space.

Casement and the Commission had come to Occidente at just the
right time: the next day, in celebration of the ending of the present
fabrico, the Indians, perhaps as many as a thousand, were expected to
attend a dance. It would be the first time that the visitors could see so
many Indians in one place.

As they watched the spectacle, Bishop told Casement that while
the festivities were habitual – there were about four in each year,
corresponding to the number of *fabricos* – this dance seemed to him
to be quite different. It was being staged for the benefit of the visitors.
Normally, Bishop revealed, the 'Indians were cuffed and kicked, and
at night . . . the *blancos* [would] go out, excited with drink, and commit
abominable orgies with the women and girls by force – even raping
prisoners in the *cepo* [the stock]'. The Spanish word *blanco* was often
used generally to refer to white people but, as Bishop and others used it,
blanco also connoted power over indigenous people.

The staging could not, however, disguise the evidence of abuse. The
Mark of Arana was all around him. 'One small boy, a child, quite recent
red weals unhealed & many other small boys show marks of flogging',
noted Casement. 'I never saw anything more pathetic than these people.
They move one to profound pity.'

Casement could only observe the Indians – he had no right to
question them; but he knew that everything in the place depended on

them. 'They paid for it all', Casement told Tizon when he welcomed Casement as his guest to the celebration of the *fabrico*. 'The food we ate, and the wine we drank, the houses we dwelt in, and the launch that conveys us up river – all came from their emaciated and half-starved, and well flagellated bodies.'

Casement wanted to persuade all of the Commission members, as well as Tizon, to think as he did about the Indians. He worked on them both individually and as a group. Louis Barnes and Seymour Bell (Bell spoke perfect Spanish), Casement believed, would agree with him eventually: Walter Fox he was less concerned about, since he had little to do with the Company per se; Henry Gielgud, in his position as Company secretary, might prove to be a major stumbling block.

A few days into their stay in Occidente, Casement had a conversation with Louis Barnes on his return from one of the Commission's botanical and commercial forays into the forest. Their exchange showed very clearly the distance between Casement and the Commission members in their understanding of the situation they had all come to examine. 'The Commission returned about 1 o'clock [pm]', recounted Casement.

> They had found two Indians, rubber tappers only, and had seen, Fox said, only three rubber trees. They seemed quite surprised. I said to Barnes I was surprised at his surprise. I asked Barnes had he not yet grasped that this story of Indian labourers was a lie. There were no labourers – there was no industry on the Putumayo. It was simply a wild forest inhabited by wild Indians, who were hunted like wild animals and made to bring in rubber by hook or by crook, and murdered and flogged if they didn't. That was the system.

Barnes seemed surprised that none of the white employees knew where the rubber trees were located or where the Indians were working. Casement, almost rebuking him, pointed out that trees were of no concern to the employees: all they cared about was that the Indians did not escape. The Company was forcing Indians to bring in more and more rubber, and to search over ever larger areas for trees. 'The system was one of sheer piracy and terrorization', Casement reiterated, 'and if you lifted the lash you stopped the supply of rubber.'

In Occidente, Casement became increasingly frustrated with the

Commission members. One moment he believed he had succeeded in making them see the system for what it was; a moment later they seemed to fall back into thinking of it as an ordinary commercial operation. Casement was beginning to think that it might be better for the Commission to proceed without him. He had already heard and seen enough to make up his own mind.

As it turned out, however, the present *fabrico* had been delayed, and the *Liberal*, which would be taking the rubber down to Iquitos, was now not expected in La Chorrera until early November. Casement had no option but to continue with the Commission to the rubber stations they intended to visit. But before they did so, he arranged with Tizon to have all the remaining Barbadians assemble at La Chorrera to await his return. He would interview them all there.

On 6 October, the party of visitors and the Barbadians in their entourage continued their trip up to Ultimo Retiro, which they reached the next day. As its name – 'Last Retreat' – suggests, this rubber station was the furthest from La Chorrera. At this point, the Igaraparaná was very narrow – a mere thirty yards wide – and it was not practically navigable beyond it. The station house, as Casement described it, stood 'like a fortress stoutly stockaded on the apex of the rising ground some 50 or 60 feet above the water. The house [was] built like a ship, with its bows facing the river.' The Indian *maloca* was small. There were women and children around, but no men. Casement concluded that the women were concubines of the station staff.

Here Casement found just one Barbadian, a man called Edward Crichlow, who had been in the employ of the Company since late 1904. Crichlow fed Casement stories of armed commissions into the forests (including an illegal foray into Colombian territory in the area of the Caquetá River, to the northeast), floggings, torture and murder: a litany of horrors with which Casement was becoming all too familiar. Crichlow also provided Casement with more information about two station chiefs in particular: Alfredo Montt and Armando Normand.

Casement considered the stocks at Ultimo Retiro to be the most vicious he had seen. The leg-holes there were considerably smaller than the ones in Occidente:

The ankle-holes were so small that, even for a well-built Indian, when closed the wood would often have eaten into the flesh. For an ordinary-sized European or Negro the top beam could not close upon the leg without being down upon the ankle or shin bone.

Whole families could be held in the stocks for any amount of time, each confined in all the different imaginable ways that the design of such an instrument of torture allowed.

While Casement and the Commission members were examining the stocks, Casement had his first close encounter with an Indian. A 'fearless skeleton' aged between thirty-five and forty started without warning to speak to Casement in Huitoto. Fortunately, Sealy and Chase, both of whom were nearby and knew some of the language, helped with the translation.

> Waiteka [the man's name] turned his thighs and buttocks, and showed us the broad weals on both, right down the back of the thighs, and he said he got this for not bringing *caucho* [rubber], and that they were put in this *cepo* here and starved to death – that they died in it; that many, that all of them there had been flogged. Many had died in this *cepo*.

Once they knew Casement's plans to interview the Barbadians in La Chorrera, the Commission decided on an itinerary for their journey that would get them back there on time to catch the *Liberal* to Iquitos. On 11 October, after a stay of four days, the visiting party left Ultimo Retiro for the interior of Arana's territory, to visit the rubber stations of Entre Rios, Matanzas and Atenas. This would take them more than a fortnight, and they would be trekking through the forest until they returned to the Igaraparaná for the short river trip back to La Chorrera.

Entre Rios, as the name suggests, was located between the Igaraparaná and the Caquetá rivers – the northern boundary of Arana's empire. It took the party most of the day, 12 October, to get there through the forest from Puerto Peruano, where the launch had dropped them off. The path was extremely well kept; but Casement was quick to see the wretchedness that lay behind it. 'The land rises 100 feet or more', he wrote, and then sinks again to another stream – often with steps and big trees and stakes laid – all the work of the Indians. Every stream is well bridged. Some have five big trees laid parallel and notched so the feet won't slip – and often a liana rope banister. This road is a big work – seeing too that the wretched workers on it are drawn from far-off homes, many hours away, and get no scrap of pay and only just the food to sustain a starved existence.

There were no Barbadians at Entre Rios. The Commission had arrived there to interview the station's chief, Andres O'Donnell. Casement was struck by the man's Irish name. When he asked him about his roots, O'Donnell, who spoke Spanish and Huitoto, told Casement that his grandfather had emigrated to Spain from Ireland. Casement's opinion of the man, even though he had read and heard about his criminal activities (from both Bishop and James Chase), was not as negative as his views of the other station chiefs he had met. It seems that this opinion was tempered by the Gaelic connection, no matter how distant.

Four days later, the Commission – with the exception of Walter Fox, the botanist, who remained to make a more detailed investigation of the *Hevea* species growing in the locality – moved off to Matanzas, a rubber station due east of Entre Rios. They reached Matanzas, which had the reputation of being one of the worst stations (it literally means 'slaughters' or 'massacres', and it was the station referred to most frequently in the Hardenburg depositions) in about twenty hours. Armando Normand, the chief of the station, whom they were expecting to meet, was away at La China, a rubber station ten hours away. He was perhaps hoping to avoid the visitors, but if so, he failed: a messenger was sent to fetch him.

Casement expressed a kind of morbid fascination with Normand. In his absence, Casement was given his sitting-room to stay in. If he did not know it already, Casement soon learned that his host was English. The sitting-room was a giveaway:

> . . . it is pasted round with pictures from the *Graphic*, largely dealing with the Russo-Japanese War of 1904. There are also certificates from the London School of Book-keepers of 1904, giving him a certificate as 'book-keeper' and a certificate from some senior school of earlier date.

No sooner had Casement inspected the place than Normand himself arrived,

> a little being, slim, thin and quite short, say, 5' 7" and with a face truly the most repulsive I have ever seen, I think. It was perfectly devilish in its cruelty and evil. I felt as if I were being introduced to a serpent. All through dinner he spoke Spanish only, but whenever by chance a word came to me, I answered in English. As soon as dinner was over, he bowed and left us.

There was a lot of activity in Matanzas, since the *fabrico*, one of two that year, was almost ready to move to La Chorrera. That evening, after Normand had excused himself, Casement turned in early. In the middle of the night, he and the other Commission members were suddenly awoken by the patter of small feet and low voices calling out, 'Normand, Normand'. A man with a rifle and a lantern was leading a group of women around the veranda. 'I jumped from bed. Some voices shouted down the passage and they all bolted to the room Normand is sleeping in. It was the arrival of the Harem', Casement concluded, 'making for the room where they presumed their sleeping lord was lying . . . They looked like tiny little things . . . poor little creatures pattering all day and night through the forest after this beast.'

The next morning, 18 October, Casement told Tizon that he intended to leave Matanzas to return to Entre Rios on his own, without waiting for the Commission to wind up its business. He said he would leave just as soon as he had spoken to James Lane, a Barbadian working at Matanzas, and Westerman Levine, another Barbadian, who was due from La China. Lane was interviewed immediately. Stories of floggings – one only a month before – and murders came pouring out of Lane's mouth, but Casement broke off the questioning for the time being, intending to resume it at La Chorrera. Later that afternoon Levine turned up, and he too provided details of floggings, beheadings, burnings and shootings. Many of the floggings – some of the most brutal – he had committed himself under orders from Normand. Casement gave strict instructions to Tizon that Levine should be immediately dismissed from the Company's service and brought down to Entre Rios with the Commission.

On 19 October 1910, about fifty Indians headed out of Matanzas, laden with some seventy pounds of rubber each, in the first of ten trips they would have to make to get the whole of the *fabrico* to La Chorrera in time for its shipment to Iquitos. Casement, together with Bishop, Sealy and James Lane, headed out a little later. After walking for most of the day and staying overnight in an abandoned *maloca*, the party arrived in Entre Rios after noon on 20 October. Fox and O'Donnell met them on their arrival.

Several hours later, the rubber-carrying Indians arrived in Entre Rios. They had been marching since the morning and, as they began to arrive in the station, their driver, a man called Negretti, pushed them onwards, not allowing them any rest. Casement was appalled. Just before this train had departed Matanzas, Casement had tried to carry a load of rubber, to see what it was like. 'I could not walk three paces with it – literally and truly', he wrote.

> My knees gave way and to save my life, I don't think I could have gone 50 yards. Yet here they were, coming in from 8 to 10 hours away, 25 to 30 miles, and with 45 miles through the forest before them to get to Puerto Peruano . . . The little boys, some of them of five or six . . . were coming along too, often with 30 lbs or more on their tiny backs.

Now, as they struggled by, Casement and Fox tried to take photographs of the burdened Indians. The fading light made it nearly impossible. In exasperation, Casement remarked that he had seen nothing as bad as this in the Congo: 'It is indescribable and makes me positively ill.'

Casement spent the next day in conversation with Fox – who had by now come to see the situation as Casement did, and declared that unless something was done to end the atrocities immediately, he would kick up a stink on his return. A day later, the rest of the party that had remained at Matanzas began to straggle in. First came Normand, then the Commission members, together with Tizon. A little later Normand's harem turned up.

As in his first meeting with the man, Casement made a great deal of Normand's face as a guide to his inner being.

It is a perfectly atrocious face – but there is no doubt the brute has courage – a horrid, fearful courage, and endurance, and a cunning mind too. He is the ablest of these scoundrels we have met yet, and I should say far the most dangerous. The others were murderous maniacs mostly, or rough, cruel ignorant men . . . This is an educated man of a sort, who has lived long in London, knows the meanings of his crimes and their true aspect in all civilised eyes.

Entre Rios was full of people; but Westerman Levine, whom Tizon was supposed to bring along to the station, was nowhere to be seen. Casement was perplexed by his absence and, as he mulled it over, began to fear that a plot was being hatched to undermine his work in the Putumayo. There were plans, he concluded, to tamper with the evidence.

It occurred to Casement that the Barbadians, who had been gathered together in La Chorrera to await his return, would be a soft target for both Normand and Macedo, the chief of La Chorrera. Casement was convinced they would try to bribe the Barbadians – not difficult, given that most of them were deeply in debt to the Company. In that event, it would be the word of eight men (the number who were expected to assemble in La Chorrera) against three – Bishop, Sealy and Chase – whose depositions and evidence were water-tight.

Casement had to act quickly. In order not to arouse suspicion, he decided to dispatch Bishop to La Chorrera to make sure that the Barbadians who were waiting there for Casement were 'not tampered with'. 'As I am playing with the Devil', Casement commented, 'I won't take any risks. I'll not go spades and let him double when I have such a good hand of Barbados clubs.'

Casement was getting ever more anxious that his grand plan for evacuating the Barbadians might fail. He hoped that his pre-emptive strike would work, but only time would tell. In the meantime he busied himself in Entre Rios, learning more about the details of the *fabrico*, of the kinds of weights the Indians were expected to (and did) carry. He also spoke to Bell and Barnes of his fears about the La Chorrera plot, and discussed with them the possibility, which he had already raised with Cazes in Iquitos, that he would leave La Chorrera with all the Barbadians and drop them on the Amazon in Brazilian territory, where they would await a steamer on its way to Manaus. Casement was certain that if the Barbadians appeared in Iquitos, they would be jailed immediately on trumped-up charges. He had put them in this dangerous situation, and he was determined to get them out of it safely.

Several days later, after the Commission had gone to visit another nearby rubber station – its name, Atenas (Athens), must have evoked a wry smile – the party was ready to return to Puerto Peruano to pick up the launch downstream to La Chorrera, which they reached on 28 October.

On 29 October Casement heard the best news possible: Tizon had agreed to let the Barbadian men go even though they had admitted to crimes themselves. The only condition was that Casement would have to pay their debts to the Company.

The *Liberal* was due on or before 5 November. There was no time to waste. Bishop had managed to get to the men before Macedo and Normand did, and they agreed to tell Casement everything. Over the next few days, on 31 October and 1 and 2 November, Casement met and took depositions from nine men. Each one of them, in their own way, confirmed all that he had heard. 'The list of horrors', Casement commented with a degree of satisfaction,

> has grown every hour to-day and yesterday and Monday. So completely are the Barbados men now vindicated that Tizon actually to-day asked me 'as a favour' – his own words – to let him have a list of the names of all the Agents of the Company incriminated by the men. High and low – he asks now they shall be judged by the blackmen! What a change from the first days of my coming to La Chorrera.

La Chorrera was abuzz. The *fabricos* from throughout the area administered by the La Chorrera headquarters continued to flood in, carried on Indian backs. Casement and Fox watched a *fabrico* arrive from a station a fair distance away; in the line of carriers were two young boys, one of whom was carrying about 50 pounds of rubber – almost his own body-weight. The other boy was carrying more than his own body-weight in rubber. 'Fox and I watched this confirmation of so much – it told its own tale – with a sort of grim joy.'

Over the next several days Casement pored over each of the Barbadians' accounts, checking wages paid against items purchased from the Company store and gambling debts. Everything appeared greatly, arbitrarily, overpriced – the Barbadians had been forced to part with their wages in a major swindle. But there was little time for argument, and no point, as he had already agreed to the Company's condition for letting the Barbadians go.

On 9 November, after Casement had been in La Chorrera for almost a fortnight, the *Liberal* finally arrived. Casement caught the air of celebration as the ship's white funnel poked above the bush as it approached. Some people cheered, and the ship let off a rocket. At six in the evening it anchored, and passengers started disembarking. Bishop, who went aboard when the ship tied up, returned excitedly to Casement with the news that John Brown, Whiffen's guide and Casement's hope as an interpreter, was aboard the ship, and had finally answered Casement's call. What would Casement do with him now that the job was done? He would have to go back to Iquitos with them on the *Liberal*.

Casement received letters and news from home. One piece of news struck him in particular. Dr Hawley Crippen, the notorious murderer who had managed to escape the authorities in Britain, had been caught. 'But what a farce it seems', Casement remarked,

> a whole world shaken by the pursuit of a man who killed his wife – and here are lots of gentlemen I meet daily at dinner who not only kill their wives, but burn other people's wives alive – or cut their arms and legs off and pull the babies from their breasts to throw in the river or leave to starve in the forest – or dash their brains out against trees.

The public was fascinated and preoccupied with a gruesome murder in polite society, while the systematic extermination of a people held little interest for them. The public's duplicity sickened Casement, while at the same time it showed him how alone he was in trying to right serious wrongs. 'Why', Casement asked, 'should civilisation stand aghast at the crime of a Crippen and turn wearily away when the poor Indians of the Putumayo, or the Bantu of the Congo, turn bloodstained, appalling hands and terrified eyes to those who alone can help?'

Rumours in La Chorrera were rife among the Barbadian men that there was a plot underway to have them 'disappear' before they reached their destination. When Casement heard of the rumours, he knew that, whether they were true or not, he had to make sure that the Barbadians avoided Peruvian territory. Fortunately the Brazilian customs officer on the *Liberal* agreed to drop the Barbadians off in Brazilian territory on some pretext. Casement was mightily relieved.

On Wednesday, 16 November 1910, almost two months after arriving in La Chorrera, Casement was on his way out. 'Thank God!' he exclaimed.

> I left La Chorrera and the Peruvian Amazon Company's 'Estate' to-day. I am still their involuntary guest on their steamer *Liberal*, with the eighteen Barbados men, four Indian wives of these and the children of John Brown, Allan Davis, James Mapp and J. Dyall.

On 20 November, having steamed down the Igaraparaná and the Putumayo, the *Liberal* entered the Amazon River. The next day, the captain and Casement agreed on the spot where they would drop off the Barbadians – a small place called Esperança, on the Brazilian Amazon. Apart from Bishop, Casement had not told the Barbadians of this plan; when it was made known, almost all of them agreed to it. Only Bishop, John Brown, his wife and child, and Philip Lawrence, who had been a cook at La Chorrera, opted instead for Iquitos.

With a decent of supply of food from the ship's stores, fourteen men, four women and four children disembarked. They would now wait for a passing Booth steamer from Iquitos to take them to Manaus. Casement had written letters to the captains of the ships he expected to pass this way, explaining the situation and telling them that they could claim the passage money from the British vice-consul in Manaus. With all arrangements made, Casement and the others continued on to Iquitos.

11

Godforsaken Hell-Haunted Wilds

After setting the Barbadians on their way to safety, Casement could relax and enjoy the journey back to Iquitos. The shimmering riverscape, which had escaped his attention on the way to the Putumayo, now prompted comment and reflection. Instead of being immersed in documents, he had leisure to appreciate the ebb and flow of one of the world's great waterways. 'A beautiful natural history store' is how he summed up what he saw. Instead of the dark, menacing forests of the Putumayo, there were wonderful vistas of fruitful trees and shrubs, 'a vegetable profusion'. The Amazon personified bountiful nature, fertile as the Nile, laden with silt from lands stretching up to the Andes, rich black soil which formed islands that dissolved in the next flood, only to reform again. Were it not for rubber, Casement concluded, the indigenous people would live in 'absolute clover'. There was no felling or clearing of timber required:

> The great river does that. It just piles up millions of tons of gleaming drift, washed clean and harrowed and shining as the water subsides from the crest, and leaves them stretched out for miles to sun and rain for enough time annually to raise two crops each year.

It was the Garden of Eden.

Yet, as Casement surveyed the scene and imagined the benevolent possibilities it offered its inhabitants, he recalled the horrible actuality of the Indians' lives that his questioning of the Barbadians had revealed. Everything that sustained them and gave them pleasure in this remote forest – the plants, the animals, and the rivers – had been ripped from their grasp. It had been stolen from them not by a Government, as in the case of the Congo pillage, but by an association of vagabonds, the scum of Peru and Colombia, who have been assembled here by Arana Bros and then formed into an English Company with a body of stultified English gentlemen – fools, or worse – at their head.

As if that was not criminal enough, these 'cut-throat half-castes' turned the women and children into playthings, while their husbands and fathers

> are marched in, guarded by armed ruffians, to be flogged on their naked bodies . . . bearing the indelible marks of the lash over their buttocks and thighs, and administered for not bringing in a wholly lawless and infamous toll of rubber.

Casement's sympathy for the Indians, and his profound understanding of their oppressive exploitation, led to a plan to take back to England an Indian boy who, through the good offices of the Anti-Slavery and Aborigines' Protection Society, or the Missions, might persuade some wealthy and well-intentioned people to buy shares in Arana's company – not for rubber, but to save the Indians. His idea was that well-disposed English shareholders, hearing of what was happening from one of the victims, would be able to curb Arana's greed and force him to end his henchmen's reign of terror.

To this end, Casement looked around for a suitable candidate, and eventually at La Chorrera, while waiting for the boat to take him back to Iquitos, he spotted 'a dear little chap' and invited him to England. As the child was willing, and both his parents and his older brother had been killed by the rubber ruffians, his tribal chief accepted a present of a shirt and trousers in return for his agreement that the boy go with Casement. This virtual sale of the child, and the whole plan of using a native Indian to elicit help and sympathy for his fellows, may seem repugnant to us now, but at the time it was a recognised mode of behaviour. And for Omarino, as the boy was called, it must have been a welcome release from almost incredible exploitation. Casement weighed Omarino at twenty-five kilos, while the load he had carried to the Company's scales was twenty-nine and a half kilos.

On the same day, a young Andoke man begged Casement to take him away with him. His name was Arédomi, and he was desperate to escape the Putumayo. Both young Indians accompanied Casement to Iquitos.

When they arrived on 25 November 1910, Casement went to stay with Cazes, while the remaining Barbadians and the Indian youths were placed in rented accommodation. Casement's relationship with Cazes was never warm. He felt that Cazes had failed to help the Barbadians when they had complained to him years earlier about their treatment by agents of Arana's company. He also suspected that he had known much more about what was going on in the Putumayo than he was prepared to admit, particularly to the Foreign Office. Moreover, he was afraid that the relationship between Cazes and Arana would compromise the Commission's investigation. Casement knew of the letter Arana had written to Cazes in which he had stated that the Company's commission had only a commercial purpose, and that the investigation of crimes was a matter for the Peruvian government only. Casement's understanding was that the letter was meant to keep Cazes quiet.

Back in Iquitos, face to face with Cazes, Casement was certain that the consul had been withholding information.

> Every time he opens his mouth he shows how very much more he knew about it all than he admitted to the FO when asked for information. He was cheek by jowl with Arana in London at that time. He knew heaps and heaps of things and yet in his letter to FO he pretended he knew practically nothing.

Despite his distrust, when Casement went to see the prefect of Loreto, Dr Alayza Paz Soldan, he had to take Cazes along to translate. There, Casement suspected Cazes of mistranslating, and of speaking for himself instead of on behalf of Casement.

In spite of this, once Casement had related all that he had seen and learned in the Putumayo – including the names of the worst offenders – the prefect assured him that justice would be done. He also confirmed that the Peruvian government had already begun to make plans for its own commission of investigation into conditions in the Putumayo. The attorney general of Peru, José Salvador Cavero, had successfully applied to the Supreme Court in Lima to instruct the court in Iquitos to investigate the alleged crimes. Cavero was moved to do so after reading a disturbing letter printed on 7 August in the Lima newspaper *El Comercio*, by Enrique Deschamps, a distinguished member of a newly founded and influential intellectual association in Barcelona, the Sociedad Libre de Estudios Americanistas, who repeated the allegations made in *Truth* and implored the Peruvian government, whose reputation was at stake, to investigate the matter.

Despite Paz Soldan's assurances, Casement was unconvinced that any real investigation would take place, let alone that justice would prevail: Arana's grip on the town and the region was just too strong. As he was about to leave his office, Paz Soldan told Casement that the Peruvian government had only consented to his visit, and that of the Peruvian Amazon Company's commission, because they regarded the allegations as unfounded, and therefore attached no importance to the investigations.

When Casement went to say goodbye to Paz Soldan at the beginning of December, he was informed that the Peruvian government's own commission would be on its way to the Putumayo by the end of the month. Casement was appalled to learn that the *Liberal* was heading back to the Putumayo next day, and that on board would be Pablo Zumaeta, Arana's brother-in-law, and Benjamin Dublé, a senior manager in the Iquitos office of the Peruvian Amazon Company. Ostensibly, they were travelling to La Chorrera to dismiss the worst section chiefs. Casement, who was convinced that the Company would do everything in its power to hoodwink its own government, concluded that Zumaeta and Dublé were on their way to interfere with the witnesses. He was contemptuous of the prefect's weakness in allowing the two men to pre-empt the investigation.

He was now even more determined that the truth should prevail, and that the actions of the Peruvian government in trying to cover up the atrocities, as well as the atrocities themselves, would be revealed. He realised that all that was left to him was to 'try and move the civilised world to action'.

When Casement had returned to Iquitos from the Putumayo, and saw the Booth steamship *Atahualpa* tied up at the pier, he was overjoyed. His feelings of delight and relief that he was back safe and sound were tinged, however, with the ambivalence of seeing, in the ship's English flag, a

symbol of fairness and decency and, at the same time, an impediment to
the independence of his own land.

> Hurrah, I'll welcome the sight of the English flag . . . since there is no
> Irish flag – yet. I am glad to think there is a flag – red and all – that stands
> for fair dealing and some chivalry of mind and deed to weaker men.

During his time in the Putumayo, Casement had become increasingly
sympathetic to the Indians, and outraged by their plight. Although
dispatched by the Foreign Office to investigate conditions in the lands
belonging to the Peruvian Amazon Company, he only had authority
in respect to the Barbadians, who were British subjects. As he admitted
privately in 1913, he had gone way beyond his remit: had he failed or got
into trouble with the Peruvian authorities, he could have been disowned
by the British government for exceeding their instructions. Casement's
sense of outrage at greed and injustice, and his humanitarian sympathy
for the victims, led him to take great risks, both with his career in the
Foreign Office and with his life – he knew how easily people disappeared
in the Amazon.

Casement's experience of conditions in the Putumayo led him to
side emphatically with the Indians against their Hispanic oppressors.
While catching up on the news that he had missed during his time in
the Putumayo, Casement noticed in the 12 November edition of the
newspaper *El Oriente* that the Huambisa Indians, who lived some 400
miles to the west of Iquitos, had killed sixty-seven people, presumably
Peruvians. He read the article with glee – his only regret was that it was
not 6,700 people. As he remarked, 'these gentlemen went to conquistar
the Huambisas, but apparently they found that tribe still a pretty tough
nut to crack, and able to do some conquistaring on its own account'.
This was in line with his earlier reactions in the Putumayo; when Andres
O'Donnell told him of the murder of the Colombians by the Indians,
Casement had replied that his sympathy was with the Indians. Later, in
his diary, he added, 'I have more than sympathy – I would dearly love
to arm them, to train them, and drill them to defend themselves against
these ruffians.'

Later, of course, when he came to see the Irish as the Indians of the
British Isles, and tried to put these sentiments into action, he paid for

them with his life and reputation. But already, in 1910, it is clear that he was willing to risk his own life to expose oppression and exploitation, and to help its victims defend themselves.

On the day of his departure from Iquitos, Casement bade farewell to his friend the French trader Marius Vatan, who reminded him how dangerous the area was. 'It was only because [you] had come in an official character that [you were] allowed out alive . . . Your death would have been put down to Indians.' At about eleven o'clock on the morning of 2 December 1910, just a few days beyond the three months since his first view of Iquitos, the *Atahualpa* cast off from the Booth Company's pier.

> This is the last view I shall ever have of the Peruvian Amazon – of the Iquitos Indians and their pleasant cheerful faces – of the low line of houses fronting the wide, bold sweep of the [Amazon] as it comes down from its throne in the Andes – the mightiest river upon earth bathing the meanest shores.

But Casement was wrong about never seeing the Peruvian Amazon again. Less than a year later he would be back, Vatan's chilling message echoing in his mind.

12

A System of Armed Extortion

Casement arrived back in London on 4 January 1911. He was now free of the responsibilities and charges he had undertaken in the Putumayo. He had extended protection to twenty-one Barbadians. Of these, three decided to remain working for the Company, two remained as guides and interpreters for the Commission, ten headed off to work on the construction of the Madeira–Mamoré railway, and six, including Frederick Bishop, decided to return home. The Indian youths, Arédomi and Omarino, were sent, in Bishop's care, to Barbados to learn British ways, before proceeding to London.

Casement lost no time in getting in touch with his superiors at the Foreign Office and his supporters at the Anti-Slavery and Aborigines' Protection Society. He had already primed the Foreign Office to expect revelations. He told Sir Edward Grey that his investigations fully supported the charges made against the Peruvian Amazon Company, that the Commission members all agreed with his findings, and that the prefect in Iquitos was convinced also.

The following day, Casement met with Louis Mallet, the assistant under-secretary of state at the Foreign Office. The gist of their conversation was forwarded to Sir Edward Grey. Mallet stated that Casement had confirmed everything that Whiffen had told the Foreign Office in November of the previous year, and that 'the cruelties practised on the Indian tribes exceed in horror the Congo atrocities'. Casement promised an immediate report, and warned that the Peruvian Amazon Company would probably try 'to clear out but that their duty is to remain and put things right'.

Two days later, Casement sent a preliminary report. It was short and to the point, conveying succinctly the abysmal horror of the Putumayo.

He stated that his conclusions were based on voluminous evidence, and that he would be submitting a more detailed report in time; for now, he wanted his superiors to know the seriousness of the situation. His evidence came not only from the testimony of the Barbadians, but also from his own eyes:

> The marks of the lash were not confined to men or adults. Women, and even little children were more than once found, their limbs scarred with weals left by the thong of the twisted tapir-hide, which is the chief implement used for coercing and terrorising the native population of the region.

Appended to this preliminary statement was an annotated list of what Casement called the worst criminals in the Putumayo. They included six section chiefs he had met during the investigation, and he singled out two of them as being particularly vicious – Augusto Jiménez, the boss of Ultimo Retiro, and Armando Normand, the boss of Matanzas, 'a man of whom nothing good could be said'.

The report was eagerly received at the Foreign Office. Its preliminary nature was recognised, as was the fact that it dealt in the main with the Barbadians and their experiences. But, as one clerk noted, 'the report only gives one an idea of the condition of the natives, but one gathers enough to realise that it cannot be much less bad than that which prevailed in the Congo'. The main arguments were summarized and distributed around the office.

Even in its preliminary form, the report was a damning piece of evidence. Sir Edward Grey understood perfectly the publicity potential of the documents. He was happy to have its content passed on, confidentially, through Lucien Jerome, the British chargé d'affaires in Lima, to the Peruvian government; and, through James Bryce, the British ambassador in Washington, to the United States government. He did not want to share Casement's draft report with the Peruvian Amazon Company. Rather, he wanted to use the threat of publication to force them to reform their operations.

On 31 January Casement delivered his first complete report. Longer and more detailed than the preliminary version, it ran to nineteen foolscap sheets in its printed form, and focused on the experiences of the

Barbadians who had been interviewed. Casement described how they had been recruited in Barbados, the nature of their contract with Arana, and how they had been hood-winked: having been promised work as labourers, they found themselves rounding up Indians at gunpoint and 'acting as armed bullies and terrorists over the surrounding native population'. He reported how, because of extortionate prices and their own gambling, they had fallen into debt and thus become peons in the service of the Company, with little prospect of buying their way out. Casement provided detailed accounts of cruelty and murder as related to him by the Barbadians.

The report did not, of course, omit the condition of the Indians, although collecting testimony from them had been outside his brief. Casement was careful to make sure that his readers understood precisely what was going on in Arana's territory. His key point was that rubber-collecting in the Putumayo was not a commercial operation, as that term was normally understood: it was an exploitative operation aimed at the Indians. 'The true attraction from the first', Casement wrote, 'was not so much the presence of the scattered *Hevea Brasiliensis* trees throughout this remote forest, as the existence of fairly numerous tribes of docile, or at any rate of easily subdued Indians.' The '"civilised" intruders' came to subjugate (*conquistar* in Spanish) the Indians, not to annihilate them. The exploiters kept repeating that they were extending civilization to the Indians in the shape of profitable occupations. This was a travesty. Searching for words that might convey the true essence of the system, Casement chose 'brigandage' and 'a system of armed extortion'.

News of Casement's report had leaked out, and its existence soon became a matter of public record. On 8 February 1911, the Liberal MP Joseph King questioned the Foreign Office. Was there a report from Consul-General Casement? Were Barbadians employed in the Putumayo? Did they carry out acts of barbarity? The answer was simply that a report had been received and that it was being considered. Two weeks later, King returned to the issue. He now pressed the government: When did the government receive Casement's report? When would its contents be revealed to parliament? Had there been any communication about it with Peru? Questions like this – in particular about when the government intended to publish the report – were raised repeatedly for the rest of the year and into the next.

The Foreign Office's answer was anodyne, and would continue to be so for some time to come. The parliamentary under-secretary of state, Thomas McKinnon Wood, simply answered that the government had received Casement's report, and that communications with Peru had revealed that the government there had ordered a judicial commission to proceed to the Putumayo. Privately, however, the Foreign Office, which had the right to publish the report, decided not to reveal any more. As in the case of their dealings with the Peruvian Amazon Company, the Foreign Office decided that, in its relationship with the Peruvian government, the threat of publication was currently a more effective weapon than publication itself. 'If we were to publish', as Louis Mallet wrote in a departmental memo, 'it would deprive us of our chief lever with the Peruvian Government.'

Without the support of the United States, which did not seem to be forthcoming, there was little else the Foreign Office could do. As Grey pointed out, Arana's territory was not British – the British had no jurisdiction there, just a few British subjects. All they had was Casement's damning and deeply embarrassing report, and the implicit threat to name and shame.

Behind the scenes, Casement continued to influence the Foreign Office through his confidential correspondence with Louis Mallet. In one of his early letters to Mallet (dated 8 January), Casement was blunt about what he had seen in Arana's territory. There was evidence everywhere that Arana had the area under his thumb; that his crimes were well known but that no one dared say anything – including the prefect, Paz Soldan: 'honest but weak – all around him at Iquitos are rogues and villains'.

Casement suggested that it was the duty of the British government to make the Peruvians aware of what they had to lose by supporting Arana's empire. Peru needed to attract and retain foreign investment. It could not afford a scandal and, as Casement argued, 'Once these Putumayo atrocities were publicly vouched for and the shocking detail of the infamous treatment of the Indians made public all sources of foreign investment in Peru would dry up'.

Casement was furious about the treatment of the Indians, and assumed all right-minded folk would feel as he did. 'If only one of the ruffians were hanged', he exploded, 'or imprisoned even, for a very long time –

but hanging [is] best – it would go far to end their dastardly acts.' Even the four members of the Peruvian Amazon Company's commission – Barnes, Bell, Gielgud and Fox – had come around to Casement's way of thinking: '[I]t wasn't hanging they wanted to inflict – that was far too mild – they wanted torture by their own methods to be inflicted on Mr Arana's principal agents and year-long friends'.

Casement ended the letter with an anguished cry. 'I will make any personal sacrifice in the world to help you', he wrote to Mallet, 'and if it should come to wanting evidence I will get you the living personal witnesses of those on the spot at my own cost if needed.'

While producing his first report, Casement was painfully aware that the sufferings of the Indians that had so aroused his compassion were not what the investigation was about. He was distressed that he had to leave out so much about the Indians, and to include so much about the Barbadians and their ill-treatment that was comparatively trivial, though 'mean enough' in itself, as he put it. He began to write a second report 'giving chapter and verse as far as I can' on the condition of the Indians in the Putumayo, but it was slow and gruelling work. Towards the end of February, he wrote, 'I am "full up" with atrocities and horrors at times – and it is only the thought of those poor, hunted, gentle beings up there in the forest that keeps me going.' He finally dispatched it to the Foreign Office on 17 March 1911 – St Patrick's Day.

'I have the honour', Casement began his report, 'to transmit herewith a report dealing with the methods of rubber collection and the treatment of the Indians in the region dominated by the Peruvian Amazon Company on the Putumayo affluents of the Amazon.' In some 25,000 words, Casement detailed the horror of the Putumayo. He began by dispassionately laying out the region's geographical and historical context, but a simple statement of the fall in population after the arrival of white folk revealed the true and dreadful story. From an estimated 30,000 Huitoto Indians (the largest group native to the area) there seemed, he wrote, to be only about 10,000 left. Even allowing for the depredations of disease and warfare, which were fairly constant, it seemed that the arrival of the *caucheros*, and in particular the rubber-collecting system favoured by the Peruvian Amazon Company, had depleted the population by nearly two-thirds; it was, as Casement had remarked on previous occasions, even worse than the Congo. Paternoster had not been far off when he remarked in his first *Truth* article that the population of the area had been reduced by tens of thousands.

Once the reader had absorbed this dramatic drop in the population, Casement began the catalogue of what he termed 'continuous criminality'. He detailed the regime of violence, discussing the use of the gangs of *muchachos de confianza* to terrorize the Indian rubber collectors; the employment of Barbadians and others to round them up; the ritual nature of the *fabrico*; and the ubiquitous penal system – horrible floggings, sometimes to death, the use of the stocks, and deliberate regimes of starvation. Casement spoke about the Peruvian Amazon Company as operating with complete impunity, outside civil authority; and of the perpetrators, the chiefs of sections, as being a law unto themselves, addicted to a cycle of criminality. 'The freebooter on the Putumayo had [no care] for the hereafter to restrain him', Casement wrote.

> His first object was to get rubber, and the Indians would always last his time. He hunted, killed, and tortured to-day in order to terrify fresh victims for to-morrow. Just as the appetite comes in eating so each crime led on to fresh crimes, and many of the worst men on the Putumayo fell to comparing their battues and boasting of the numbers they had killed . . . Such men had lost all sight or sense of rubber gathering – they were simply beasts of prey who lived upon the Indians and delighted in shedding their blood.

Casement recounted the story of one Bora Indian, a young cacique or chief referred to in the Barbadian depositions as Katenere, 'the bravest and most resolute opponent the murderers had encountered'. The story went that Katenere, like so many other Indians, consented to bring in rubber for Armando Normand, the chief of the Matanzas section, but because he was being badly treated he fled into the forest. After some time, Katenere and his wife were captured and returned to the station, where he was put into the stocks. One day Bartolomé Zumaeta, another of Arana's brothers-in-law and a senior agent of the Company in Iquitos, arrived and raped Katenere's wife in front of him. Somehow Katenere escaped with his wife. He managed to get hold of some Winchesters, and with a small band of supporters began to wage an offensive against the Company's agents. This was some time in 1908. For the next two years Katenere's mission was successful, including a major triumph when he personally found and shot Zumaeta dead. However, on one of the Company's expeditions to hunt him down, Katenere's wife was captured and taken to the station, and when he tried to rescue her he was shot down. So ended the only resistance to the Company's ruthless system.

About a week later, Casement sent the Foreign Office verbatim transcripts of the thirty interviews with the Barbadians that he had recorded. Readers could immerse themselves in all of the horrible details, recounted by real voices, which had to stand in and speak for the missing voice of the Indian. This completed Casement's work. Mallet's first reaction was to the point: he warned Sir Edward Grey, 'The details are so sickening that you may not care to read them.'

Meanwhile, Arana's family had taken up residence in London, in a spacious house near Hyde Park. No sooner had Casement disembarked in England from Iquitos than he received the first of a series of letters from Arana asking to meet him and discuss his ideas for the reform of the Company. Casement thought the communication very cheeky; he simply wrote back to say that he had been on official business in the Putumayo, and was not at liberty to discuss it. Still, Casement was curious – 'it may do good to meet the rascal', he wrote to Mallet; but at this stage it went no further.

Several months passed. Arana had left London. Casement heard no more from him, but he then resurfaced. He had been selected as the Peruvian representative at the International Rubber and Allied Trades Exhibition, scheduled to open in Islington's Agricultural Hall in late June. When, in early March, the Foreign Office first heard of this appointment, Louis Mallet, who learned of it in a telegram from Lucien Jerome, the British chargé d'affaires in Lima, was absolutely livid. He had never heard of the International Rubber Exhibition; but on the matter of Arana's presence at it as a representative of Peru, he was not short of words: 'It is an outrage', he commented in a memo on the subject, 'that Arana should be sent here as Peruvian representative to any exhibition.' He continued:

Can we object to Arana's appointment or move the promoters to do so? The Prince of Wales is a Patron of the exhibition and we have called the attention of foreign governments to it. Arana is a criminal of the most appalling type and ought to be hanged.

A discussion then followed among a number of Foreign Office clerks as to the best course of action. The matter was taken so seriously that they asked Sir William Davidson, the Foreign Office legal adviser, whether there was any possibility of charging Arana with murder once he stepped onto British soil. His answer was entirely in the negative. So Arana could not be apprehended but, Mallet suggested, if he did come to represent his country at the exhibition, 'the King should be asked to withdraw his patronage'.

Algernon Law, a senior clerk, came up with the most useful suggestion. The manager of the exhibition should be sent for and told that they should telegraph Peru to say that Arana was not a 'persona grata' to them or to the delegates from other countries, and that he could not be received. So the machinery of government began to move. Mallet met Mr Staines Manders, the managing director of the International Rubber Exhibition, near the end of March. Three weeks later, Manders let Mallet know that Arana had resigned his post as his government's representative at the exhibition.

Arana, always wanting the final word, told his London board a completely different story – an indication of the extent to which he deceived his own directors. The minutes of the Peruvian Amazon Company recorded that Arana had declined to accept his government's wish to be the country's representative on the grounds that he had pressing business in the Putumayo.

13

Deus ex Machina

After Casement left the Putumayo, the Commission continued its work visiting stations in and around the Caraparaná, which were under the control of El Encanto, in addition to those controlled by La Chorrera. Finally leaving the Putumayo on 22 February 1911, and after a stay in Iquitos and Manaus, the Commission sailed for England on 12 April – except for Gielgud, who remained in Manaus to attend to business matters there.

Since he had returned to London, Casement had from time to time received news from and about the Commission and its progress. Cazes kept him informed, but the Commission members themselves also wrote with news, and their sense of what was going on and what could be done. Louis Barnes, the Commission's head, wrote to Casement from El Encanto towards the end of December 1910, shortly after he had left Iquitos for England. If Casement had any doubts that the members shared his views, then this letter dispelled his uncertainties. Using language that Casement would have found very familiar, Barnes informed him that at Santa Catalina, a rubber station to the east of La Chorrera, he 'had the great pleasure of shaking by the hand a Bora who was present at the despatching to a warmer land of Bartolomé Zumaeta, and I was told he took part in it'. Barnes was referring to that heroic incident, as Casement himself had put it, when Katenere killed Zumaeta in revenge. Barnes further endeared himself to Casement in the next sentence: 'After seeing the terrible way the poor wretches have been treated one can only wonder how they left a Blanco [a Spanish-Peruvian] alive or allow one to live.' Barnes brought Casement up to date on where they had gone and whom they had met, and suggested new names to put on the so-called blacklist of criminals. He ended the letter on a note of solidarity: 'Rest assured', he told Casement,

> we shall be no party to any attempt at white-washing or hushing things up in any underhand way, what you told the Prefect . . . is correct and if necessary I will drive it home to him and I know the others are with me.

So they were. Walter Fox, the rubber specialist attached to the Commission on the recommendation of the Royal Botanic Gardens at Kew, was a soft-spoken, gentle man, and the oldest member of the Commission. Fox did not mince his words when he reported back to Colonel David Prain, the director at Kew. Most of Fox's communication, naturally, concerned the flora of the region, and particularly the botany of the rubber trees, but he was so outraged by what else he had seen that he could not withhold a stinging and shocking assessment: 'I wish not to anticipate our reply to that further than that I should like to exterminate 5/6 of the employees here who are placed over the unfortunate aborigines. The whole system of management is wrong from top to bottom'.

Even Henry Gielgud, the secretary of the Peruvian Amazon Company, and the individual in the Commission that Casement had had the most trouble persuading that they were witnessing a crime and not a commercial system, had come around. He, too, had written to Casement, commenting on the fact that Abelardo Agüero, the chief of Abisinia section, and the man accused of unspeakable acts of torture, maiming and murder as an agent of the Company, had fled towards Colombian territory to the north with his retinue of *muchachos* in tow when he got wind that charges might be on their way. Before he departed, he and his men had set fire to the Boras' *chácaras* (garden plots where they grew their food) as his final act of evil. Gielgud recounted this, adding that it was a pity that the Indians 'couldn't tie [Agüero] up in one of the *chácaras* with his friends – it would have been an acceptable holocaust'. Casement sent Mallet these choice quotes in order that the Foreign Office should know, in advance of its arrival back in England, that the Commission's views of the Putumayo were no different from his own. Casement's persistence had scored a singular victory.

* * *

The idea that the Indians could be saved only by a British public company subject to British regulations – which would introduce a system of exchange to replace the one based on terrorism, exploitation and quotas – had started to form in Casement's mind while he was still in the Putumayo. Whatever he might have felt about British rule in Ireland, no well-regulated British company, he believed, would resort to exploitative practices in its operations. It would pay a fair wage for a fair day's work, Casement was convinced. He did not believe in turning the clock back. He had made this perfectly clear when discussing colonialism and Africa with Morel. 'A gentler humanity' is what he believed in, and a British company founded on sound commercial and legal principles was now the only way to save the Indians.

The Foreign Office was keenly aware of Casement's deeply held view that the best future for the Indians lay with a reconstituted British company. Sir Edward Grey made this the goal of the Foreign Office as well. The scene was now set for a battle for control of the Putumayo. There were two possible outcomes. One was a reconstituted Peruvian Amazon Company, with headquarters in London, which appeared to be the best solution for the Indians. The second was a private company run by Arana and his men as a continuation of the same old system of terror and violence. Casement hoped that the Peruvian government could be urged diplomatically to prosecute Arana, making the second possibility less likely.

Casement's report was a major part of the Foreign Office's arsenal in its battle with Arana. In early March, Grey had asked Casement for his opinion on whether he agreed that his first report 'might be communicated confidentially to the company at once with an intimation to the effect that the Secretary of State assumes that steps will be taken to put a stop forthwith to the practices disclosed'. Casement's opinion was that it would be better to await the Commission and their report before transmitting a copy of his own. On 29 April the Commission disembarked back in England. Within a short time they would be delivering their report to the Company. Grey agreed that timing was critical, and waited for the right moment to strike. Grey's other plan was to have Casement attend those board meetings at which reform measures were under discussion. Confidentially, as he told Casement, he wanted to know the Company's intentions, and 'to some extent impose [my] wishes on them through you in an unofficial manner'.

On 4 May, Casement went to the Foreign Office and agreed to attend board meetings on the terms that Grey had outlined. Knowing that the Commission's report would be delivered any day, Grey's plan was put into action. On 13 May, Grey wrote to the Peruvian Amazon Company. In an attempt to get a positive response, Grey began by reassuring the board that it was not being accused of anything – he was convinced, he told them, that they were ignorant of the 'appalling state of affairs' – but that, in return for this absolution, they should put in place a set of reform measures which would prevent the abuses ever happening again. He then played his trump card.

> To help the Company in this object he would be willing to place at the disposal of your Directors unofficially and privately the services of Mr Casement who from the knowledge gained from his recent tour and his previous experience in such matters would, it is confidently expected, be in a position to offer the Company valuable assistance. Mr. Casement has expressed his willingness to do all he can in helping to draw up a scheme of reform and to attend, if desired, any meetings which your Directors may hold with this object in view.

Though he agreed to attend board meetings, Casement was shocked to learn that Grey had exonerated the directors. Some were ignorant, he admitted to Mallet, but Arana was not, and 'none of them *should have been ignorant*' (my emphasis). In a particularly astute reading of the situation, Casement reminded Mallet that, from the outset, the directors had chosen to accept Arana's word without question, and proceeded to hide behind 'this error of judgement' in order to claim ignorance. 'Support them in the future to do right as far as possible, and to repair the terrible wrongs of the past but don't think you are called on to explicitly champion their past ignorance.'

Casement's criticism of Grey's hasty exoneration – what he termed the 'unnecessary professions of faith' – found favour with Mallet. In a memo to Grey he echoed Casement's view. Grey, clearly embarrassed, answered that he only had the 'British' directors in mind. Grey had to backtrack and so, on 31 May, he wrote to the Company, under the pretence of asking for the Commission's report, to clarify his position on the ignorance of the directors in respect of the abuses in the Putumayo.

What came out was a bit of a fudge: 'In expressing his opinion that your Directors were in complete ignorance of the appalling state of affairs revealed in Mr Casement's reports Sir E. Grey is to be understood to refer only to the British members of the Board.'

The Commission's report, presented at a board meeting of 17 May, was very wide-ranging but, as was expected from the brief given to its members, touched mostly on commercial and financial matters. It was mild compared to Casement's, a Foreign Office clerk noted. Nevertheless, though the report's details were sparse, its analysis shallow by comparison, and its main concerns commercial rather than humanitarian, the Commission came remarkably close to Casement's view in its conclusions. The management of the operation, the Commission concluded, was hopeless, producing 'abominable results from the commercial as well as from the humanitarian point of view'. They hardly ever visited the area, and let the chiefs of the rubber stations do more or less what they pleased as long as they got the rubber; and as their remuneration was based solely on how much rubber they got, they would resort to any method to get as much rubber as possible in the shortest time. The Indians were treated as the chiefs' property. Not collecting the required amount of rubber became a heinous offence, and was treated accordingly. 'The ultimate welfare of the Indians did not interest him, and such important matters as the planting of the 'chácaras' [garden plots for growing food] and conservation of rubber were allowed to go by the board.' The report then went on to repeat an observation that could be traced back to Saldaña Rocca in Iquitos in 1907, and to Casement more recently, that the Putumayo was a haven for convicts, and that 'unfortunately, too many of the Company's employees were recruited [from that class]'. The chiefs of the rubber stations were, in the Commission's opinion, totally unfit for the job – they were uneducated, lacked character, and had not the slightest idea about rubber. 'One chief, who had been in the Putumayo for seven years, frankly admitted that he only knew a rubber tree when he saw it bleeding, and only a few even knew the native names for the trees', the report noted.

Getting straight to the point of the nature of the labour system that the Company followed, the report concluded that 'labour supervision as carried out by such men under the conditions above described and in the absence of any Governmental control rapidly became indistinguishable from slave-driving.'

As Grey had hoped, Casement was invited to a board meeting to discuss the Commission's report, set for 1 June. He insisted that the Foreign Office provide him with a shorthand writer to take accurate, detailed, notes of what was said. 'I am not going to leave anything to chance', he told Mallet,

> and to the 'recollection' of anyone after the event. A great deal is possible, to my mind, with men in such a desperate hole as these men are in, and my remarks might be misinterpreted, or misunderstood afterwards – so it will be as well to have a trusty record kept of anything I say apart from the desirability of a record of what they say.

The directors were all present, with the major exception of Arana, together with the members of the Commission. The meeting lasted two hours and, according to Casement, accomplished nothing. Casement was dismayed that the board's directors were 'all at sea' and did not seem to 'know what to do or have any ability to carry out a scheme of reforms. They are in the hands of Julio C. Arana and his informal gang of robber cousins and brothers-in-law out there.'

At the meeting, Casement read out a letter he had just received from Arana. In it Arana expressed complete astonishment that, as he put it, 'there existed a state of affairs which one could hardly expect of mankind'. He continued to thank Casement for all that he had done 'to all concerned and especially to the natives of that region'. Arana devoted most of the letter to congratulating himself for already having taken the necessary steps towards reform, and excusing himself, because of financial problems with the Company, for being unable to pay as many 'visits of inspection' to the Putumayo as he wished.

Casement's reaction to the letter was clearly evident in his annotations to it, which included phrases such as 'liar' and 'wholly untrue'. While he may have acted diplomatically at the meeting, Casement made it quite clear to the directors that Arana was culpable and that 'no sincere reform was possible with him on the Board'. Casement went on to suggest that reform might begin by sending

a member of the Commission or one of the British directors to El
Encanto and another to La Chorrera to work with Tizon on changing
the system. The board accepted this proposal.

A second meeting was called for 28 June. By then, however, King
George V had ascended the throne after the death of his father, Edward
VII, on 6 May 1910. The honours list accompanying George V's
coronation on 22 June 1911 included the conferral of a knighthood on
Roger Casement. Sir Edward Grey, on whose recommendation the
honour was conferred, was the first to congratulate him, Sir Roger
Casement, 'in recognition of your valuable services in connection with
your recent Mission to the Putumayo District.'

Casement was deeply troubled by the honour – even more than he
had been six years earlier when he was made a Companion of Saint
Michael and Saint George for his Congo investigation. Then he had
felt that accepting an honour from the British would be frowned on in
Ireland; now he was sure that accepting a knighthood would be seen by
the Irish as traitorous. He certainly felt a traitor himself. The tension was
increasing between his sense of the injustice of British rule in Ireland and
his allegiance to the British state, in whose service he had come face to
face with gross injustices in the Congo and the Putumayo. His problem
with the new title was evident in a letter he wrote to Gerald Spicer,
head of the American Section at the Foreign Office, a few days after his
knighthood had been announced. 'Thank you for your congratulations
and good wishes', it began, innocently enough, and then the tone
changed abruptly:

> . . . altho' if you ever attempt to 'Sir Roger' me again I'll enter into an
> alliance with the Aranas and Pablo Zumaeta to cut you off someday in
> the woods of St James' Park, and convert you into a rubber worker to
> our joint profit.

Like the earlier award, Casement's knighthood was only grudgingly
accepted.

Arana was absent from the second meeting. The board explained that
it 'had not invited him, thinking his presence would not be welcome to
Sir R. Casement'. Casement responded by pointing out that

as Senor Arana was a Director, and the most important one too, it might be well for the Board to ensure his presence at their further meetings, since their decisions must be largely dependent on their ability to carry him with them, or else on their power to compel his acceptance.

Then the directors dropped a bombshell – the Company had no money left and was struggling to carry on the business. Rubber output from the Putumayo had fallen in 1910 by 20 per cent on the previous year's figure, and world prices had taken a severe tumble, thanks largely to the appearance on the market of cheaper plantation rubber from the Far East. Added to that, the Company's level of debt had risen to dangerous levels. There was panic among some of the rubber station chiefs in the Putumayo following Casement's visit, and they were demanding their commissions. In addition, Pablo Zumaeta, having mortgaged the Putumayo estates to his sister Eleanora (Arana's wife) for £60,000, now claimed, with his power of attorney, the repayment of the principal plus interest on her behalf. The Company's British bankers had refused to extend any more credit.

Once Arana saw that the Company's own commission was not going to whitewash conditions in the Putumayo, and when he found out, as he must have done from Tizon, that Casement's findings were utterly damning, he must have realised that he had exposed his operations to unnecessary scrutiny, and that floating his company on the London Stock Exchange had been a big mistake. Though it had seemed at the time to make him a player on the world commercial stage, thanks to Hardenburg, Whiffen, Casement and the Company's commission, the true nature of his operation had been exposed, and the Peruvian Amazon Company was now a liability. He had to retrace his steps and withdraw his rubber empire from the limelight. Behind the scenes, Arana sought a solution to his problems by financially draining the Peruvian Amazon Company, leaving it with as few assets as possible, and effectively killing it as a going concern. Pablo Zumaeta's insistence on the payment of the mortgage was a major step in that direction. The Company was to be 'robbed left, right and centre by Arana and his gang', as Casement put it. What was left would not suffice, Casement feared, to serve as the foundations of the hoped-for British company.

It was evident that there was little hope of anything positive being done, because every reformative action, such as sending out people from England to the Putumayo, depended on funds that the Company no longer had. As Henry Read – one of the directors and a highly experienced Latin America hand – put it when pressed by Casement to commit to some action, and soon: 'You cannot get blood out of a stone; we have no money to carry on anything unless something turns up.' The meeting broke up, but not before deciding on a further meeting, set for 5 July, at which Arana would be present.

Casement was despondent. After talking it over with Louis Barnes, he decided to suggest to Read and to the others that their best option now lay in raising money themselves to pay for someone to travel out to the Putumayo and put the reforms in place. But Casement saw little hope that this quite desperate measure would succeed. As he remarked to Spicer,

> Their efforts seem hopeless. The business incapacity at this end has been on a par with the criminal neglect at the other (Manaos [*sic*] and Iquitos). The only men equal to their task were the murderers. They killed effectually and got rubber too, which the Zumaeta-Arana family seem to have appropriated in one way or another between them. Everything since the Company was formed has been left to J.C. Arana in London and Pablo Zumaeta in Iquitos.

A week later the board met again, and this time Arana was present. It must have been quite a scene – Casement glaring at Arana, suspecting him of trying to break up the Company but not being able to prove it or even voice his suspicions; Arana continuing to act as though the problems had nothing to do with him. The meeting failed to solve the Company's problems, and it soon became clear that its finances were in an even worse state than they seemed. Arana cynically offered to help by halving his directorial salary, bringing it down to £1,250 per annum.

Casement left the meeting with the distinct impression that the Peruvian Amazon Company as currently constituted was unlikely to survive, something that was corroborated by a letter from the chairman of the board, John Russell Gubbins, asking for a private interview at Casement's home. At the meeting Gubbins told Casement that the news was very bad: the Company had outstanding debts exceeding £100,000.

Furthermore, the board believed, and had evidence in support, that Arana and family were determined to oust the British directors and liquidate the Peruvian Amazon Company as now constituted. Such a liquidation would mean that the Company would cease to be a public concern and as a consequence the cloak of protection that Casement hoped a British public company would provide to the Putumayo Indians would disappear.

Time was now of the essence. Something had to be done to retain a civilized presence in the Putumayo, for the sake of the Indians and to stop Arana getting his way. Money was the only answer. As Casement told Spicer at the Foreign Office in the wake of his interview with Gubbins, Arana wanted the Putumayo to himself, and 'when the company breaks up (which Gubbins thinks will be the 17th instant, if some Deus ex Machina does not offer £100,000 to start with) they may exploit the last rubber trees and last Indians to their private profit'. Casement put it bluntly: '[T]hey and their Iquitos pals would want such a lot of bribing to get them out of the Putumayo that only a Carnegie, or some unusually philanthropic person, could afford to purchase their retirement'.

At its next meeting, on 14 July, the board turned, remarkably enough, to Casement to find money from among his 'humanitarian friends' to buy out Arana and save the Company. Casement had these contacts – to people such as William Cadbury, the Quaker chocolate manufacturer and philanthropist, and Charles Booth, the chairman and owner of Booth Steamship Company and a great social reformer; and, through other contacts, to the great industrialist of the age, Andrew Carnegie. Casement immediately threw himself into a frantic round of fundraising.

But despite his heroic efforts, by the end of July most of Casement's attempts had failed. The reason he heard most often for not investing funds was that the time was not right for wild rubber. Rubber harvested mainly on British and Dutch plantations in the Far East, and which had first begun to arrive in European ports in significant volumes in 1909, looked as though it would soon outstrip wild sources. The output of plantation rubber had doubled in one year, and was set to do the same again, while that of wild rubber had stagnated.

Amid the drama of trying to save the Company, and thus, it was hoped, the Indians in the Putumayo, Arédomi and Omarino, the two Huitoto youths Casement had brought out of the Putumayo with him, had arrived in Southampton. Their stay in Barbados, which was only to prepare them for the English leg of their experience, had lasted longer than expected. Now, on 26 June, they were at last on English soil.

As he had planned, Casement used the two youths as publicity for the Putumayo as often as he could. It would not be unfair to say that he used them as exhibits. They were taken to the Foreign Office and shown off at various gatherings, some at the homes of close friends, at an Anti-Slavery and Aborigines' Protection Society meeting, and at the Universal Races Congress, which met in London between 26 and 29 July.

Not long after that, the wider public was introduced to Arédomi and Omarino. On 1 August, the *Daily News* printed an article with the title 'Inferno In A Paradise'. The bulk of the article took the form of an informal interview with the two Huitoto youths. It was a unique moment. Readers were drawn straight into the lives of the Huitoto people with an immediacy they could never have got from the reports already in circulation, such as the earlier articles in *Truth* and the parliamentary questions and answers printed in newspapers such as *The Times*. 'It is already known in this country', the article began,

> that the rubber merchants of Peru have exploited the Indians of the forests in the north-east of the country, and are forcing them to work by diabolical cruelty. Yesterday I heard from the lips of two young Indians who have escaped from this 'inferno in a paradise' a plain tale of the sufferings of their people, the Witota [*sic*] tribe . . . I met them in the studio of an artist who is painting their portraits, and found them in native dress, a loin-cloth of white bark. Their brown bodies are finely built, and their faces bright and intelligent. They may be savages: they are certainly gentlemen. Their home is a forest on the banks of the Igara Parana, a tributary of the Putumayo, in that wild tract of country in the north-east of Peru.

The interviewer went on to ask the youths about the frightful abuses the Indians had been suffering in the Putumayo. Omarino told of how he had witnessed his own mother's beheading on the order of José Fonseca, the chief of La Sabana rubber station. He also recounted that women were taken from their families and forced into harems for the rubber station chiefs, and that his people suffered terribly carrying the extraordinary loads of rubber through the forest, and were dying of starvation.

'There was no doubting the lads' sincerity', the article continued.

> They told their hideous tale in a simple, straightforward way. They have escaped; others are being tortured and done to death. The rubber districts of Peru are far away from the civilized parts of the country. Iquitos, the headquarters of the rubber trade, is filled with adventurers lusting for rubber – godless men who hold nothing sacred. There is no church and no religious influence in the town.

Casement had wanted to use Arédomi and Omarino to publicize the horrors of the Putumayo, and the article in the *Daily News* certainly did that. But Casement had more long-term ideas for them, which included having them educated in Ireland at St Edna's, a bilingual school (Gaelic and English), begun and run by Patrick Pearse, the Irish nationalist and political activist – a plan which did not materialize. Casement probably realized that taking the youths to Ireland was unlikely to be in their best interests, and that it would be difficult since he would not be with them. It was, as he told his friend William Cadbury, an idealistic rather than a practical proposition: 'I fear with me gone they might not understand things and give great trouble – and there is the far off, later future to think of.' He would have to return them to Peru.

The final blow to the attempt to find a buyer for the Company came on 3 August, when Casement's last hope was disappointed: Andrew Carnegie failed to register an interest. With Gubbins also failing to raise funds, there was no doubt that the Company was going into liquidation; it was only a matter of time – and of weeks rather than months.

Then good news reached London. The Foreign Office learned late in July that the Peruvian government's own judicial investigation of conditions in the Putumayo was underway in Iquitos. Several chiefs of rubber stations had been arrested in Iquitos for alleged atrocities, and warrants had been issued for more than 200 people. With the Peruvian Amazon Company on the verge of liquidation, Casement hoped that the

Indians might be saved through the judicial system, with some kind of protection afforded them against oppression and exploitation.

Perhaps it was a vain hope, but Casement was determined to find out more and to be on the spot. On 5 August 1911, he wrote to the chairman of the board of the Company with the news that he would no longer 'be at liberty to attend further meetings . . . I am leaving this country at an early date.'

14

The Veil over the Putumayo Mystery

It was near the end of July, as Casement realized his fundraising efforts had come to nothing, that he suggested to Gerald Spicer that he return to Iquitos. The Peruvian Amazon Company, he wrote, was on the verge of collapse; and recent telegrams had convinced him that events in Iquitos, including the judicial investigation, were moving quickly. These developments made it imperative, Casement argued, that 'we should have someone at Iquitos with as little delay as possible to watch and as far as may be guide events locally.' 'I am quite willing to go out at once', he continued, 'if it is thought I could be of service in this direction. I think I might be.'

The tenor of Casement's letter became more insistent as it progressed. 'I am quite ready to go', he wrote, 'and should be glad to try and put a square ending to what has begun and carried so successfully to this length – and were I in Iquitos I could influence things a good deal in the right direction.' It was also clear that Casement saw his return to Iquitos as a covert operation. He suggested that the Foreign Office should let it be known that he was returning to ensure that the authorities were not questioning the Barbadians who had decided to remain in Iquitos. Casement's real intentions – 'to influence the authorities to take sincere and effective measures on the Putumayo' – were to be kept quiet.

Spicer agreed with Casement's suggestion and pressed it on the department. 'Sir R. Casement's idea is a good one', he urged:

> There would be considerable advantage in his being at Iquitos to watch the course of events . . . Sir R. Casement's knowledge of all the circumstances is so extensive that he will be able to find out easily how the trials are conducted & what is now the actual state of affairs on the Putumayo.

On 3 August 1911, Casement visited the Foreign Office to make final arrangements with Spicer. He would leave London for Iquitos on 16 August. The word was put around the department that he was returning to Iquitos on public service in his position as consul-general for Brazil. A telegram containing Casement's plans was sent to Lucien Jerome, the British chargé d'affaires in Lima, who had authorization to pass the information on to the Peruvian government and to David Cazes, still the honorary British consul in Iquitos.

Henry Gielgud, Seymour Bell and Louis Barnes, members of the Company's commission, were given to understand that Casement was returning to Rio de Janeiro. He did not want anyone on the board knowing his true destination; he wanted his arrival in Iquitos to be as much of a surprise as possible.

Casement's close friends, however, knew where he going and what he was up to. To his ally and fellow humanitarian Edmund Morel, Casement was particularly frank:

> I go *again* to the forest . . . it is only a mission, a continuance of my work
> of last year and I hope to make a clean sweep this time. We have got the
> Peruvian govt. on its mettle and I am going to try and keep it clean and
> bright.

Casement admitted to Morel that the Putumayo had been consuming all his energies. His return to Iquitos, a town which he hated, filled him with moral purpose: 'I shall here be an instrument of good, and maybe the means of ending a ghastly system of wrong-doing.' However, he also told Morel, he had not forgotten his primary objective in life. 'This is my last external effort on behalf of others. Henceforth & for aye I shall concentrate on Ireland alone – & neither Congo, nor Hindu nor Inca shall haul me aside'.

In fact, as it turned out, the Putumayo would occupy Casement for longer than he intended.

In June, the subject of the Iquitos consulate came up in the Foreign Office. Casement had commented when he was previously in Iquitos that the situation of an unsalaried consul could lead to conflicts of interest. David Cazes was an example; he supported himself in Iquitos

Roger Casement on the deck of one of the ships he used
on the Amazon to get to Iquitos in September 1910

The Devil: Julio César Arana, 1907

The *Liberal* on the Putumayo, 1910

The headquarters of the Peruvian Amazon Company at
La Chorrera, 1912 (photograph by Stuart Fuller)

A Barbadian with two *muchachos de confianza*, the Company's hired guns (below); Captain Thomas Whiffen's exploration party, setting out in search of the missing Eugène Robuchon, 1908 (above)

The Peruvian Amazon Company's commission, La Chorrera,
1910; (left to right) Juan Tizon, Seymour Bell, Henry Gielgud,
Walter Fox, Louis Barnes and Roger Casement

Three Indian youths carrying substantial loads of
rubber, 1910 (photograph by Roger Casement)

Image and reality: Cartoon printed in *La Felpa* of an Indian being flogged in La Chorrera (above); source photograph by Eugène Robuchon, 1903 (below)

The Mark of Arana: This photograph, taken by Henry Gielgud in 1910, shows the scars on an Indian boy who was flogged at Ultimo Retiro for not bringing in enough rubber. Casement had sent a copy of it to the British Embassy in Washington to help it put pressure on the State Department to become actively involved in the Putumayo issue.

Slavery and the 'civilising mission' on the Putumayo. Above left, a terrified
Huitoto woman. Above right, Carlos Rey de Castro stated that fifteen years
before this woman was nude and tattooed; now she made her own clothes
on the latest model of the Singer sewing machine (Silvino Santos, 1912).
Bottom, chained Indian rubber-gatherers in stocks (W. E. Hardenburg, 1912)

Adolfus Gibbs, one of the Barbadians that Casement
interviewed in Iquitos in September 1910 (photograph
probably taken by Silvino Santos in Manaus in 1913)

One of the many political cartoons in the British press
following the publication of Roger Casement's report
in 1912 (*Westminster Gazette*, 18 July 1912)

as a trader, and since rubber was the main and most lucrative product, it was inevitable that his operations would involve the rubber trade. The time had come, Casement argued, to place the Iquitos consulate on a salaried, rather than an honorary, footing.

Spicer agreed, as did Mallet, to whom it fell to write to the Treasury for the necessary finance. Mallet told the Treasury, briefly, about the background of the Putumayo issue, stressing in particular the point that the process of getting reforms in the area was at a sensitive stage, and that the Foreign Office was working closely with both the Company and the Peruvian government to make progress. Explaining why he was writing to them, Mallet pointed out – as Casement had urged him to do – that the Foreign Office thought that reforms in the Putumayo would be neither far-reaching nor permanent unless they were supervised by a salaried British consul. Because of the difficulties of operating in such a distant part of the world, the Foreign Office requested a salary and allowances in excess of the normal rate.

It was essential to find the right man and install him as quickly as possible. Casement insisted,

> You should choose a good man for the Consul at Iquitos, a young man (not too young of course, but one who can stand the climate and the heat) – a man . . . with brains, intelligence and a good, honest nature, who can put two and two together.

– and he knew the man. George Babington Michell, at that time posted in Paris as acting consul-general, had begun his diplomatic career in 1902 with a first posting to Morocco, where he remained for the next few years until, in 1905, he was posted to the Congo. He stayed in the Congo for two years, and it was because of their shared interest in the Congo that he had become acquainted with Casement. They had recently met in Paris, after Casement's return from the Putumayo. Michell was forty-seven, the same age as Casement – not exactly a young man – but he had 'tropical' experience, and this counted for a great deal in the circumstances.

Three days after petitioning the Treasury, the Foreign Office learned that their request to fund a salaried consul in Iquitos had been granted. On 21 July, Casement heard that Michell had secured the appointment.

Although Michell was prepared to leave for Iquitos as early as late September, on Casement's insistence his scheduled departure was taken out of Foreign Office control; it would instead depend entirely on the situation in Iquitos, something Casement himself would assess first-hand. Once Casement gave the go-ahead for Michell to go to Iquitos, the Foreign Office would terminate Cazes's appointment as honorary consul.

All was now set up. On 16 August 1911, after a flurry of letter-writing and shunting between England and Ireland, Casement arrived at Waterloo station to board a train for Southampton. With him were Arédomi and Omarino. Seeing them off that day was William Rothenstein, one of the country's leading painters, and his wife. Casement had commissioned Rothenstein to produce a double portrait of the two Huitoto youths. The first sitting had taken place in Rothenstein's Hampstead studio in the middle of July, both youths dressed as they had been in the Putumayo: for authenticity, Casement presented Arédomi with a richly plumed head-covering he had brought from the Putumayo. Rothenstein had had them to his studio several times, but on 15 August Casement told him that there would be no more sittings. He was taking them home, but not to the Putumayo – 'I shall not leave them in the forest again', Casement wrote to Rothenstein,

> but with a good friend in Iquitos where they will be happy and cared for and have some decent future – and I have no doubt, in many days to come they will think and talk of you and of the 'picture'.

Later that day in Southampton, Casement and the Huitoto youths boarded SS *Magdalena*, bound for Bridgetown, Barbados. 'I return when Providence permits me', Casement wrote to Rothenstein, 'but they, poor forest spirits, never again!'

So far as the Foreign Office was concerned, Casement was going to Iquitos to keep his eye on events there, to help ensure the success of what seemed from a distance to be a genuine move for reform in the Putumayo. But his decision to go to the Amazon via Barbados suggests another plan. He was going to try and persuade one of the Barbadians, presumably Frederick Bishop, to act as his interpreter. Casement was intending to go to the Putumayo – 'to the "twilight"', as he put it in his parting letter to Rothenstein.

Casement knew Barbados well, having spent two months there in the summer of 1908 recuperating from illness shortly after taking up his post as consul in Pará. 'The place is so small a mouse could not hide' is how he summed up the island. To his enormous surprise, upon his arrival in Bridgetown on 28 August, Casement was greeted by none other than Andres O'Donnell, the chief of the Entre Rios rubber section in the Putumayo, who, Casement had felt, possibly on account of his Irish connection, had not plumbed the depths to which the other chiefs had sunk. O'Donnell had been living on the island for the past six months. He was owed quite a bit of money by Arana, but had no hope of ever getting it back. Casement commented that 'he looked abjectly miserable'.

Although Casement had initially been quite generous in his assessment of O'Donnell, he was not about to conceal O'Donnell's presence from the authorities. 'I don't think he killed Indians for pleasure or sport – but only to terrorize for rubber – a thing he was appointed to do by his superiors,' he wrote to Spicer from Bridgetown. Although 'he had a very well kept and well planted station and his Indians seemed happier than any others I met' – O'Donnell had served Arana for seven years – 'it was just the same infamous regime of extortion and terrorism there as elsewhere – but without the hideous torturings and indecencies of many of the other posts'. Even if he was the 'least criminal of the chief agents', Casement wanted Spicer to let the Peruvian government know that O'Donnell was in Barbados, so that they could take the necessary steps to have him extradited to Peru to face charges there.

Casement, Arédomi and Omarino did not remain long in Barbados. Aside from O'Donnell, Casement did not encounter any other Putumayo Barbadians, and left the island without the interpreter he had hoped to enlist.

On 4 September, they boarded their ship bound for Pará. Although he had failed to find an interpreter, Casement had met Herbert Spencer Dickey, an American medical doctor who was recuperating from an attack of yellow fever. It turned out that Dickey had been the medical officer in the Putumayo, working for Arana between July 1908 and

June 1909, based in El Encanto. Dickey knew South America well. After qualifying as a doctor, he had set out for Colombia to work for the Tolima Mining Company, a London-registered gold and silver prospecting and mining concern, where he remained for seven years. From Colombia Dickey transferred to Peru and the Putumayo. After his spell with Arana, Dickey had moved to Brazil to work for a rubber concern on the Javari River, to where he was now returning. Quite by accident, Casement found in Dickey an extremely useful resource: he could speak Portuguese, Spanish and the Huitoto language, and also knew a great deal about the rubber trade, and about the Putumayo and the people who worked and slaved there. How much more he knew would emerge on the voyage.

They reached Pará on 9 September. After a fortnight's stay waiting for the next available ship to take them upriver, Casement's party, including Dickey, left the port on 23 September on the *Hilda*. Dickey recalled the trip many years later. Casement, he remarked, was one of the most unusual and interesting people he had ever met. His singular choice of clothing said a lot about him.

> Embarking on the river steamer from Pará that day in 1911, when the temperature was floating around ninety-six in the shade, he wore a thick and very dark brown suit of Irish homespun. How he stood it I do not know, but then the rest of his costume was at least as strange. His straw hat looked quite as if it had been taken from an ash can years before. He wore a heavy flannel shirt, but did recognize the tropics to the extent of wearing white canvas shoes the soles of which were rubber. The final touch was a tremendous and very knobbly walking stick – a shillalah that must have been two inches in diameter at the very least.

Casement did just as he pleased, even if it offended others. At one point, Dickey remarked, Casement kicked off his shoes and removed his socks. The ship's captain was aghast at Casement's behaviour – it did not

> to his mind, go very well with the Irishman's post as British Consul General in Rio. I quite agreed with my friend the captain, but when I spoke to Casement as the captain had suggested, I was told to tell the captain to go to hell, that my companion's feet were hot and that he had

no intention of putting on shoes and socks until he felt cooler. And he
didn't. He went barefoot until we reached Manaos.

Dickey revealed that he knew quite a bit about what had happened in
the Putumayo after Casement's departure at the end of the previous year.
He had picked up titbits of information while working in the Brazilian
rubber district. He had heard that two men on Casement's most-wanted
list – José Fonseca and Alfredo Montt – had been tipped off and escaped
into Brazil, forcing a number of Bora Indians to go with them. Casement
had accused Fonseca of innumerable crimes against the Indians; Montt's
alleged atrocities were, in Casement's estimation, even worse. Fonseca
and Montt had gone to work rubber in an area on the Javari River at a
place called Santa Teresa, some forty miles from its confluence with the
Amazon. Dickey, by a strange coincidence, was working nearby.

Casement made plans to get as close to Santa Teresa as possible on
his way upriver to Iquitos. He wanted to get the Brazilian authorities
in Manaus to expel the two 'wretches' and escort them to the Peruvian
border, at a point where Casement would arrange to have police officers
arrest them and send them back to Iquitos to face the law.

In Manaus, while the ship was prepared for its final leg to Iquitos,
Casement had a meeting with the governor of the State of Manaus,
Colonel Antônio Bittencourt, who, according to Casement, had agreed
to do what he could to catch Fonseca and Montt and, to that end, had
released one of his own men, a Brazilian police officer, to join the ship.

Nine days later, the *Hilda* reached the border town of Benjamin
Constant, a little way up the Javari River from its mouth at the
Amazon, and not more than a few hundred yards across the river from
the Peruvian border post. The Brazilian officer, José de Campos, had
promised Casement that he would be going at once to Santa Teresa
with a sufficient force of men to arrest Fonseca and Montt. The *Hilda*
remained in Benjamin Constant for less than twenty-four hours, during
which time Casement heard nothing more from de Campos. Casement
did, however, see him in company with another police officer and one
Senhor Serra – the other partner of the firm that employed both Fonseca
and Montt.

Fonseca and Montt slipped through the net and escaped arrest. De
Campos, despite his reassuring words, was clearly corrupt, and Dickey

even went so far as thinking that the two criminals had been tipped off by the Peruvian consul in Manaus, Carlos Rey de Castro – a name Casement knew well from Robuchon's posthumously published book.

The *Hilda* was ready to depart for its final destination. Several days later, on 16 October, and two months after leaving Southampton, Casement was back in Iquitos. He, Dickey, Arédomi and Omarino left the ship.

For a short time, Casement's faith that he could influence the course of events for the good in Iquitos was rewarded; within the first week of his arrival, *El Oriente*, which during Saldaña Rocca's days was very pro-Arana, had printed an article eulogizing his work in the Putumayo; and the prefect, Alayza Paz Soldan, had said that 'the honour of lifting the veil over the Putumayo mystery' was entirely Casement's.

Then Casement had a meeting with the man behind the arrest warrants and arrests he had heard about in London. His name was Rómulo Paredes. He had recently returned from the Putumayo, having been appointed in March by the attorney general of the Supreme Court in Lima to head up a commission of enquiry into conditions there. Paredes had no legal training and was not the court's first choice. That had been Carlos Valcárcel, who had been made a judge in Iquitos in July 1910. Valcárcel fell ill just before his planned investigation in the Putumayo, and had retreated to New York to seek medical help. Paredes was thirty-four years old, and had come to Iquitos in 1907 from Lambayeque on Peru's northern coast, where he had begun a career as a journalist. He had continued his work in Iquitos and had recently purchased *El Oriente*.

Events had moved very quickly while Casement was in London. The commission of enquiry, which Paredes headed, was large and well prepared. Aside from Paredes, there was a physician, two interpreters and a military escort of nine men. The commission had visited all of the rubber sections in the Putumayo. Paredes took depositions from chiefs of rubber stations, lesser employees, and many Indians, which he had gathered into a dossier of 3,000 handwritten pages that he used to write his report to the prefect. Paredes imparted the results of his investigation in the Putumayo to Valcárcel, who was now back in his judicial post following his medical treatment. Immediately Valcárcel issued arrest warrants for 237 people.

Casement enjoyed meeting Paredes not least because of the compliments he was paid. 'Says if it had not been for my prior journey', Casement commented in a letter to Spicer,

> he could not have succeeded – it was my going that broke up the gang and [made] everyone else alert and 'ready to tell the truth' . . . He said openly that he had blushed with shame to be a Peruvian – and had he not known that I had been there and would report it all to my govt. he would not have gone on with it – the crimes laid bare were too atrocious.

Compliments and Paredes's good work notwithstanding, it soon became clear that the real situation in Iquitos bore little relationship to Paredes's optimistic picture. For one thing, only nine of the 237 warrants issued by the Iquitos court had led to an arrest, and almost all of the men charged were minor agents of the Company. Paredes's list of warrants had included the names of some of the worst perpetrators of atrocities – men such as Victor Macedo, Carlos Miranda and the Barbadian Armando King – but all of these men were still working and living in the Putumayo. Secondly, early in August Valcárcel had issued an arrest warrant for Pablo Zumaeta, the managing director of the Peruvian Amazon Company in Iquitos and brother-in-law of Arana, but no arrest had taken place, although he was living quite openly in Iquitos. The Superior Court in Iquitos then quashed the warrant, and instead issued Valcárcel an order of dismissal, arguing that he had earlier abandoned his post by going to New York. Other arrest warrants made during the time Casement was in Iquitos also came to nothing, as the authorities always seemed to arrive just a little too late: many chiefs escaped into the forest, taking with them considerable numbers of Indians, either to work new rubber stands or to sell on to other *caucheros*. Too many people with authority in Iquitos were under Arana's influence. Justice was not being done.

Casement's confidence soon dissolved into frustration and despair. From several quarters he learned that many of the chiefs of rubber stations who had had arrest warrants issued against them were still working in the Putumayo, and walking around freely as though nothing had happened. His own failed attempt to get Fonseca and Montt arrested, he now realized, was not just bad luck but part of a larger conspiracy against the implementation of justice.

While in London, Casement had clearly thought that he could make a difference by going to Iquitos. Was he simply naïve? It is hard to believe that he had failed to grasp the political situation in Iquitos and the degree to which Arana had the town under his control. Whatever explains Casement's misguided beliefs, he now realized how illusory they were. Casement's reports back to the Foreign Office reflected his disappointment. On reading one of his dispatches, a Foreign Office clerk noted that they

> reveal a hopeless state of affairs. There seems no doubt that the authorities are in connivance with the criminals, & that things are still about as bad in the Putumayo as they can be – in fact it is not improbable that the last state of the district will be worse than the first. The control now seems to be entirely in Arana's hands . . . & as long as the rubber is collected at the present rate there will always be money for purposes of bribery.

There was little more Casement could do in Iquitos. Arana had many friends in the Amazon who had helped to keep the true state of conditions in the Putumayo concealed. Carlos Rey de Castro, the Peruvian consul in Manaus, who watched over Arana's business in the city, was particularly instrumental in this, Casement learned: 'This man's reputation for venality in connection with the Putumayo is so well known in Iquitos that I have heard him referred to by Peruvians there as a disgrace and discredit to their service.' Paredes confirmed that Rey de Castro was 'one of those primarily responsible for the ignorance in which the government at Lima had been wilfully kept of the true state of things on the Putumayo.'

Another particularly vile person whom Casement learned about was Benito Lores, a man who had been appointed by the Peruvian government as a special commissioner for the Putumayo. Lores, Casement discovered, had been the captain of the launch *Iquitos* when it had been involved in the massacre of the Colombian *caucheros* at La Unión in January 1908: and it was this same Lores who had been involved in imprisoning and then kicking Walter Hardenburg when he was forced on board the launch after witnessing the atrocity.

Paredes also warned Casement off trying to go back to the Putumayo, on the grounds that there was little he could accomplish. Worse still, without the protection of the Commission, which he had enjoyed on his previous trip, his life would be in great danger.

On 30 November, Paredes called on Casement and handed him a copy of his own confidential report, which he had completed and submitted to the prefect on 30 September. Paredes had no authority to hand the report to Casement, and no one, it seems, knew that he had done so. Casement read it with great care.

Several days later, Paredes went to see Casement again, and surprised him with the news that he would be leaving Iquitos very shortly for Lima and for Lambayeque, his family home. He expected to return to Iquitos in April. He was becoming increasingly uncomfortable in town. One of the local papers, *El Heraldo*, began a series of attacks on Paredes, on the prefect, and on the Lima government. The British government, Sir Edward Grey and Casement himself did not escape censure. The British government was charged with having acted improperly and with having issued secret instructions to Casement to remove from the jurisdiction of Peru the 'sole criminals . . . the Barbados negroes, who alone had committed reprehensible acts'. In the same article, Pablo Zumaeta and his cohorts were lauded as 'heroes and patriots who only advanced the interests of their country'.

Casement remarked that the situation in Iquitos was now the same as it had been four years before, when allegations of the crimes committed in the Putumayo first appeared in *La Felpa* and *La Sancion*. Then the local newspapers had attacked Saldaña Rocca, before turning on Walter Hardenburg; now, Casement argued,

> the people assailed are the Peruvian Government itself, the special judge sent by that Government to the Putumayo, and the foreign Government charged with fomenting the conspiracy against the local patriots who have done so much and suffered so many things in advancing the cause of Peruvian civilization in the wilderness.

It was time for Casement to leave Iquitos for good.

On 7 December, Casement boarded the Booth liner *Ucayali* for its voyage downriver to Manaus. This really would be the last time he would make the journey.

The despair he had felt in Iquitos at the situation there stayed with him on his voyage down the Amazon. To add to his misery, he now learned that the Peruvian Amazon Company had gone into liquidation. The decision had been taken on 12 September, after consultations with Sir Frank Crisp, the Company's solicitor and one of the most influential company lawyers in Britain. On 27 September, at an extraordinary general meeting, the board unanimously agreed to appoint Julio César Arana as the Company's liquidator. There could be no more cynical a ploy than this. Arana could do exactly as he pleased. The shareholders in London were now entirely at his mercy, as were the Indians in the Putumayo.

Arriving in Manaus on 11 December, Casement wrote to Spicer summing up the situation as he saw it. The criminals had all escaped, some of them into Brazilian territory; and now that the heat was off, they were regrouping. Victor Macedo, the chief of La Chorrera, had gone to Iquitos – 'the Superior Court will probably go down in a body to greet him & have him to dinner', Casement commented caustically. He would not be surprised, Casement noted, if the chiefs of rubber stations with arrest warrants out for them all returned to Iquitos and brought criminal libel charges against Paredes, so pervasive and powerful was Arana's grip.

Casement now understood more clearly than ever the extent to which Arana and his henchmen had lied, and how ruthless they were. He told Spicer that Dickey had been in the Putumayo when Whiffen passed through in the summer of 1908 trying to solve the mystery of Robuchon's disappearance. Dickey was disgusted to learn of Arana's accusations of blackmail against Whiffen. 'Whiffen acted all the time on the Putumayo like a gentleman', Dickey said, '& the whole thing was a put up game to blacken his character when they found he knew too much'. Pablo Zumaeta, Casement believed, was the worst of the pack. Apparently he had even kidnapped three Peruvian soldiers, his own countrymen, and sold them into slavery to work rubber in Brazil. 'Pablo is to me the essence of all that is contemptible. If you saw the little fat, cowardly, pale-faced beast you would want to kick him right away.'

As if all this were not depressing enough, when Casement reached Manaus, he was greeted by the arrival of none other than Julio César

Arana himself, fresh from his triumph in London at having been appointed official liquidator to the Peruvian Amazon Company. Arana made straight for Casement's hotel, but Casement refused to receive him. Casement was most likely motivated by a sense of disgust, as well as being careful to maintain the distance that was required of him as an official of the British government.

Two days later, on 17 December, Casement boarded the *Hubert*, another Booth liner, for the final leg of the downriver voyage to Pará and the mouth of the Amazon. The next day, still some distance from Pará, Casement completed a summary of Paredes's report updating the situation in the Putumayo. He wanted to get it to Grey and the Foreign Office as quickly as possible.

On arriving in Pará, Casement changed his onward plans. He decided not to return to London as intended. Instead, on 24 December, he boarded the *Denis* for Barbados, and arrived at Bridgetown on 29 December. One of the first things he discovered was that Andres O'Donnell was not only still on the island, a free man, but that two days earlier he had married Miss Stella Bruce Turney, the daughter of the superintendent of Queen's Park. The news grated on Casement as yet another reminder of how little justice had been done. O'Donnell had become a highly respected member of Barbadian society. No one had arrested him or asked for his extradition, as Casement had hoped would happen. The local press referred to the marriage as one of the chief 'fashionable events' of the week. Attending the celebration, Casement noted, were a number of the British residents and a 'strong contingent of the local Peruvian "colony" who form now an appreciable element of Barbados social life. These Peruvians are mostly from Iquitos and more than one of them Putumayo murderers.'

It was not Casement's intention to stay in the colony any longer than he had to. On the day he arrived, he learned that there was a ship scheduled to leave on 31 December, and he booked himself onto it. At three in the afternoon the SS *Terence* cast off from Bridgetown. It was not heading for Europe; its destination was New York. Someone had to make the Americans put pressure on the Peruvian government to save the Indians. Who better than the Irish Knight himself?

PART IV

15

Publish and Be Damned

When in late November 1909 James Bryce, the British ambassador in Washington, asked the US government for help in putting pressure on the Peruvian government to investigate conditions in the Putumayo, the State Department replied that it was involved in delicate negotiations with both Peru and Ecuador about their common border, and could do nothing that might jeopardize those talks. Bryce accepted the American position, but since then he had kept the State Department fully informed of developments in the investigation, and had shared Casement's reports with it. Now that Casement had turned up in the United States, Bryce wanted to introduce him to State Department officials, to impress upon them the need 'to co-operate energetically' in this humanitarian effort, as he termed it.

On 10 January 1912, Bryce wrote to Huntington Wilson, the assistant secretary of state, to arrange a meeting with Sir Roger Casement. The two men met and talked. Casement also had a few minutes with President Taft at a dinner. Recalling the president's meeting with Casement a few years later, George Young, the first secretary at the British embassy, left a vivid description of that encounter, when, in a quiet corner of the British embassy, the two men had first met. 'A queer picture they made – the tall Celt haggard and livid from the Putumayo swamps, fixing with glittering black eyes the burly rubicund Anglo-Saxon. It was like a black snake fascinating a wombat.' Casement explained to the president, and later to other State Department officials, that he was convinced that 'no really serious efforts are being made to prosecute those responsible for atrocities in the Putumayo'. American help was needed urgently.

Casement had come away from his second trip to Iquitos despondent. His efforts, and therefore those of the Foreign Office, had hit a wall.

There was nothing more that it could do. Only the US government, he was convinced, could move things along. 'So I went off to Washington', Casement later recalled,

> entirely off my own bat – without a hint that such a move was on – without letting the F.O. know and got . . . the thing taken up from there by a sort of personal assault on Taft and the State Department. Grey was delighted when he knew & spoke in the warmest terms to me.

Following on directly from Casement's meeting with State Department officials, US secretary of state Philander Knox sent an urgent message to the American minister in Lima, Henry Clay Howard, informing him that he should make the details of Casement's concerns known to the Peruvian government; to impress upon them that they should take drastic and effective action in the region; to emphasize that the British government was intent on publishing the reports of Casement's investigations; and that this exposé 'might induce public opinion of the world to believe that Peru has shown herself unable effectively to exercise sovereign rights over the disputed region'.

Casement also suggested to the State Department that it should reopen its consulate in Iquitos, which had been effectively closed down in 1908. The State Department agreed.

It now looked as though the US government was at last getting involved in the Putumayo cause.

Casement's trip to the United States was short, but extremely fruitful. He was back in England on 20 January 1912. Partly because of his success in Washington, where he had 'worked up the State Dept. to a high pitch of feeling in the matter', and partly because of his now unassailable knowledge of the politics of the Putumayo, Casement had put himself in the role of gate-keeper at the Foreign Office in London: nothing was decided at the highest levels without first finding out his opinion. Almost as soon as he disembarked in Southampton, he was at the Foreign Office consulting with his superiors, and particularly with Gerald Spicer.

Energized by his American detour, Casement's opinion was that time should not be lost, and that the Foreign Office should 'strike while the iron is hot': his reports should be published as soon as possible.

Leaving anything to Peruvian justice alone, he felt, would be a mistake. Casement's bitter experience in Iquitos several months earlier had now convinced him that initiatives from the Peruvian authorities, whether in Iquitos or in Lima, meant nothing. When, for example, the president of the Iquitos court made a judicial order at the end of December 1911 to accelerate the criminal procedure against the men being held in an Iquitos jail awaiting trial, Casement had become so mistrustful of justice in Iquitos that he remarked to the Foreign Office,

> They are put forward merely to deceive, and give the impression that the matter is being dealt with in due process of law. If we were to await the development of the proceedings, it might well be that the nine men in custody would die in jail before the final stage of investigation were reached – but I fear the remaining Indians on the Putumayo would also be dead – or killed.

Casement had also learned that Arana was saying in Peru 'that as soon as what he called "this fuss" was over, the natives would be set to work again'. To Casement, this meant the extermination of the Putumayo Indians.

The Peruvians needed to face up to their responsibilities in the Putumayo, and the best weapon the Foreign Office had to put pressure on them to act was publicity. Casement began his campaign of pressuring the Foreign Office. In early February he prepared a memorandum outlining his vision for the steps that should be taken following publication of his report. Publication, he insisted, would show to the world 'how Peru has used her primitive, defenceless, innocent populations in this greedy rush for rubber'. 'The surest check against continuance of these cruelties', he continued, 'is to drag into daylight and hold up to universal reprobation the authors and abettors and criminals of the Putumayo slavery'. Concentrating on punishment was not, he argued, the best way forward, for that would allow the Peruvian government to drag its heels, as it had done already, and open the British government to a charge of duplicity. He was thinking here of Andres O'Donnell, who was now living the life of Riley in Barbados, where the authorities were turning a blind eye to his presence. 'We should look rather foolish', Casement remarked,

with one of the criminals marrying 'with pages in white satin' and
English girls as bridesmaids in 'pink voile' dresses (they should have
been crimson!), at a British church in a British colony, with a 'highly
fashionable' colonial gathering, and nothing said by us.

At the same time, Casement presented the Foreign Office with a
report of his findings from his most recent trip to Iquitos. The report
showed that nothing had been done to stem the atrocities perpetrated
against the Indian population. Paredes had taken thousands of pages of
evidence on the Putumayo and, according to his calculations, the Indian
population had fallen to a new low. 'Human bones,' Casement wrote,

> the remains of lost tribes of Indians, are so scattered through the forests
> that, as one informant stated, these spots 'resemble battlefields'. One
> Peruvian officer, who had been through the Putumayo since the date of
> my visit in 1910, said that the neighbourhood of one particular section
> he had visited recalled to him the battlefield of Miraflores – the bloodiest
> battle of the Chilean war [the War of the Pacific].

Casement also took the opportunity to remind the Foreign Office that
Britain should take the moral high ground and concentrate its efforts
on improving conditions for the Indians. Anything that deflected from
this purpose, such as insisting on punishment or raking over the past,
could backfire. It might also give the Peruvians a moment to reflect on
the salient fact that Britain's stake in the Putumayo rubber trade and its
impact on the commerce of Iquitos was substantial – 'the whole of the
rubber output of the region, it should be borne in mind, is placed upon
the English market, and is conveyed from Iquitos in British bottoms
[ships]'. If the Peruvians countered with an observation such as this, it
would be difficult to get the argument back to the issue of the welfare of
the Indians. It might seem a little hollow for Britain to contend that it
was a champion of Indian rights.

Casement also wanted the Foreign Office to impress on the Peruvian
government that it, too, should concern itself with reforms, and that
those that Paredes had recommended to the Iquitos court should form
the basis of an overall plan. Of course, Casement had already seen
Paredes's report in Iquitos, and now he handed over his summary of

it to the Foreign Office so that his colleagues could see for themselves the reforms being suggested, the most important of which was that the Peruvian government should begin to administer the area responsibly by having salaried magistrates installed in four rubber sections, with full powers of investigation and arrest.

But the Paredes report had not yet appeared in Lima, despite having been sent – or so Casement was told – four and a half months earlier. This was further proof that the Peruvian government, left to itself, would do nothing. The delay, if that was what it was, in getting Paredes's report from Iquitos to Lima prompted Casement to remark cynically,

> Had I not gone back to Iquitos it is pretty clear we should never have known anything of this document at all. Probably it would never have left Iquitos. Its existence would have been denied – that is to say we should have been told only of the 'Expediente' or dossier forming the judicial part of Paredes' work while the other, or political report, he compiled on his return to Iquitos would have been omitted from official reference.

Casement worked feverishly to try to convince everyone with influence that the reports needed to reach the public. In addition to colleagues at the Foreign Office, Casement turned to his friends and to the officers of the Anti-Slavery and Aborigines' Protection Society – 'The gang of ruffians need frightening I assure you & the only weapon is the fear of publicity.'

Casement was not alone in pressing for publication. Members of parliament, such as Joseph King, who knew that Casement had completed a report as early as February 1911, kept asking the government for a date of publication; but all they got from the foreign secretary was that he was giving the matter his careful consideration. In July of the previous year, when Josiah Wedgwood, Liberal MP for Newcastle-under-Lyme, asked the same question, he had received the same reply; and on 5 March 1912, eight months later, when Noel Buxton, Liberal MP for North Norfolk, raised the issue yet again, Sir Edward Grey simply said that he was not in a position to give a definite answer.

Grey was holding back on publication. His hands were tied: the Monroe Doctrine meant that he could do nothing without consulting the State Department. Grey was pleased that Casement had been so warmly received in Washington, and that the Americans seemed to be on board, but he felt unable to publish the reports on his own. He was holding back until he had heard what Henry Clay Howard in Lima would report back to Washington. The waiting now began.

Casement, however, was not as sanguine as Grey. He had his own contacts both in Washington and Lima who were providing him with off-the-record information suggesting that the American position was both more complicated and contradictory than was understood in London. One of Casement's informants, George Young at the British embassy in Washington, suggested that there was 'backsliding at the State Department', and that it might not be as willing to involve itself in the Putumayo as Casement had been led to believe. Casement responded to this worrying news by sending him a batch of Putumayo photographs to pass over to Huntington Wilson, the acting secretary of state. These pictures, together with accompanying notes, Casement hoped would stem the 'backsliding'. But Casement had little confidence in Henry Clay Howard. Lucien Jerome, the British consul-general in Callao and Casement's close confidant, who had a finger on the pulse of the diplomatic scene in Lima, had little good to say about Howard. Whether this was because of his lack of diplomatic experience – Lima was his first and only post – or for some other reason, or because he did not seem to take warmly to the British, Howard made a poor impression on Jerome: 'The USA Minister in Lima', he wrote, 'is a kindly old ass who believes all they tell him – and we have the clearest proof that they have lied to us again & again – & of course to him.'

Casement was growing increasingly agitated about the situation. He fired off a salvo to James Bryce in Washington. 'I hope most sincerely', he wrote,

> that the State Department will not try to prevent us from publishing the Putumayo papers. If they do it will be a sin – and a sin of selfishness that God will not forgive. Our wrong doing will be one of weakness if we give way to their deprecation – but theirs will be something more than weakness.

Only compulsion and international pressure could move the Peruvian government to act, Casement argued: it had already shown that its promises lacked any substance. 'The USA', Casement continued, 'will be doing a grave disservice to humanity and civilisation if they, for purely selfish ends, oppose the letting in of light upon this den of thieves and murderers.'

Casement's fears were well-founded. Early in March, Charles des Graz, the British first minister in Lima, passed on information to the Foreign Office that Howard was going to tell his superiors in Washington that, in his opinion, publishing Casement's reports would 'do more harm than good by its effect on the Peruvian Government and check any present endeavour or future practical scheme of reform when devised'. Howard believed that pushing the Peruvian government by embarrassing them publicly was counterproductive.

Casement feared the worst: that the Foreign Office would not publish without the State Department's support. So Casement stepped up the pressure. He started feeding his Foreign Office colleagues with as much information as he could honestly garner from his contacts in Peru and Washington, so as to undermine the hold that the United States had over decision-making in London. Casement was no great fan of the Monroe Doctrine, and he took every occasion he could to criticize it, while putting the civilizing position of Britain – and, for that matter, of Germany – on a higher moral level. If the United States wanted exclusive influence in Latin America, it also had to take the responsibility that went with that position, and this included chiding its neighbours in cases of humanitarian abuses, such as the Putumayo.

Casement repeated that Howard was being fed a pack of lies. The Peruvian government, Casement emphasized, depended on Arana in the Putumayo, since his presence there guaranteed their claim to this territory. At the same time, Peru depended on foreign investment, and only a threat to that flow of capital would make its government cut its ties with Arana and improve the lot of the Indians. Both the British and the American governments had a moral duty to their publics to warn them off investing in 'such coffin ships as the Peruvian Amazon Company'. Publication of his reports was essential, since 'to purify the Putumayo through Peruvian official agency alone would be like referring the keeping of Lent to a jury of butchers!'

At the end of March, Casement's pressuring received a substantial

boost when the London *Morning Post* broke the silence. On 25 March
it printed an interview with Seymour Bell, the merchant who was one
of the members of the Peruvian Amazon Company's Commission to
the Putumayo. Whether the members of the Commission were under
some code of honour to keep quiet is not clear, but Bell's interview
came out of the blue. The article recounted the cruel conditions under
which the Putumayo Indians collected rubber for the Company, many
of the details of which closely adhered to Casement's own reports. That
Casement had accompanied the Commission, and had already written
reports for the government that had still not seen the light of day, was
emphasized by Bell in the interview. The article ended with a challenge
to the government. Now that 'the light of publicity has been shed upon
the situation by Mr Bell's statement', the government was obliged to
publish Casement's report.

Several days after the *Morning Post* story, *Truth* waded into the fray
by pressing Bell on his observations. Could he be clearer on whether the
cruelties he documented were a thing of the past, or was he implying
that they were still continuing?

At this point Bell turned to Casement for assistance, and they
exchanged ideas about how he should answer the question in *Truth*.
On 17 April, under the banner of 'Peru and Her "Congo"', *Truth* had
its answer, telling its readers that hardly anything had changed in the
Putumayo, and that the Peruvian government had not established the
rule of law in the region. 'Englishmen', it stated, 'were justly indignant a
few years ago at the diabolical atrocities perpetrated in the "Red Rubber"
days of the Congo. This is a far stronger case.' The British government,
it argued, had a duty to bring an action against the Peruvian Amazon
Company, which, though in liquidation, was still in existence as a British
company. 'As a preliminary step towards that end', the article continued,
'the publication of Sir Roger Casement's report to the Foreign Office
should be pressed for.'

Public pressure on the Foreign Office was growing. The newspapers
were doing their part, as were the parliamentary questions about the
government's plans to publish the report, which had been repeatedly
fired at the Foreign Office since February of the previous year. On 28
March, just a few days after Bell had spilled his story in the *Morning Post*,

James Bryce finally informed the Foreign Office that the news from Washington was not as bad as they had feared. Howard, it was true, was against publication, but Huntington Wilson, the acting secretary of state, had used his influence, and replied that the United States had decided that it would defer to the judgement of the British government regarding publication of the reports.

The ball was back in the British court, and it was becoming clear that it would now be impossible to resist the clamour for publication. So plans were rolled out to publish Casement's reports, together with dispatches and telegrams, in what was termed a 'Blue Book' – an official publication whose name derived from its rich blue paper cover. But then, in early April, the State Department looked as though it was about to change its position again. It had heard from Lima that the Peruvian government was about to appoint a committee to study the administration of the Putumayo and make reforms to guarantee the rights of the Indians. Everything was up in the air again.

The Foreign Office seemed pleased with the news from Lima and concluded that, if it was correct, the publication of Casement's damning report would be harmful, as Howard had warned. It decided to hold off on the decision to publish for the time being. But Casement was not so easily taken in. Over the next month and more, he continued his campaign to undermine the trust that the two governments were placing in Peru. He pointed out, for example, that one of the members who was going to be appointed to the Peruvian government's committee, Senator Julio Ego-Aguirre, representing the department of Loreto in congress, was a legal adviser to the Arana brothers. Senator Ego-Aguirre – who, incidentally, had been one of Hardenburg's students in Iquitos – had also come out publicly in a Lima newspaper accusing Hardenburg of blackmail. To Casement, at least, appointing Senator Ego-Aguirre to study conditions in the Putumayo was tantamount to planning a whitewash. As if that was not enough to cast doubt on the Peruvian government's true intent, Casement also learned that Arana had been buying political favours in the capital – 'spreading a lot of money in Lima', as he put it. As for Henry Clay Howard, Lucien Jerome had told Casement that he was not taken seriously in diplomatic circles in Lima, preferring to drum up business for American companies rather than worry about humanitarian issues.

He carries no weight here . . . He never goes to his office but spends his
time in the different business houses in Lima trying to work up business
for the American exporters for the Panama Canal. He is certainly
energetic about that line.

Jerome also mentioned that Howard was not sympathetic to the British.

Perhaps the most worrying news for Casement was that the Putumayo
was now producing more rubber than it had in the previous year, and
he feared that Arana's system of terror and violence was, if anything,
getting worse. While the American and British governments dithered,
time was running out for the Indians.

At the end of May, the State Department's pursuit of Howard's advice
became official: it was giving the Peruvian government time to initiate
its own reforms. Bryce, in Washington, took a dim view, and expressed
his concern that the United States wanted to remain 'at our expense as
the benevolent guardian of Peru'.

Throughout June, news filtered back to London to the effect that the
Peruvian government was simply playing for time. Casement had had it
right all along. It had, for example, made everything more complicated.
In addition to its own committee, the government had created an
auxiliary commission, to be headed by Paredes, who was to return
to the Putumayo for more information, and then report back to the
committee in Lima to consider its next move. When he learned of this,
Casement was incredulous – after all, Paredes had already supplied the
government with all the facts it needed. The composition of the auxiliary
commission, moreover, was simply a farce, as Casement pointed out.
One of its members, Dr Don Julio Maradiegue, had actually worked as
an advocate for the Aranas. This new tier of organization would mean
that, instead of producing concrete proposals for reform by the end of
July, as the Peruvian government had promised the State Department, a
delay until the following January was now inevitable.

Everything seemed to be conspiring against the publication of
Casement's reports. Eduardo Lembcke, the chargé d'affaires at the
Peruvian legation in London, began bombarding the Foreign Office with
dispatches reporting that Lima had already undertaken to reform the
rubber regime in the Putumayo, and that conditions for the Indians had
already improved. Publication, Lembcke repeated, should be withheld.

Lembcke then proceeded to place all the blame for the atrocities squarely on the shoulders of the Barbadians, and accused Casement of perverting the course of justice by spiriting the criminals away from Peru.

The Foreign Office was in a quandary. On the one hand, from a diplomatic point of view, it had to submit to Washington's reading of the political situation; on the other, it was convinced by the evidence that the Peruvian government was playing for time – or, worse, that it had no intention whatever of intervening in the Putumayo. Early in June, Pope Pius X had issued a papal encyclical, *Lacrimabili statu*, which deplored the conditions of the Indians and called for a missionary presence for the first time in the Putumayo. Public opinion in Britain, too, was pressing hard for publication. But what to do? Diplomacy or action? The crunch came at the end of June, when the Foreign Office learned that the auxiliary commission would not be meeting its deadline of reporting by the following March – and, more worryingly, that Paredes had changed his tune, and while spending time in Lima had fallen under Arana's spell, publicly blaming the British for what had happened in the Putumayo.

That was too much to bear. As far as Louis Mallet was concerned, Paredes's defection was the final straw. Mallet urged immediate publication of Casement's report.

On 2 July, the Liberal MP Joseph King asked in the Commons whether Arana had been arrested and when he would be brought to justice. Sir Edward Grey replied that this was beyond his jurisdiction, and made no further comment. Moments later another Liberal MP, Noel Buxton, rose and asked, 'When will the Report of Sir Roger Casement on the Putumayo rubber atrocities be published?' For the first time since early 1911, Grey gave a straight answer to that question: 'I propose to lay the Papers before the House very shortly – at any rate before the end of the month'.

On Saturday, 13 July 1912, the Blue Book was finally published. The British government had gone out on a limb and followed Casement and its own instincts, rather than the Americans. 'I've blown up the Devil's Paradise in Peru', Casement exclaimed with glee when he heard the news.

I told you I should – and I've done it. It is a good step forward in human things – the abetters of cruelty are not so secure as they were – & their tenants are getting very scared. Putumayo will be cleansed – altho' nothing can bring back the murdered tribes – poor souls.

16

An International Scandal

Monday, 15 July 1912, was a very hot day in London. The temperature reached 90 degrees Fahrenheit. There, in *The Times*, was the shocking headline that said it all: 'The Putumayo Atrocities: A South American Congo – Sir Roger Casement's Report Published'. Readers were instantly transported to the steamy jungles of the Amazon, to a vast territory 'within a square formed by the Equator, 5 deg. South lat., and 70 deg. West Long, the sovereignty of which is in dispute between the three Republics of Peru, Colombia, and Ecuador.'

No sooner had they been taken through the geopolitics than readers were thrust into harrowing details of flogging, torture and murder reproduced from the report. At one point in the article, the editor broke off, remarking:

> Far more terrible examples of cruelty are quoted on the direct evidence of witnesses of the crimes. We cannot reproduce them. It must suffice to say that all of the Indians of such a district, without discrimination of age or sex, became the helpless victims of the lust, cupidity, and savage cruelty of its conqueror.

The article reminded its readers that the story of the dreadful events of the Putumayo had first been brought to the public's attention by an American engineer and published in *Truth* in the latter part of 1909; and that his allegations were fully borne out by the investigations of Casement, whose evidence came from a group of Barbadian men who had been forced by Company superiors to carry out heinous acts against the Indians. At no time during Casement's questioning of the men, the article noted, were their claims disputed by the agents of the Peruvian Amazon Company who were present at the time.

The article concluded thus: 'No one who reads Sir Roger Casement's Report can fail to wish it means and power to extend its civilizing influence. The existing system cries aloud to Heaven'.

On the following page, readers could continue to digest these revelations with the help of the editorial. There, under the banner 'Slavery in South America', the writer took a broader view of the whole story. 'Systematic slavery' was the key term used: 'enforced by the lash and the bullet and enforced by every excess of cruelty and lust'. The result was that the Indian population had declined from 50,000 in 1906 to 8,000 in 1911. There was no evidence that their conditions had improved: indeed, judging from the level of rubber exports that were leaving the region, the real fear – and this was attributed to Sir Edward Grey – was that they were worse.

The editorial did not dwell on the details of the atrocities. Rather, it emphasized the lack of reform, and that the consequences, for Peru, of failing to act, could be substantial. The article pointed out that, though the authorities had issued warrants galore, virtually none of them had led to arrests. Many of the worst criminals were living openly in Peru, and excuses were still being made about the impossibility of policing such an out-of-the-way region at the same time as claiming sovereignty over it. The editorial praised Sir Edward Grey and, especially, Sir Roger Casement, who 'has deserved well of his countrymen and of mankind by the ability and zeal with which he has investigated under very difficult conditions an appalling iniquity'. It ended with a reminder that governments have responsibilities. 'It is for the Peruvian Government', the editorial remarked,

> to remember that sovereignty has its duties as well as its rights. It is for the Governments and peoples of this country and of the United States to stimulate them to the discharge of those duties, to lend them moral support in the task, and to bring home to them that failure to perform it must fatally compromise their credit and their future.

Soon most newspapers in Britain were carrying the story. The *Daily Chronicle* provided a little more information than most, in an article written by Reverend John Harris of the Anti-Slavery and Aborigines' Protection Society. Harris reminded readers that it was Walter Hardenburg, who had arrived in London at the Society's offices in the summer of 1909 with a manuscript of a book entitled *The Devil's Paradise*, who had first exposed the horrors of the Putumayo. In the following weeks, most of Britain's periodicals, with titles such as *Truth*, the *Saturday Review*, the *Spectator*, the *Economist*, and the *Nation*, and specialist magazines such as the *India Rubber Journal* and the *Anti-Slavery Reporter and Aborigines' Friend*, carried considered pieces on the Putumayo.

Thanks to the world's extensive telegraphic connections, and its use by a core group of news agencies – Reuters, Associated Press and Agence France-Presse – news of the publication spread very rapidly. Most papers reported along the same lines as *The Times*, though sometimes with much more sensational details. One such was the New York *Sun*, which published attention-grabbing headlines such as 'Butcher Natives To Get Rubber', 'Negroes of British Company Commit Terrible Crimes', 'Enslaved, Burned at Stake and Maimed – Just a Few of the Horrors', and 'One Tribe Decimated'. The *New York Times*, too, publicized the story, with the headline 'Rubber Atrocities Spared No Victim'.

The Blue Book – or, to give it its full, official title, Command Paper 6266, 'Correspondence Respecting the Treatment of British Colonial Subjects and Native Indians Employed in the Collection of Rubber in the Putumayo District' – was a hefty document. It ran to 165 pages, and nearly 100,000 words. The volume contained both of Casement's reports, written after his visit to the Putumayo; statements from thirty Barbadian men, which covered about half the total length of the publication; and a list of those Casement considered to be the worst offenders in the employ of the Peruvian Amazon Company. The book concluded with Casement's report concerning his recent visit to Iquitos. Interspersed with these pieces were dispatches from British consular officials in Peru, and from James Bryce and his colleagues in Washington, providing information on the diplomatic position of the United States leading up to publication. Alfred Mitchell Innes, of the British embassy in Washington, suggested that the Blue Book should include a photograph of a young Indian boy which vividly showed innumerable lesions on the back of his body – the Mark of Arana.

When he showed this photograph to James Bryce, Innes recalled that he 'nearly wept and, to tell the truth, so did I'. However, Sir Arthur Nicolson, the permanent under-secretary of state, felt that it was inappropriate for a Blue Book to have photographs in it. The Blue Book was put on sale, as were similar government publications, at a reasonable price of one shilling and five pence, equivalent to about £5 today.

The Blue Book presented a wealth of detail on all aspects of the Putumayo rubber trade: how rubber was extracted; how collections were organized around the *puesta* and the cyclical *fabrico*; how systems of oppression worked and were enforced to work; about the history of a region of which hardly anyone had ever heard; and so on. Besides exposing the atrocities, the volume gave a unique insight into the underbelly of one of the world's newest and most important industries, and one of the world's most remarkable materials.

Part of the lasting impact of the Blue Book is that the horror is related through intimate stories. Sometimes Casement let the men tell their own stories; sometimes he presented their stories in the form of a narrative. But in most instances the statements were a mixture of narrative and near-verbatim conversations. It was presented very personally and directly. Everyone had an identity – name, age, place of birth and length of employment in the Putumayo. Frederick Bishop, Casement's guide and interpreter, was here; as was James Chase, the twenty-three-year-old who gave evidence 'under a sense of fear; his agitation was plainly marked, and he was greatly disconcerted', and whom Casement found in La Chorrera. His substantial statement, the longest of the thirty such statements, was enough in itself to provide Casement with all the evidence he needed of criminality. Chase also told Casement the heartening story of the fatal revenge of the Indian chief Katenere against his oppressors. Never before had colonial subjects had their voices heard in a public document like this.

These thirty Barbadian men made history within the Blue Book, and their names became known the world over. The Blue Book also gave rise to spin-off stories such as the one carried by the *New York Times*. In early August 1912, Robert Isaacs, an elevator operator in a New York apartment building, contacted the paper and claimed that he, too, had worked in the Putumayo for Arana.

Isaacs's story appeared a day later, on 4 August, under the headline 'Saw Wholesale Murder in the Amazon'. It strongly resembled the Barbadian statements recorded by Casement.

> Over and over again, [he] has cut into its almost impenetrable jungle lands, with his Winchester on his shoulder and his machete in his hand, on the search for Indians; who at the command of cruel Captains, has burst into peaceful Indian villages, helped round up the inhabitants, helped drive them back along the trail to slavery.

Isaacs told of how he was enticed to sign up with the Aranas in Bridgetown; how, when he got to the Putumayo, 'he suddenly found himself not a rubber hunter but an Indian hunter, not a laborer but a warrior, armed to the teeth, flanked by murderous companions, doomed to live in a hell of bloodshed and torture'; and how, finally, after witnessing and taking part in such horrors, he managed to get away from the Putumayo, and ended up working for three years in the engineer's mess on the site of the Madeira–Mamoré railway building project, before coming to New York to work running an elevator in an apartment building. 'I'm speaking the truth', he exclaimed at the end of the piece, 'I can go back to the Putumayo forests and show anybody heaps of rotting skeletons at the places where we surrounded and massacred the Indians.'

Casement had left England for the Putumayo in August 1910, and had delivered his final report at the end of March 1911. After a gap of fifteen and a half months, the story was finally in the open, an international scandal. But now what?

By the time of the Blue Book's publication, Iquitos had become home to two new consuls. The British consulate had been there since the latter half of the previous century, but now, it was to become for the first time a salaried post. George Michell, the man recommended by Casement, was the consul now fully representing British interests. The Americans also had a new consul – thirty-two-year-old Stuart Jamieson Fuller.

Fuller received his first instructions from Huntington Wilson early in April 1912, while he was en route to Iquitos. By this time, the State Department had laid its hands on Charles Eberhardt's reports, when he had been the first American consul in Iquitos in 1907 and 1908. Where the reports had been for all these years, or whether they were for some reason suppressed, is not known.

Wilson remarked that, when Eberhardt visited the Putumayo in 1907, he reported that the Indians were being exploited to such an extent that he feared they might soon be extinct. Fuller was told to keep in close contact and to cooperate fully with Michell – the first such Anglo-American collaboration in the region – and to get to know the rubber district of the Putumayo, 'to visit, at intervals which may appear . . . advisable, the rubber stations along the Putumayo region in order that the department may have before it your views based upon personal observation'. The rather vague language veiled a specific question: Had the cruelties so graphically described by casement ceased? The Peruvian government still insisted, as it had been when the allegations first appeared in the September 1909 issue of *Truth*, that the cruelties described were 'historic', having happened before 1907. Conditions for the Indians, the Peruvian authorities contended, had vastly improved since then.

Fuller arrived in Iquitos near the end of May 1912. He immediately contacted Michell, who was about to leave for a tour of inspection of other major rivers that joined the Amazon. Like others before him, Fuller learned very quickly that this river town was far from a paradise. His first dispatch caught something of his desperation. Iquitos was a difficult place to settle in, he told his superiors; prices were impossibly exorbitant.

Aside from the difficulty of settling in, Fuller soon learned that, in his own words, 'the Putumayo question proves on examination to be considerably more complicated than would at first sight appear'.

There was little sign locally of much overt concern, or indeed appetite for reform. Casement had the same impression: most people thought the storm of international attention would soon pass. This attitude was exemplified by the case of Pablo Zumaeta, the head of the Peruvian Amazon Company's Iquitos operations, and Arana's brother-in-law. He was still under indictment, but that did not prevent him from being a well-respected man in town to whom others looked up. Fuller observed that he enjoyed

most of the local honors, vice alcalde [vice mayor of the municipality],
vice president and acting head of the chamber of commerce, president of
the benevolent society, etc., to all of which he was elected subsequent to
his exposure.

Fuller soon discovered, as had Casement, that the Aranas were not only
among the wealthiest and most influential families in Iquitos and Loreto,
but that their influence stretched all the way to Lima. Their grasp on
local politics was absolute. Fuller continued: '[T]hey would bring
pressure to bear on many people who might otherwise strongly support
a movement to protect the Indians and improve their condition'. Fuller
had learned what Casement and Hardenburg knew well: that Arana and
his family were not just a local power, but had strong connections with
the Lima political elite. Indians did not figure in their thinking, except as
expendable commodities.

There were many obstacles to overcome, but Fuller and Michell wanted
to get to the Putumayo as soon as possible. In late May, Fuller reported
to Washington that he and Michell were planning to visit the Putumayo
either in late July or early August on a government vessel – 'a launch
other than those belonging to the parties responsible for the atrocities'.

Chartering a vessel was out of the question, he wrote, the rates being
astronomical. This left two possibilities. They could go by the Peruvian
Amazon Company's launch, which headed up the Putumayo at the time
of the *fabrico*, visiting both La Chorrera and El Encanto; but that posed
the problem, as Fuller put it, that 'anyone who went up in this way
would be allowed to see exactly what the Company wished him to see
and no more'. The government launch, which made the trip every four
or five months taking supplies for the garrison, would allow them more
freedom; but since it only went to La Chorrera, this option would limit
the scope of their investigation.

By the end of July it had become clear to both Fuller and Michell that
the departure of the government launch would be indefinitely delayed.
No one seemed willing to explain the delay; Fuller suspected that the
Peruvian government was behind it, as it did not want Fuller and Michell
poking their noses into the region, not wishing anyone to challenge their
proclamation that conditions there had already improved. Disappointed,
Fuller and Michell had no choice but to take passage on the *Liberal* – the

Company launch with which Casement was so familiar – which they were told would leave Iquitos on 6 August.

As the day of the scheduled departure approached, both Fuller and Michell did all they could to avoid dependence on the Company once they got to the rubber stations. 'To see anything at all of the local conditions', Fuller explained,

> it is going to be necessary to do some travelling in the interior, owing to the fact that the dispatch of the company's launch is to be only to single ports and to each of these on separate voyages from Iquitos.

To get around on their own, they would need to take everything with them – a tent, food, cooking equipment, a cook, an interpreter and Indian bearers. To pay the bearers, Fuller and Michell would have to stock up on merchandise – 'cheap clothes, sugar, salt, knives, and handkerchiefs' – because 'there is no money in the whole district and the Indians do not know what money is and would have no use for it'.

The interpreter they hired was John Brown, who had appeared too late to be of any use to Casement when he went to the Putumayo, but had stayed on in Iquitos. His connection with the Putumayo went back a long way, and he had travelled with both Robuchon and Whiffen. He could speak the Huitoto language, as well as other local languages. The consuls could have found no one better. The cook was a Barbadian named Simeon Ford.

As they were packing their bags, the day of departure was put back by twenty-four hours, in order to accommodate a contingent of twenty-five gendarmes. They were being dispatched to the Putumayo ostensibly 'to keep order and protect the Indians', and were under the command of Benito Lores, the special commissioner appointed by the Peruvian government for the Putumayo district. Lores was known only vaguely to Fuller and Michell; what they did know was that he had business and political interests in Iquitos unrelated to his official duties: not exactly an impartial government official.

On the evening before departure, Fuller and Michell learned from the acting prefect of the Department of Loreto that Carlos Rey de Castro, the Peruvian consul in Manaus, was going to meet the *Liberal* at the mouth of the Putumayo and join them on their voyage. The Peruvian government had commissioned Rey de Castro to undertake an investigation on its behalf in the Putumayo 'for the purpose of ascertaining the fulfilment of the measures taken, with the object of observing the manner in which the instructions issued to the authorities of that zone were being carried out'. Both consuls knew something about Rey de Castro's relationship with Arana: they had read a report that Casement had written for Sir Edward Grey in November of the previous year, in which he produced evidence that the Peruvian Amazon Company had advanced the vast sum of £5,000 (£380,00 in today's money) to Rey de Castro – who, as Casement put it, had thereby been 'purchased'.

If they had previously had any doubt that the authorities and Arana were conspiring against their investigation, now they knew for certain that a stitch-up was underway. But they still had no idea how far Arana would go to keep prying eyes out of the Putumayo.

17

The Old Gang

In London, Casement followed closely the events unfolding on the Amazon. He was in constant touch with the Foreign Office – he wrote to Sir Edward Grey and others at least once a week commenting on the constant dispatches that were arriving from the British legation in Lima. He also heard frequently from Lucien Jerome, the British consul-general in Callao, who fed Casement with local stories, rumours and newspaper cuttings. Casement knew all too well what lay in store for the two consuls, and the nature of the people with whom they would have to contend.

It was going to be a charade; Rey de Castro's appearance was proof of this. When Casement learned that Rey de Castro was on his way to the Putumayo, he could not withhold his incredulity: it was a scandal, pure and simple. Casement had heard more than enough on his previous trip to Iquitos of the extent to which Rey de Castro had misinformed Lima concerning the true state of affairs in the Putumayo.

Lores and his troop of special police was further evidence of the cover-up. Casement suspected that they were being sent to the Putumayo to

> scare the Indians so that the two Consuls will see none! . . . These poor beings will be alarmed at the soldiers & this domineering bully will take good care to have news sent round to all the Sections so that . . . the Indians with any grievance will be kept out of the way.

Casement was also convinced that the rubber station chiefs would even go so far as selecting 'parties of specially selected "muchachos de confianza" in pants & shirts etc. [to] play the role of the native population.'

When Rowland Sperling, an assistant clerk at the Foreign Office, read about Rey de Castro and Lores, he concluded that

the Arana gang are already doing all they can to prevent the Consuls discovering the true state of affairs now existing, but we can do nothing until we get the Consul's report. They may be able to get behind the scenes in spite of Arana.

Fuller admitted that, when he learned on the evening before the *Liberal* left Iquitos that Rey de Castro would be accompanying them, he had seriously considered cancelling the trip, but 'decided to continue in view of the arrangements already made at considerable expense and the doubt as to facilities for going up at a future date'.

What he thought when the *Liberal*, on 11 August, four days out of Iquitos, pulled up at Colonia Riojana, an Arana outpost in Brazil (named after Arana's birthplace of Rioja) where the Putumayo meets the Amazon, we can only imagine. Waiting for the *Liberal* was the *Napo*, a Booth steamship heading for Iquitos from Manaus. Getting off the *Napo* and transferring to the *Liberal* ahead of Carlos Rey de Castro was Julio César Arana. Some ten days later, the news of Arana's appearance at Colonia Riojana reached Casement. If Rey de Castro's involvement was a scandal, then how would one describe Arana's?

Everyone at the Foreign Office agreed that this consular tour of inspection was a farce. Casement summed up what they must have thought in a lengthy memorandum he wrote to the Foreign Office from Belfast towards the end of September. Arana's objective was to get two favourable reports, one from each consul. Casement painted the scene for his colleagues:

The Consul General at Manaos [*sic*], an old hand at the game – gets instructions to intercept the two Consuls and accompany them on their journey – and the better to ensure the success of this scheme Arana himself returns in supreme control while a special police force is hurried to the spot which will be at his disposal to impede the Consuls' enquiries and intimidate the wild Indians from approaching them.

He expected a whitewash. The two consuls would be forced to see everything through Rey de Castro's eyes; they would conclude that the Putumayo was tranquil and that the Indians were not being forced to work. All sorts of promises would be made 'and the entire region will be closed again for years to the world and we shall never know how the Indians are faring under "the change to humanitarian methods"'. In reality, Casement continued,

> everything will be done to aid [Arana] in profitably exploiting the patient native race. The leopard does not change his spots; and the Aranas and Zumaetas have no more feeling for Indian humanity today than when they began their career of murder and pillage on the Putumayo.

Transferring to the *Liberal* that day, as well as Arana and Rey de Castro, was a whole contingent of people including Dr Herbert Spencer Dickey, who was now back in Arana's employ as medical officer for La Chorrera, and seven others: Rey de Castro's personal servant; an agronomist; an accountant; an Italian telegraph engineer; Marcial Zumaeta (Arana's brother-in-law); a Huitoto woman called Julia, whom Zumaeta had brought from Barbados to return her to the station of Entre Rios (she was reported to be Andres O'Donnell's Indian 'wife'); and a photographer, Silvino Santos.

The party consisting of Fuller, Michell and the ten others arrived in La Chorrera on 17 August. As Casement and others in the Foreign Office had already anticipated, Rey de Castro and Arana did everything they could to manage the two consuls, to prepare the ground for their various visits, and to prevail on them to see everything through their eyes: 'Señor Rey de Castro', Michell remarked on recalling watching the Indians at work, 'kept pointing to their fat and prosperous condition, and expatiating on the happiness and obvious contentedness of the people.' Fuller's version of Rey de Castro's interference differed little from Michell's. 'He insisted on stopping at unimportant places', Michell wrote,

> where he apparently did nothing but take meaningless photographs of Indians. He continually attempted to take direction of the whole thing into his hands and ordered the company's men about to suit his

convenience, apparently with the intention of conveying the impression
that this was an inspection tour under his sole direction.

The two consuls were hardly ever free of their hosts. Conversations
were monitored; itineraries changed without warning or reasons
given; and delays were the norm. Rey de Castro was their constant
companion. 'Under a pretence of allowing us a complete freedom of
action', Michell reported that Rey de Castro did everything he could
to impede their progress, partly by foisting the agronomist and the
photographer on them, pestering them with questions, and insisting on
taking photographs.

> His anxiety not to lose sight of us was amusingly evident. Though totally
> unfitted physically for severe exercise, he followed us over fatiguing
> roads, through heat and storms, wherever we went, while Señor Arana,
> a heavy man, no longer young, and suffering acutely from sciatica, also
> accompanied us, uncomplaining but indefatigable.

Hemmed in, the consuls saw far less than they wanted to see. Arana and
Rey de Castro excelled at keeping Fuller and Michell from seeing too
much. They hardly caught a glimpse of any Indians – except during a
three-day period when they managed to slip away with the connivance
of one of the Barbadians who had remained in the region – and visited
fewer stations than they had hoped. In the end, they were only in the
area for just over a month – far less time than Casement on his tour.

When they returned to Iquitos on 6 October, both consuls retired to
write their reports and both came to the same conclusions – namely that,
from their limited vantage point, conditions seemed to have improved in
that 'no evidence of cruelties now being perpetrated came to our notice'.
Most of the personnel who were alleged to have committed the worst
crimes had vanished, replaced by new faces, yet the old system of quotas
and percentages were still in force. The consuls' key finding, however,
was that there was no evidence that the government was taking any
interest in the region: 'The fate of the Indians', they concluded with some
trepidation, 'lies almost wholly in the hands of a commercial concern.'

Casement's fear of a complete whitewash was not fully realized.
To their credit, Fuller and Michell did not fall into Rey de Castro's

trap, and used their ingenuity to see as much as they could without his interference. On the other hand, the reports seemed to conclude that the worst of the excesses were over and that the Peruvian government took little interest in the Putumayo. The Indians' fate was not in their own hands, but still in those of the Company.

Arana had won this round of the war. The old gang – Arana and the Zumaetas – was still in charge, the region even more tightly in their grip than before. Despite the fact that Paredes's arrest warrants had been issued almost a year before, and despite the boast that the jails in Iquitos would not be big enough for all the criminals they were going to arrest, no one was being held in custody. The old station chiefs had scattered to other parts of Peru, other parts of South America, or even further, and no one was trying to bring them back to face charges. Fonseca and Montt were living openly in Brazil. The Brazilian authorities were reluctant to get involved, as there was no extradition treaty between Brazil and Peru.

Andres O'Donnell managed to reach Panama safely, even though he had been arrested. A legal quibble over the extradition papers had led the chief justice of Barbados to order O'Donnell's release from custody, and he promptly made his way to Bridgetown's wharf to get out on the next available ship. Armando Normand had escaped to Bolivia, was living in Cochabamba, in the centre of the country, and was appealing to the Peruvian courts to quash his warrant. Victor Macedo, according to Consul-General Lucien Jerome, was living quite openly in Lima; when the police went to the address they were given, there was no sign of the man, though he had been there until very recently. Jerome suspected that Macedo had been given a tip-off.

Arana was ensuring that none of the station chiefs would appear in court. Their silence was important, but Arana went beyond evasive measures. Not for the first time, he turned to the press to attack his enemies directly. A perfect example of this strategy was an interview given by Abel Alarco, Arana's brother-in-law and the man behind the recruitment of the Barbadians in 1904, to the Lima paper *El Comercio* on 22 July 1912. In the interview, Alarco, sensing that Peruvian pride was under threat, played the nationalist card. Colombians, he insisted, had been behind all of the attempts to discredit his country, including the publication of the Blue Book, because they would stop at nothing to get the Putumayo and its wealth. Alarco accused Hardenburg and Perkins of being puppets of Colombian President Rafael Reyes who, for the sum of £4,000, had purchased their services to spy on the operations of the Peruvian Amazon Company, and to start a propaganda campaign against Peruvians by selling stories of atrocities in London. According to Alarco, when Hardenburg got to Iquitos he made a proposition to Arana's solicitor, Julio Ego-Aguirre, that for £8,000 he could be persuaded to write very favourably about Arana's operations in the Putumayo. When Ego-Aguirre refused, Hardenburg set off for London with his defamatory dossier, and 'sold' his story to *Truth*. Alarco maintained that Peru was only doing in the Amazon what European powers had been doing for centuries worldwide: subduing local populations, often by force, and deriving great commercial benefit therefrom. 'For we need not hesitate to declare,' he remarked, 'we who have opened the Putumayo to commerce and the world, that we have used force when force was indispensable. One does not conquer by caressing.'

The world, and especially Britain, owed a great debt to Peru, Alarco argued. Peruvians had laid down their lives in order to defend themselves against the 'savage, an unintelligent and unproductive being' to deliver rubber, 'a product which is quoted in Liverpool as if it were gold'. The 'Englishman who spends his mornings speeding along the broad dusty highroad in his 40 horsepower "Argyll car"', asked Alarco, '[does he] know not or does [he] not wish to know how great the daring of the Peruvian who produces the rubber for the tyres of his car?' 'The issuing of arrest warrants against innocent, brave men', Alarco thundered, was 'bleeding the Putumayo dry, as these heroes of commerce are forced to disappear into the "depths of the forest" to escape rough justice.' 'One more act of complacency from our Government', Alarco concluded, 'and the Putumayo will be finally lost to Peru.'

Giving interviews to the press, especially those that stirred patriotic emotions, was an excellent way for Arana's people to get their message across in Lima. But not everyone in Lima saw it Arana's way. *La Prensa* was one paper that tended more towards an anti-Arana position. On 8 July, just days before the Blue Book's publication in London, *La Prensa* launched a major attack on Arana and his methods of guaranteeing silence. In an article that was part obituary and part editorial, *La Prensa* announced that Benjamin Saldaña Rocca had died recently 'in a state of cruel abandonment'. It was Saldaña Rocca, the paper reminded its readers, who had first brought attention in Peru to Arana's dark world in the Putumayo:

> His efforts were completely wasted because, in those quarters where he did not find the gold of the Firm of Arana in his path sealing the lips of the Government officials, the circumstance that the frontier controversy with Colombia as to the ownership and possession of the Putumayo had at that time been rekindled, forced honourable men to observe a patriotic silence. And that humble defender of Right and Humanity had to fly from Loreto and died miserably in a wretched hole in order that he should not in his turn be the victim of the criminal exploiters of that river.

The article continued in this vein, emphasizing the veil of secrecy and obfuscation over Arana's operations, and citing as another victim of the Putumayo silence, Eugène Robuchon:

> in that obscurity which covered up the investigations, the denunciations and the deaths – in that same Putumayo – of the French explorer Rebuchon [*sic*] whose photographs reproducing the 'macabre' orgies of the servants of the Firm of Arana even now pass from hand to hand.

The exposure of conditions in the Putumayo represented not, in *La Prensa*'s opinion, a challenge to Peruvian patriotism, as Alarco had suggested in his article in *El Comercio*, but a 'great National shame'.

A newspaper, *La Voz del Oriente*, soon appeared, published by a club called the Centro Loretano – an organization founded to promote the interests of the Department of Loreto in the political life of Lima. Its very first issue signalled that it, too, was joining in the battle of words over the Putumayo. It carried an attack on the 'blackmailer' Hardenburg, and the editor vowed to his readers that he would continue to publish the truth of the events in the Putumayo, and that the paper would make the Putumayo a central feature of its concerns. Subsequent issues carried vicious attacks on both Casement and Whiffen, accusing both of attempted blackmail and extortion.

In Iquitos, the Arana gang continued to fight back against its critics. On 4 November, Consul George Michell reported that the municipality had thrown a lavish banquet in the 'Hall of Mirrors' in the Hotel Continental in honour of their favourite son, Julio César Arana. Local merchants and public officials applauded the master of ceremonies, the merchant Luis Morey, when, in eulogistic tones, he reminded his audience that Arana had brought civilization and work to the Putumayo. Arana replied that words failed to express his gratitude for the sympathy and understanding of the guests, 'all men of honour and sound judgement'. The banquet in his honour, he said, had inspired him with greater courage in his struggles.

Arana then turned briefly to Luis Morey and repeated that, as far as his countrymen were concerned, his name and the Putumayo were synonymous. Arana then explained to the audience that he had sacrificed much to bring civilization to the Putumayo.

> It is a region, watered by the river of that name, which has remained unexplored until a few years ago, and which, with part of its forests inhabited by *cannibal natives* [my emphasis] has for a long time resisted every attempt at civilization. It was necessary to establish enterprises strong and powerful in capital and resources in order to achieve the domination over the tribes which were an obstacle to the march of progress.

Peru, though, had its enemies, and they were intent on besmirching Arana's good name. 'Elsewhere, to the foreigner, the Putumayo is a vast region which has become celebrated through attacks and criticisms of which it has been and still is the object.' Then, taking the moral high ground, his speech of thanks ended on a rousing patriotic note:

> I do not defend nor shall defend those who, calling themselves civilized, have perpetrated cruelties through degeneration or greed, but I shall do all in my power that light should be shed and that the name of those men should be rehabilitated who acted in defence of the National territory, contributing to assuring our sovereignty. I do not know if perseverance in work and faith in the destiny of my Country, stimulated by our valuable and benevolent friendship, will lead me on to commercial success, but

in exchange I am certain that [against] all adverse vicissitudes of fate, I must preserve stainless the name left me by my fathers and which, with fortune or without, I wish to leave equally pure and clean to my children.

Whether Arana really believed that patriotism justified his exploitation of the native population, or was just cynically manipulating his audience's jingoism, is not clear: probably both. He certainly knew how to appeal to his fellow *blancos*. Who would stand up for the 'cannibal natives' when the defence of national territory was at stake? Arana's florid rhetoric echoes that of colonial exploiters like King Leopold in the Congo; the Peruvians' independence from Spain had not changed the Hispanic attitude to the indigenous people.

PART V

18

The Canon and the Board

On 4 August 1912, on a cool and overcast Sunday morning, Canon Herbert Henson took the pulpit in Westminster Abbey and, in a fiery sermon, named and shamed the British directors of the Peruvian Amazon Company. Until now the public knew only that the Company had British directors, not who they were. Thanks to Henson, they would soon be in the public spotlight and become household names.

Henson had a fierce reputation as a preacher and polemicist. Canon of Westminster Abbey, he used the pulpit, not just at Westminster but at other sacred venues, principally to address religious issues of the time: concerns such as nonconformity, communion, Christian socialism and religious education received a thorough examination in sermons that he carefully timed to last thirty-five minutes. He was no stranger to political controversy, using the letters page of *The Times* to give vent to his views on themes as widely diverse as the Irish Land Bill, the Education Bill and women's suffrage, to which he was strongly opposed.

A few days after the Blue Book's publication, Henson expressed in a letter to *The Times* his outrage at the atrocities that had taken place on the Putumayo. It gave a clear sense of his stand on the issue. He began by attacking what he called the 'gainers', whose 'gains are dyed deep with innocent blood'. 'Not the least painful feature of the Blue-book', he wrote, 'is the repeated reference to the truly humiliating fact that a great British company has been the cardinal criminal in this miserable business.' 'Who are the directors?' he asked, 'Who are the shareholders? Perhaps some of your readers conversant, as I am not, with mercantile affairs and affinities will tell us.'

He pleaded that the British public should rush out to buy copies of the Blue Book, and, for the petty amount of one shilling and five pence, see for themselves the extent of 'commercial greed in the twentieth century'. He then turned his attention to the United States. 'If the "Monroe Doctrine" carries to American minds any moral connotation', he pointed out, 'then the great Republic which fought the greatest civil war of modern times in suppressing slavery cannot stand idle while the dependent Republic of Peru fails in the alphabet of humane government.'

On past performance, Henson would have taken his politics no further than *The Times*, but on this Sunday morning he daringly brought politics into Westminster Abbey. His preparation for this sermon was meticulous – nothing was left to chance. He had already preached a trial run a fortnight earlier, at Shrewsbury School, and only a week before at Westminster Abbey's adjoining parish church of St Margaret's, where he was also rector.

The congregation was packed that morning – American tourists and visitors from the provinces joined regular London worshippers, according to the *Manchester Guardian*'s correspondent. Perhaps they knew in advance what was coming their way. For them, Henson had prepared an uncharacteristically long, forty-five-minute 'passionate sermon' – a full ten minutes longer than he usually allowed himself – to expatiate on the Putumayo atrocity.

In his 'Sermon on a Blue Book', Henson began by reminding his congregation that it was Sir Roger Casement's report – 'this black record of painful and violent crime [which] will form part of that literature in which perplexed and undone races confess their mysterious and inscrutable anguish' – which had exposed the 'most infamous oppression that has ever served the interest of cupidity or stained the record of despotism'.

Basing his sermon on the text of the Blue Book, Henson went on to describe the barbaric methods of collecting rubber in the Putumayo, and demanded that the 'employers of the malefactors' – they are among us, he proclaimed – 'should be arrested and brought to trial. Justice demanded no less'. He also demanded that some international agreement should be put into operation by the Great Powers to save the Indians from their misery.

This was pretty strong stuff, but then Henson ventured into even more dangerous territory. After referring to the 'Arana brothers' as adventurers, 'able, uncommissioned and uncontrolled, to set up over a great territory an infamous despotism, and destroy in a decade the greater part of the native inhabitants', and to Arana himself as 'the arch-organizer of the whole tragedy', he then turned on the

> great financial syndicates of Europe and America, wealthy companies and individuals, who gain the double advantage of moral anarchy in the rubber yielding forests, and legal security in the civilized communities which provide their markets and revere their wealth.

A little later Henson did what no one else had done. He named the directors: 'Mr Henry M. Read, Sir John Lister-Kaye, Bt, and Mr John Russell Gubbins'. Henson rounded on these men. What had they done for their remuneration? he asked his congregation. Surely, he answered, they had assured the shareholders that the Company 'was an honourable business, earning an honest profit'. And when the allegations first appeared in *Truth*, he continued, did these same men try to find out the truth? 'Far from it', he answered.

As Henson put it in his memoirs, he 'resolved . . . to pillory the British company which had brought such great disgrace on the British name, and lent itself (either in conscious collusion or in indefensible ignorance) to such infamies'. Writing to *The Times* was one way to do it. Another way was to buy up a great many copies of the Blue Book and distribute them freely, which he also did – but using the pulpit was the most audacious strike of all.

Neither in the letter to *The Times* nor in his two previous sermons had Henson named names. According to his own memoir, it was not until after the sermon at St Margaret's that he learned the names of the British directors, and he decided there and then to preach, as he recalled it, 'with the gloves off'. Large parts of Henson's sermon, especially the names of the British directors, appeared in the British press over the next few days. Now that the names were out, Henson demanded that the directors should be arrested and brought to trial, and that

> the time has come for such change of commercial law as shall render it impossible for those who make money by the oppression of native races to wash their hands of all responsibility for the crimes of their agents in those regions, however remote, where their wealth is gained.

Henson later said that he made these defamatory remarks deliberately to force the directors to proceed against him – in other words, to get it all out in the open. The Peruvian Amazon Company's firm of solicitors, Ashurst, Morris, Crisp & Co., lost little time in replying to Henson. They were indignant – 'The statements which you made . . . in regard to our Clients can only be characterized as absolute untruths and they constitute an outrage upon every aspect of fair play and justice' – but they did not threaten nor initiate any legal action. Rather, they stated that the directors knew nothing of what had gone on in the Putumayo, and that as soon as they had learned from *Truth* what was alleged to be taking place there, they dispatched a commission of enquiry to find out the truth. They demanded to know from Henson what measures he was going to take to amend for conduct which 'our Clients are justified in describing as unworthy of a Clergyman of the Church of England – unworthy of a Gentleman – unworthy of a man.'

Henson was not one to be cowed. In response, he refuted each and every one of their 'facts', and ended his letter with the following remark:

> I differ so completely from your Clients in their view of what is befitting a Clergyman, a Gentleman, and a man, that you will not be surprised to learn that I think nothing is required from me in any of those characters which would abate anything of the severity of the censure which I conceived myself called upon to pass on the Directors of the Peruvian Amazon Company preached in the Abbey Church on the 4th of August last.

More exchanges followed. Henson then decided to make the correspondence public. On 19 August, he read the letters from the solicitors and his answers at a meeting of the Anti-Slavery and Aborigines' Protection Society. He told Reverend John Harris that he was free to keep the correspondence and get it published.

Readers of *The Times* were treated to a remarkable public display of acrimony when, on 24 August, the newspaper published the exchange of letters between Henson and the directors' solicitors. Henson had staged a significant publicity coup. The public mood was already unsympathetic to the directors' plea of ignorance. The newspaper's editorial, which chastised the solicitors for the tone and temper of their letter, came down firmly on Henson's side and turned on the directors, asking them to explain how they were so 'innocently misled as to the character of the enterprise in which they recommended the public to participate', how they were kept in the dark about how the profits of the Company were made, and what they had done 'to stop the atrocities and to make amends to the victims'.

Henson took the bold step of naming the directors, but his was not the only pressure on them. Before Henson's sermon, on 19 July, Michael Reddy, an Irish Parliamentary Party MP, had asked the foreign secretary bluntly whether the government intended taking action against the Company's British directors. Francis Acland, the parliamentary under-secretary of state and Foreign Office representative that day, sidestepped the question; but when pressed by another MP, he admitted that the government hoped that their actions were 'amenable to English law'. Another MP managed to squeeze a cautious affirmative answer to his suggestion that the government should publish the names of these directors and bring them to justice.

The following day the parliamentary exchange was printed, as usual, in *The Times*. Reading his newspaper in his fine Georgian home in London's Manchester Square that day was Sir John Lister-Kaye. Sir John had been a director of the Peruvian Amazon Company since its foundation. The parliamentary questioning unsettled Sir John. If the government were to publish the names of the directors, as they seemed likely to do, his good name would be forever associated with a horrible atrocity. Taking advice from the Company's solicitors, Sir John and the other directors decided on a pre-emptive strike. They prepared a letter for circulation in the press, which recounted the setting-up of the Company's commission to the Putumayo, and Casement's attachment to it. It then stated that, after the return of the Commission, Sir Edward Grey had written to the Company with these words:

> The Secretary of State is convinced that your Directors were in complete ignorance of the appalling state of affairs now revealed and that they will lose no time in elaborating a scheme of reform which will effectually prevent the recurrence of these grave abuses.

(At the time when Grey wrote the letter, Casement had been appalled by the exoneration.) The directors' letter now suggested that, in light of Sir Edward's statement, Acland should retract his own.

Lister-Kaye used his excellent connections to pull strings. Personally contacting Sir Arthur Nicolson, the permanent under-secretary of state, he explained that he would prefer Sir Edward Grey to clear his and the other directors' names in the House of Commons, rather than sending the letter to the press. Grey replied that the matter would be cleared up in a further round of parliamentary questioning.

In parliament on Tuesday, 23 July, just a few days after Lister-Kaye's meeting with Sir Arthur Nicolson, the Liberal MP Joseph King opened the questioning, asking the foreign secretary whether the directors might face criminal charges. Sir Edward Grey answered robustly:

> [When] the matter was first brought to their notice the British directors made it clear that they had no knowledge of the state of affairs; they appointed a Commission, which was evidently sent in good faith to inquire on the spot. I am not aware of any ground on which His Majesty's Government could take action respecting them.

This statement was not precisely the same as was contained in his letter to the Company in 1911: in parliament, Grey did not say that he was convinced of their ignorance, but rather that they claimed ignorance. Though this was not quite the same thing, it seemed to assuage the directors, and their threatened letter was never sent to the press.

As soon as Grey sat back on the bench, Douglas Hall chimed in with a question about responsibility. He asked: 'Is not the principal responsible for his agents?' Grey did not answer the question, and it was Joseph King's turn again: 'May we take it', he continued, 'that the directors fully recognise the validity and truthfulness of Sir Roger Casement's Report?' 'Oh yes', answered Grey.

> So far as I am aware the directors have never disputed the state of affairs which was disclosed. What they have contended was that they were

entirely ignorant of the state of affairs before Sir Roger Casement's and their own Commission went there.

But Grey's answer still did not satisfy the House. The next day, King pushed further by asking whether the Blue Book had been sent to the director of criminal prosecutions, to see whether they considered that there was a case to answer, whether charges could be brought against the directors 'who have profited financially from the cruelties practised in collecting rubber in the Amazon basin'. Sir Rufus Isaacs, the attorney-general, thought that the English court would not entertain such an indictment.

The questioning had reached an impasse, but on 1 August, thanks to pressure from the MPS who had been most insistent upon it in the Commons, the Putumayo atrocity came to be debated in parliament for the first time – instead of being subject to questions, as had been the case until now.

Liberal MP Joseph King, who in February 1911 had first raised the issue of the publication of Casement's report in parliament, spoke eloquently and pointedly. This was essentially a British matter, he emphasized; the location of the Company's operations was not germane to the situation. 'British honour and policy are deeply concerned', King stressed. He then went on to explain that a not insignificant part of the labour force was British; that the Company was British; that the rubber was shipped in British vessels; and that it was worked on by British manufacturers. Casement had made similar points. 'Under these circumstances', King continued,

it is humiliating and intolerable that we cannot bring the criminals to justice. It is also most unsatisfactory, to my mind, that we cannot with a clear conscience say that the British company which has command of this trade is clear of blame, and that its directors and officials are clear of knowing what was going on, or, at any rate, that they did not blindly pass over those methods which have been going on.

Nothing short of a proper and full investigation into the matter of corporate responsibility would satisfy the country.

Behind the scenes, preparations were already underway to satisfy King's demand. On 6 August 1912, the day before parliament adjourned for the summer recess, the pressure finally came to a head. Lord Robert Cecil, the Independent Conservative MP, turned away from asking questions of the foreign secretary and instead enquired directly of the prime minister, Herbert Asquith, whether,

> in view of the accusations which have been made against the Peruvian Amazon Company, particularly in foreign countries, the Government will consent to the appointment of a Select Committee to inquire whether any responsibility rests upon the British directors of the company for the atrocities on the Putumayo; and whether any changes in the law are desirable to prevent the machinery of the English company law being used for such nefarious practices.

Select committees, the members of which could come from either the House of Commons or the House of Lords, were appointed to enquire into specific matters of public interest. While the select committee was not a court of law, it had substantial judicial powers. It could compel witnesses of any rank to appear and to produce evidence.

Cecil had already proposed this idea privately to Sir Edward Grey, who said he would discuss it with the prime minister. Asquith was in favour of an inquiry, and replied that his government would approve the appointment of a select committee to investigate the issues raised, and that it would begin its work once parliament reassembled in October.

Not long after the House of Commons returned in October 1912, the select committee on the Putumayo was constituted, with Charles Roberts, MP for Lincoln, as its chairman. Roberts had the reputation of being unerringly impartial. His politics were firmly liberal, supporting, among other causes, female suffrage. *Truth* strongly supported Roberts's appointment, emphasizing his compulsive search for the facts. 'As a licensing justice', the magazine reminded its many readers,

> he was regarded as the Torquemada of the Trade. Like the inquisitors of old, whom he resembles in countenance, he always warmed to his victims, whom he regarded, not as deliberate evildoers, but as the unhappy creatures of an iniquitous industry . . . Mr Roberts . . . whose

giant frame and gaunt arms loom above and around . . . always had the facts.

On 30 October, the House of Commons were informed of the terms of reference of the select committee: it was to inquire whether the directors of the Peruvian Amazon Company were responsible for the atrocities in the Putumayo, and whether the law needed changing 'to prevent the machinery of the Companies Acts being used in connection with similar practices in foreign countries'.

It would soon be calling its witnesses.

19

La Selva *Returns to Parliament*

The select committee planned to meet weekly until all of its witnesses had been heard. The hearings would take place in the Palace of Westminster, in a roomy, wood-panelled, Gothic-looking room, with two full-length windows overlooking the Thames on one side, and an enormous fireplace on the other. Committee Room 11 was large enough to cope with the expected numbers: fifteen members of the Committee, including its chairman, the witness and his counsel, as well as a number of newspaper reporters and as many members of the public as could squeeze in. Reporters from *The Times* and the *Manchester Guardian* were always present in the audience – both papers carried a full report on the once-a-week proceedings. By the time the first round of hearings was complete – before parliament's Christmas break – it became clear that the weekly schedule was too infrequent to accommodate the number of witnesses. In the following year, the Committee often met three times a week, calling its final witness on 30 April.

Roberts made it clear at the outset that his committee was not there to repeat the facts of the atrocities: they accepted that these were as Sir Roger Casement had described them in the Blue Book. The Committee's job was not to judge or take action, but rather to present information and their recommendations to the House of Commons on the specific question of the responsibility of the British directors of the Peruvian Amazon Company. It was parliament's business to take the matter further, both in the specific case as well as in the more general issues that it raised. The key question that concerned the Committee was: Who knew what, and when?

To answer that required background information which neither the Blue Book nor any other public document had revealed. Roberts had a large pool of potential witnesses to draw from – the Foreign Office, the Colonial Office, the Anti-Slavery and Aborigines' Protection Society, and the Peruvian Amazon Company itself were obvious choices. Roberts hoped other witnesses, as yet unknown, might emerge from the proceedings themselves.

One of the first things Roberts did, even before the Committee had been formally constituted, was to contact Sir Roger Casement. Beginning on 24 October and continuing for the next eight months, throughout the period of the hearings, the two men kept in close touch, sharing ideas on whom to call as witnesses, what kind of questions to ask of them, and what documents to have submitted. When not writing to each other, the two men met, often in Casement's London flat or at Roberts's house in Kensington.

In this they were taking a risk, as they both realized, because it could be construed that Casement was leading the chairman. But it was a risk Roberts was willing to take in order to sharpen his investigation. Roberts clearly wanted Casement to provide him with the kind of insight into the whole Putumayo world that only he had. Simply having him appear as a witness in front of the Committee, which he did on two occasions, was not enough. Casement, on his part, saw the select committee as yet another part of the investigation, in which he had been involved for more than two years and on which he could continue to make an impact.

On 6 November, The Committee called Gerald Spicer of the Foreign Office as its first witness. As head of the American department and a senior clerk, Spicer could take the Committee through the role that the Foreign Office had played since the revelations of atrocities in the Putumayo in *Truth* in September 1909. Spicer confirmed that the department's *locus standi* – its only jurisdictional interest in the case – was the allegation that certain Barbadians had suffered at the hands of employees of the Peruvian Amazon Company. Spicer went on to acquaint the committee members with how the Barbadians had come to be employed by Arana; with details of the company's commission of enquiry and Casement's attachment to it; with the Blue Book's main conclusions; and with the relationship between the Foreign Office and the Peruvian government. Spicer's testimony was factual, providing dates and places. The exchanges with committee members were entirely amicable, and Roberts seems to have been pleased with how this first day went.

One week later, it was Casement's turn. During his hearing, Casement described what he had come to see so clearly about the Putumayo: the criminality of the forced-labour system, and how culpability rested entirely with Arana, his brother and brothers-in-law – the Peruvian directors of the Company. The system, Casement emphasized, was deliberately designed: 'It did not grow up by chance or by error or by neglect'. The Peruvian directors knew just what they were doing.

Casement did everything in his power to make the members of the Committee understand that at the heart of the entire system lay a very basic issue of human rights. Casement explained that the scheme of commission payments to the Company agents and the system of terror were

> not necessarily [connected], but they follow upon the absolute denial of all protection to the Indian by the civilised authorities in these regions. There are no civilised authorities in that part of the country. The rubber man goes out into an unknown region with his rifle and associates, and he looks for Indians rather than for rubber. The rubber is always there; the forest is full of rubber trees, but they are valueless unless you can get labour; they are hunting for labour, and the labour is that of the wild Indians; they can conquer and subdue the Indian, who is a grown-up child.

The problem in the Putumayo, as in the Congo, was quite simply forced labour. Lord Alexander Thynne, the Conservative MP who prompted Casement for this exposition, continued the questioning. 'Would it have been possible to have got the labour by other means?' 'If they chose to pay them they could, of course, get it', replied Casement.

On his second appearance in front of the Committee, on 11 December, Casement, in response to Roberts's request for him to clarify the value of trade goods the Indians received for their loads of rubber, produced 'ocular proof', as he called it. He held up examples of the meagre goods that constituted the Indians' wages, waving them in front of the members and the gathered public:

I have here a hat, a pair of pantaloons, and a shirt. These three things . . . represent 60 kilos of rubber . . . Here is a belt, I think, of cardboard. That was given for 5 kilos of rubber . . . Here is a flask of powder and some fish-hooks and some beads. They never gave a whole packet of beads, but two or three strings. They are all things of very trifling prime cost indeed, and of very inferior quality. What I have produced here represents, I am convinced, more than three years' work to an Indian; and, besides, he would have to feed himself and his wife and children all the time, in addition to which he would have to carry the heavy loads of rubber on very long journeys . . . I do not think he would voluntarily and willingly have worked for this trash except under compulsion.

Roberts urged him on. Were Indian workers, he asked, 'supposed to be in debt to the company?' In other words, were the Indians the peons of the Company working off their debt? 'No', answered Casement, 'that would relate to the more civilised regions. The hold on the Indian in the Putumayo was that he could not escape'.

These goods, Casement told Roberts, should be placed on exhibit in the museum of the Board of Trade. 'Those evidences of swindling', Casement remarked, 'are as eloquent in their way of the whole blackguard system as the brands of the lash on the limbs of the poor Indians'. As for the latter, Casement produced photographs at his second hearing, for all to see: one was of a woman starving in a hammock, taken sometime before July 1911, which appeared in a Lima newspaper; others, taken by Casement himself, showed clear proof of horrible punishments. Some showed the scars of flogging and maiming, while others showed Indians in an emaciated condition. Casement also produced photographs of Indians carrying rubber loads, demonstrating how their bodies were distorted. These were important because 'a great many deaths took place owing to the long journeys and the heavy weights imposed upon the Indians'.

Casement could provide a vivid picture of the Putumayo abuses, but he could not directly answer the committee's key question: Did the London directors know the state of affairs in the Putumayo? The only observation he could make was personal, recalling that when he returned from the Putumayo and told them what was going on there, they seemed ashamed but did not 'resent' the information.

Once he had finished giving his evidence, Casement handed over to Roberts documents that no one else had. He let him see his own annotated copy of Robuchon's book, pointing out that, even though it had been edited by Rey de Castro, certain passages, which Casement summarized for Roberts, should have warned anyone who read it that rubber-collecting was coercive, and that the Indians were always under pressure. No mention was made of payments to them. Though it described itself as bringing civilization to 'the cannibal tribes' of the Putumayo, this, Casement repeated, was no civilizing company.

Handing Roberts a number of articles from Peruvian newspapers, Casement described the kind of men who spoke for the Peruvian Amazon Company and for the Arana family. In particular he highlighted the interview that Abel Alarco had given to *El Comercio* in July, to show Roberts Alarco's 'intimate knowledge of the true state of things on the Putumayo'. Roberts learned that Alarco had accused Hardenburg of blackmail, and admitted that to get the rubber out of the wild, uncivilized, forests required coercion: 'one does not conquer by caressing' was how he had put it. Using another article that appeared after Alarco's, Casement vividly showed Roberts how widespread was the culture of denial and counter-attack in Peru. This article quoted Dr Carlos La Torre, a representative of the Department of Bajo Amazonas to the Peruvian Chamber of Deputies, accusing not only Hardenburg but also Casement of blackmail. 'In all those who came forward in the discussions of this campaign there is only revealed the thirst for gold', La Torre remarked.

Casement's appearance was followed by that of Gilbert Grindle, principal clerk of the West Indian Department of the Colonial Office, who repeated the facts of the Barbadian immigration to the Amazon, and the complaints by some of the men of ill-treatment at the hands of Arana's company that had been received in both Bridgetown and Iquitos.

Once Roberts had got as much out of the government as he could – and that was not very much – the Committee called on others in the story. The first to come forward was Horace Thorogood, then a reporter on the London newspaper the *Star*, though in 1909 he had been writing for the *Morning Leader*. Thorogood's story, which he had first recounted in his own newspaper, was sensational. On 23 September 1909, the day after *Truth* published its first Putumayo article,

Thorogood went to the offices of the Peruvian Amazon Company asking for an official reply to the allegations made in the magazine. He said that five or six directors of the Company were there, and that they denied the allegations and accused Hardenburg of trying to blackmail the Company. They were not prepared, at that time, to add more details to their denial, and invited Thorogood to return the following day. The next day none of the directors were there – just a man who appeared to be the Company's secretary. He told Thorogood that he should write no more about the allegations, and then handed him an envelope that contained a banknote. 'For how much?' asked Roberts. 'I do not know', said Thorogood,

> I did not take the banknote out; I returned it to him and I said, 'What is this for?' He said, 'Well, we are much obliged to you for the trouble you took on Wednesday', and I said, 'But you surely know that it is very improper to offer a reporter money.' He said, 'Oh, it is not a bribe; it is in recognition of the trouble you took on Wednesday.'

Other witnesses had their own reasons for appearing before the committee. Travers Buxton and John Harris of the Anti-Slavery and Aborigines' Protection Society had no material evidence, and used the occasion simply to keep the record straight, to reiterate that their Society had played a critical role in the unfolding of events from the very beginning: it was they who had not only believed Hardenburg's allegations against Arana, but had insisted that he take his amazing story to the offices of *Truth*; they had been the first to write to the Peruvian Amazon Company to seek an urgent meeting with the board of directors to discuss the allegations; and it was they who had first suggested that Roger Casement be sent to the Putumayo.

A fortnight after Buxton and Harris's appearance, the Committee took evidence from Louis Barnes, who had become the leader of the Peruvian Amazon Company's commission of enquiry after Colonel Reginald Bertie had fallen ill in October 1910. Barnes was responsible for the Commission's report, which had not been made public. It was Casement who had suggested to Roberts that the select committee should summon Barnes to give evidence. It was the first time, but not the last, that Casement would steer the investigation.

Whether Roberts would have called Barnes in any case is not known, but Casement certainly stage-managed the event. He provided Roberts with a long series of very detailed and pointed questions for the Committee to put to Barnes through which the culpability of the directors would be revealed. 'You will see the points I seek to bring out', Casement told Roberts, 'the dire neglect of what should have been a duty & the easy confidence in Arana – the line of least resistance.'

The questions were typical Casement – full of insight and drive; had Roberts used them verbatim, the source would have been obvious. Framing Casement's questions in his own words, Roberts put them to Barnes, who appeared before the select committee on 27 November. Casement had been instrumental both in getting Barnes to testify and in providing Roberts with an appropriate line of questioning.

Barnes was an excellent witness. His was the first testimony that allowed the members of the Committee an insight into how the Peruvian Amazon Company worked from a managerial point of view. Barnes made several important points. The members of the Commission had come to precisely the same conclusion about conditions in the Putumayo as had the Blue Book: it was a criminal system. Local chiefs of rubber stations did just as they pleased and were seldom visited by the managers in Iquitos. They, in turn, hardly ever communicated with the board in London, and instructions sent from London were simply ignored in Iquitos. Indeed, Barnes emphasized, the London board was wholly ignorant of the management in both Iquitos and the Putumayo. The directors in London had no idea how money was being spent – including, especially, how labour was being paid. There was no evidence that they had ever asked. The management was a shambles. Barnes concluded his testimony by stating that all of the Company's officials he had spoken to in Iquitos and Manaus had denied that atrocities had been committed, and that 'if the English directors had asked for reports from the same source no doubt they would have received the same answer as he did'. So far, then, it looked as though the directors had really been in the dark; but the Committee was still perplexed as to why they had not asked any questions of the management on the ground.

Then, on 4 December, it was the turn of Sidney Paternoster, the assistant editor of *Truth*, and the very man who had met Hardenburg and accepted his story. Paternoster reminded the Committee that he had believed in Hardenburg from the first time he met him, and it was this feeling of trust that compelled him to bring the Putumayo atrocities to public view. He assured the Committee that, had there been the slightest evidence that Hardenburg was interested only in financial gain, he would not have written and published the piece. Paternoster told the Committee that Hardenburg had come to see him in August 1909, and showed him issues of *La Felpa* and *La Sancion*, the depositions he and Saldaña Rocca had collected in Iquitos, and his own book manuscript. Roberts asked: 'Did you know nothing of him before?' Paternoster answered that he had not.

Roberts then drew out of Paternoster that he had gone to see Cazes at his London flat, where he confirmed Hardenburg's allegations. Cazes told Paternoster that

> his lips were sealed officially; that privately he had never been on the Putumayo or any of its affluents to search for himself, but he had heard all these stories; he knew that a previous American consul had been up those rivers, and that in the American consul's office he had seen a report which contained very similar allegations to these.

Cazes would be the next important witness. So far, Casement and Roberts had agreed on most things in the Committee's proceedings, but when it came to Cazes, who was scheduled to appear on 17 December, they were at odds on the issue of how he should be questioned. Casement did not want Cazes to be put through the ringer. It was not his fault that he was in such a difficult position in Iquitos. The Foreign Office was as much to blame as he was, 'for they were quite content to leave those parts in the hands of local traders, only consulates in name, until the avalanche fell'.

In the bundle of documents Casement handed over to Roberts was a copy of the letter that Arana had written to Cazes in July 1910 alerting him to the imminent arrival of the Peruvian Amazon Company's commission in Iquitos, and explaining that its terms of reference were solely commercial. Casement clearly explained how this letter had come into his possession, and what significance it had.

> Cazes behaved rightly to me as his official senior etc. & gave me a copy of the letter and any assistance he could to investigate. Arana's intention, of course, was quite clear to me. He counted on Cazes, as a local merchant,

considering his wishes as perhaps of more importance than the passing influence of a British consular officer sent to investigate and clearly implied his hope that Cazes might remember that trade friendships were of more value than a consular post valued at £21 per annum.

By sharing the letter with Casement, Cazes showed that his allegiances were to Casement over Arana. Casement did not want Roberts to use the letter in a question to Cazes – he did not really want Cazes to be dragged into a public enquiry at all. As he put it to Roberts, Cazes had

> already lost the Consulate & all its attendant prestige – and really through me and my representations on the need of an official, paid Consular officer at Iquitos. So, if you can see your way to suppress that question, all the better perhaps.

As Casement had pointed out previously, by using local British businessmen as unpaid honorary consuls, the Foreign Office put them in an impossible position.

Casement was clearly anxious about the letter, writing again to Roberts the same day setting out his argument more forcefully. 'On fuller reflection I would beg of you not to make any public use of the letter from Julio Arana to Mr Cazes. Let it be solely for your personal guidance & help.' The caution Casement urged was not only about Cazes, but also reflected his anxiety that he might be recognized as the source of Roberts's material and line of questioning. No one apart from Casement could have had a copy of this letter, and if anyone was curious about its provenance the trail would lead directly to Casement. 'My name', he concluded, 'can in no circumstances transpire as your informant on anything.'

Casement was displaying a kind of nervousness that, until now, had not been usually apparent. He was a driven man wanting to root out crimes against humanity, whether in the Congo or in the Putumayo. But the Putumayo, which had now absorbed two years of his life, was having an impact on both his physical and mental state. Casement's doctor confirmed that he was suffering from severe pain in his back and side, which may have been caused by arthritis. His friends – in whom he confided that he was growing 'seedier and seedier daily' – certainly attributed his change in demeanour to the Putumayo. He appeared debilitated, 'bent double with pain', 'suffering from severe mental strain, in a highly nervous condition and quite incapable of discussing anything but the horrors of the investigations with which he seemed obsessed'. No doubt, trying to manage the affair from behind the scenes added to his increasingly nervous disposition.

In the end Roberts did refer to the letter, but it played no substantive part in the questioning. The Committee was much more interested in what Cazes could tell it about Arana and his relationship with the London board. One of the Committee's members, the Liberal MP Hubert Carr-Gomm, took up that very issue. 'I presume Señor Arana was a very plausible gentleman, and there was apparently a great deal of candour about him?' 'Yes', replied Cazes,

> he certainly gave me that idea. I have known Mr Arana for, I think, eleven years, since I have been out in Iquitos; and I have always known him to be courteous, and he has always struck me as being a very honourable man.

Carr-Gomm continued the questioning. 'Do you think he was the kind of man who, knowing what we know now, would quite easily have turned a Board of English directors round his finger?' Cazes replied, 'I think it is quite obvious that they believed most of the statements he made, as I should have done. I should have been probably hoodwinked.'

The select committee ended its first session on 18 December 1912, just before parliament's Christmas recess. By that time, a dozen witnesses had trooped in and out of Committee Room 11, some of them appearing more than once. What they said in front of the Committee had generally been known to only a few insiders in the Foreign Office, the Anti-Slavery and Aborigines' Protection Society and, of course, Casement. But now, as witnesses spilled all they knew, ever more damning details of the Putumayo story emerged. Still more revelations would come out in the next session, after parliament's return, when the board of directors would be questioned.

Meanwhile, Casement was advised to have a well-deserved break, 'to sweep all this off my mind'. He was going to go to the Canary Islands at the end of December, he told Roberts, to recuperate. Before leaving, he

promised Roberts the rest of the documents in his possession pertaining
to the Putumayo, including the diary he had kept while there: 'The diary
makes me sick again . . . it brings up so vividly that forest of hell'.

Casement docked at Las Palmas, on Gran Canaria, on 3 January 1913.
The next day he fired off a letter to Roberts, in which he candidly
reflected on his part in the Putumayo story. He told Roberts to bear in
mind that it had been

> practically a one-man affair – my own. I must tell you the truth – so that
> you may understand – and you will acquit me, I know, from anything
> like boasting. It was really my doing from the day Grey sent me off until
> the Report was published two years later.

Recounting how the events of the past years had unfolded, especially how
he had gone beyond the Foreign Office's relatively narrow concern for
the Barbadians to look into the bigger issue of the atrocities perpetrated
on the Indians, he stated:

> Now I tell you these things because I want you to fully realize that the
> carrying through of the Putumayo question was a personal thing & once
> the personal factor goes the matter will, of necessity, relapse into the
> ordinary routine methods of diplomatic effort.

He held out no hope that diplomacy would lead to a better life for the
victims of Arana's brutality.

> The outcome then is certain. The Peruvian Govt will really do nothing.
> They will promise & leave everything as before to the men on the spot &
> the F.O. will, perforce, be required to accept this ending & so the whole
> question closes. The other blackguards will lift up their heads, & in a
> brief space the old game will go on with renewed vigour.

Casement confided in Roberts that, as far as he could see, the Putumayo
was not an isolated incident. He feared that other companies, both
British and American, were taking advantage of what he termed 'the
Peruvian ideas of the "whiteman's" claim to Indian labour'.

Meanwhile, in London, it was time for the directors to be questioned. The first to be called was John Russell Gubbins, chairman of the board of directors of the Peruvian Amazon Company until its liquidation in September 1911. Gubbins had had long experience as a businessman in Peru. He explained that when he had joined the Company, in July 1908, he was convinced that it was a sound business. Gubbins told the Committee that Abel Alarco, Arana's brother-in-law and the man responsible for recruiting the Barbadian workers, had explained to him how the rubber-collecting system worked, and that the Indians were paid in goods, cash being useless in the forest – all of which he accepted without question.

Gubbins then repeated under close questioning a version of events that had by now become familiar: that the first that he or any of his directors had heard of the alleged atrocities was upon their publication in *Truth*; that they accepted Arana's story over that of Hardenburg's, whom they thought was a blackmailer; and that, as soon as it was possible, they arranged for their own commission of enquiry to proceed to the Putumayo.

After a gruelling three-day cross-examination, the most that the Committee could get out of Gubbins was that the relationship between Arana and the British board was probably not as it should have been. Gubbins admitted that the board could do nothing without Arana; that they had responsibility without control; that they were mere figureheads; and that they relied entirely on the information that Arana supplied to them. He stressed that the atrocities had been committed without their knowledge or consent: their consciences were clear.

Once Gubbins had been excused from the hearing, Sir John Lister-Kaye was sworn in. Though he had no background in South American business, nor in rubber, and did not speak or write Spanish, he too was convinced that the Company was sound. When he was pressed on why he only enquired about the Company's creditworthiness and not about the condition in which it held labour, he simply answered that he thought 'there were plenty of labourers, and that was the main point to consider in the collection of rubber'. Like Gubbins before him, he claimed innocence on the grounds of ignorance.

For most of the time Lister-Kaye remained calm, his answers concise and to the point. But one committee member, the Liberal MP

Willoughby Dickinson, was determined to get to the bottom of one key issue: precisely when the board of directors had decided to send their commission to the Putumayo. Was it, as the directors claimed, when the article in *Truth* appeared? Or was it later, after they had been pressured by the Foreign Office? The calm was broken.

Lister-Kaye insisted that the decision had been taken in October 1909, before the Foreign Office's involvement. When Dickinson pressed him for further confirmation of that date, by asking him when the name of Colonel Bertie was first discussed, Lister-Kaye could not recall. The British directors, he said, had met frequently to discuss various matters, and the details of many of these meetings – often held privately – went unrecorded. Finally, Lister-Kaye's discomfort at Dickinson's doggedness overwhelmed him.

> We three British directors frequently met together and talked over things. Cannot you understand the immense anxiety we had in our minds, and is it not likely that we three Englishmen should meet continually and talk over them? . . . Cannot you understand the horror I felt at this hideous situation? I expected to find some sympathy, but you are combating the idea.

Lister-Kaye then apologized for his show of emotion; but, despite being questioned on three separate days, he added nothing other than what had not already been established: namely, that the directors were ignorant and eventually set up a commission to establish the facts.

The next day, 22 January, was the turn of Henry Read, the last of the British directors to be sworn in. Read had joined the Company as a director in December 1907, and had had extensive experience in Latin American business and banking.

As usual, Roberts began the questioning. One of the things he wanted Read to comment on was why the board had accepted at face value Arana's version of events in the Putumayo. Read answered: 'Because there was so much against Hardenburg and so much in favour of Arana. I do not know whether you care to go into the reasons why we had more trust in Arana than you gentlemen appear to have?' 'I think perhaps it would be well', countered Roberts.

So Read began to tell his tale. He maintained that the suggestion of sending a commission to the Putumayo came from either Alarco or

Arana, though he could not recall which. If crimes had been committed, then why would anyone they implicated suggest sending a commission to investigate, thought the directors. Furthermore, Alarco had told them that Hardenburg

> was a bad man, and . . . had tried to blackmail the Aranas . . . Then came other episodes which were in favour of Arana. Arana, instead of paying a thousand pounds [in response to blackmail], refused, and that does not look like guilt; and we knew Arana; we had been with him some time; we were very much impressed with his quiet reserved manner, but when we asked questions he appeared to speak with the greatest frankness, and Alarco as well.

Roberts, of course, had to ask Read, as he had asked the other two directors, why he had not enquired into the conditions of the Indians:

> You are English directors of a company trading in a foreign country, and, after all, the credit of England was to some extent at stake; but it never seems to have crossed the mind of any director that he had any duty to see whether these unfortunate natives were ill-treated?

Read responded:

> Why should I think anyone was ill-treated? The thing never occurred to me. When I asked Alarco he told me that the man went into the shop, took a knife or gun, and went into the woods for three or four months for rubber; and it struck me as a free-and-easy life.

Roberts, impatient with the answers he had been receiving for days, asked Read again about why the directors had never inquired into the conditions of the Indians.

> Did you, the English directors, know enough about the conditions of Peru to make you feel that it was very undesirable to inquire into the Peruvian conditions for fear you should find what you could not defend upon any British standard?

'No, sir', replied Read, 'decidedly not.'

> The only reason we did not look into the past was because we felt we
> could not, and that the Peruvian Government alone must do it. If we
> attempted such a thing we should mortally offend them, [and] instead
> of getting help from them, we should probably be met with indifference
> and difficulty.

The day was drawing to a close, and Roberts asked Read a final
question about whether he had acted appropriately, and whether the
directors had done everything that was required of them. 'So much so',
answered Read, 'that if it were to begin all over again to-day I would do
it in exactly the same way'.

When Casement read the minutes of the evidence given by the three
British directors he was enraged. He wrote to Roberts that their lack of
action was due only to cowardice and their desire to save themselves.
They cared nothing for the wrong they had done – 'they did not draw
their Directors fees from peonage – but from piracy pure & simple'
– and showed no remorse or wish to put things right. Casement also
congratulated Roberts on learning more about the Peruvian Amazon
Company in three months than all the British directors put together had
learned in four years.

A few days later, Casement wrote to Roberts again, saying that he
was not coming home as planned but had decided to continue to the
warmer climes of Cape Town to visit his brother. He would be out of
touch for at least three weeks on the long voyage south, and would not
be home until April, at the earliest.

On 29 January, Read was recalled for a second day of questioning; but
instead of one of the committee members starting the proceedings, the
Company's counsel, Raymond Asquith, spoke first, and he had startling
news: Arana had sent a cable announcing his intention to come to
London and face his accusers.

20

The Peruvian, the American
and the Select Committee

The Foreign Office had been tracking Arana's movements on the Amazon ever since Judge Valcárcel had issued a warrant for his arrest in mid-December 1912. Arana had left Iquitos a month earlier, shortly after his celebratory banquet, and headed to Manaus. The British vainly hoped that the Brazilian authorities would extradite Arana in accordance with his arrest warrant. The unlikeliness of this happening became evident when the British chargé d'affaires in Brazil mentioned to the ex-head of the Colombian delegation in Lima the sterling efforts made by the Brazilian government to expel the Putumayo criminals who had taken refuge there. The Colombian just laughed, saying no more than that Arana was the most powerful man in Peru, and that 'all these men had money and were therefore masters of the situation'.

Arana remained in Manaus for two months without any interference from the Brazilian authorities. While there he lodged an appeal in the High Court in Iquitos against his arrest, and issued a declaration to his fellow Peruvians in the form of a telegram, which he sent to the Peruvian press. Dated 30 December 1912, it appeared in Lima's *La Prensa* the following day. In it Arana provided a clear statement of where he stood on the events of the preceding years. He began by arguing that Judge Valcárcel's warrant for his arrest was proof positive that the Colombians had finally been successful in their plan 'to convert Peruvians themselves' into agents for their country. For his part, Arana had been rewarded with an arrest warrant for resisting their attempts to do the same to him. He had proof that would establish once and for all that what had been said against him had been a series of lies, and that attempts had been made to blackmail him. He would be making all of this public in a book he was preparing, and he would tell his story to the European press. The telegram ended with the following statement:

> I would proceed to Iquitos were not my presence indispensable in Europe to undo the machinations against me and to save the prestige of my Country. But I am confident that the high Tribunals of Peruvian Justice will annul the Order of Judge Valcárcel, who has abandoned Iquitos in a quasi-clandestine manner. I beg my Countrymen to suspend judgement until they know the defence I am about to make and which will produce a worldwide reaction in favour of Peru and leave my name unblemished.

The British vice-consul in Manaus was watching Arana carefully. On 12 February 1913, he reported to the British consul in Pará that on the previous day Arana and his brother-in-law Marcial Zumaeta, who was now acting as his secretary, had boarded the *Lanfranc*, a Booth liner bound for Lisbon and England.

Arana had nothing to fear. Such was his popularity and influence in Iquitos that when Valcárcel issued a warrant for his arrest, the town erupted in riot against Valcárcel, who promptly left town because of ill-health. A month later, the High Court in Iquitos quashed the arrest warrant on the grounds that the charges were too vague.

Not only was the Foreign Office tracking Arana; the British press had also got hold of the news that he was on his way to Europe. When the *Lanfranc* docked in Lisbon, on 26 February, a London *Daily Mail* correspondent was waiting for Arana and, managing to get aboard the ship, persuaded him to answer a few questions. Arana maintained that the Putumayo atrocities had been grossly exaggerated, probably by his rivals in the rubber business. No doubt, he added, natives in remote localities had been ill-treated, but not by him – he had never been to those parts.

Before leaving Lisbon, Arana issued a fuller statement, in which he explained that he had agreed to appear in front of Roberts's committee

> to give all of the explanations in my power in respect of the present state of things, having paid a visit of inspection to the region between

August and October last at the same time as the Consuls of Britain and the United States and the representative of the Peruvian Government visited the region . . . I think my conduct and innocence will be properly judged there on this occasion, my case having already been rigorously investigated in my own country, where I have been entirely freed from responsibility by the higher tribunals.

On 2 March the *Lanfranc* docked at Fishguard. Waiting for him on the quayside was a crowd of newspaper reporters. The photograph taken of him at the time shows a portly, ageing man, not the trim, youthful Arana pictured in Robuchon's book and in the Manaus *Jornal do Commercio* of June 1908. A description in the *Observer* accompanying the photograph was favourable.

He is a stoutly built man of forty-five, about five feet nine inches in height. His short-pointed beard is growing somewhat grey, but, as one would expect from a man of Spanish race, he is naturally dark. In manner he is simple and kindly, and quite free from affectation. That he is a good businessman is abundantly clear, but he is at the same time most charitable. He assists not only his friends who need help, but some who are not his friends.

A *Daily Mirror* reporter managed to get a short interview with Arana through Marcial Zumaeta, who spoke English, in the small interval between his leaving the ship and boarding the express train for Paddington. 'I have come to tell the truth', declared Arana. 'It is time it should be told'. 'There was a look in his eye', the reporter interjected,

which foretold many an hour of stonewall response to the questioning of the most bitter critics for months. Ever since the publication of Sir Roger Casement's report on cruelties . . . Senor Arana has been the most bitterly attacked millionaire in the world. But he only smiled to-day when he landed.

Zumaeta was carrying a large bag stuffed with important documents, and the weighty trunks were filled with newspapers and photographs, which 'when published would prove that the reports were grossly exaggerated'. Zumaeta told the reporter that what he had seen in the Putumayo was completely at odds with what Casement had seen.

> We were in the region where the atrocities are reported to have taken place at the time of the publication of the Blue-book, and after a journey of 1,200 miles up the Amazon we visited many of the places mentioned in the Blue-book. All we can say is that we found no trace of any atrocities at all. The natives seemed to be well treated and there were no complaints . . . in many of the villages of their territory of 10,000 square miles we asked innumerable questions of the natives and the officials. But we could hear of nothing wrong.

Arana, he said, would tell all this to the Committee: 'He has come to England to defend his honour and to justify his career. He need not have come, but he felt it was his duty.'

Arana had made the decision to come to London initially to defend himself, not before the select committee, but rather in the High Court of Justice. There, several shareholders of the Peruvian Amazon Company, with the help of the Anti-Slavery and Aborigines' Protection Society, who had initiated the action (presumably as a way of punishing Arana), were bringing a winding-up order to effect the removal of Arana from the position of voluntary liquidator, to which the board had appointed him unanimously late in 1911. He was to be replaced by an official receiver. When Charles Roberts, as chairman of the select committee, first received news of Arana's intentions to come to London, he sent Arana an invitation through the Company's solicitors to attend the Committee's hearings as a witness.

The hearing, originally set for 29 October 1912, was postponed, the judge agreeing that Arana should be given an opportunity to answer the charges made against him.

As it turned out, there were several delays in getting Arana's evidence presented. When the petition to wind up the Company came up again in the High Court on 4 March 1913, Mr Justice Swinfen Eady refused an appeal by the counsel for the creditors for yet another postponement, arguing that the appeal should be heard as soon as the select committee had had its interview with Arana. He told Arana's counsel that his affidavit of evidence should be prepared for a hearing set for 18 March.

Though Arana's counsel argued that the High Court was not the place to discuss questions of allegations of ill-treatment and atrocities in the Putumayo, Justice Eady disagreed, and referred explicitly to the report by the Company's commission of enquiry; to the conduct of the chiefs of sections; to the allegations as they were reported in *Truth*; to the culpability of the managers; to the atrocities; and, finally, to the condemnation of Arana himself. Justice Eady relied heavily on Casement's Blue Book for much of his information. The day after the affidavits were presented, Justice Eady passed judgement. There would be a compulsory order to wind up the Peruvian Amazon Company. He had no doubt that Arana was the last person who should be entrusted with this responsibility. 'In my opinion', Justice Eady pronounced,

> Arana and his partners sold a business whose profits were derived from rubber collected in the atrocious manner I have indicated, and it is impossible to acquit all of the partners of knowledge. Certainly [Pablo] Zumaeta knew, and if Arana did not know then he ought to have known. Under those circumstances I make the Compulsory order.

In case the public had missed Justice Eady's comments and judgement on the case as they were reported in the British press, the Anti-Slavery and Aborigines' Protection Society, intent on making Arana's life as difficult as possible, published a handy little booklet containing all of Eady's pronouncements on the case.

The British public had been primed for Arana's appearance. His interviews in Lisbon and Fishguard and the proceedings at the High Court in London raised expectations of a gripping hearing in Westminster. The committee members, too, were excited about Arana's arrival but, like the showman he was, Arana made them wait. On 20 March, Arana and Stephen MacAndrew, the Peruvian Amazon Company's solicitor, successfully petitioned the Committee for a postponement until early the following month, because Arana's wife Eleanora, it was claimed, was ill and undergoing medical treatment in Switzerland, and he needed to go to her without delay.

Almost three weeks later, Arana presented himself with his counsel and interpreter in front of Roberts and the Committee. The *Manchester Guardian* provided a vivid portrayal of the opening scene on 8 April.

> The much-talked-about Julius Cesar Arana came before the Putumayo Committee to-day – a heavy, yellow-faced man, with black-grey hair and beard, who gave his evidence in rapidly spoken conversational asides to the interpreter beside him, emphasizing it from time to time by a quick gesture of his fat, short-fingered hands. He had put in a printed statement of his evidence-in-chief, which was in the nature of a general denial of the case against him, and his counsel Mr Douglas Hogg [later the 1st Viscount Hailsham], sat behind him to watch his interests. He had, however, no occasion to interfere. The proceedings moved slowly, for every question had to be interpreted to the witness, and in turn his answers to the Committee, and the interpreter went deliberately about his work. Both English and Spanish shorthand writers were occupied taking down what was said.

The *Manchester Guardian*'s reporter was transfixed by the performances given by Arana, his counsel and his interpreter that day. Of the three, it was the interpreter who interested him the most, and that was partly because of the constant interventions of one of the committee members, the Liberal MP William Young. Young was a merchant with extensive experience in Mexico, and

> discovered to-day an extraordinarily fluent colloquial command of Spanish which enabled him to correct or define translations made by the interpreter, and to put fresh questions to the witness straight in his own tongue – a gift which had, of course, to be sparingly exercised for the sake of his fellow-members.

Roberts asked almost all of the questions on the first day. Arana did not deny that atrocities had taken place, But he was adamant that he had known nothing about them until the reports were published. Roberts asked Arana whether he knew of Robuchon's book. Yes, he did. He then asked him about a passage in the book which referred to the Indians' loss of liberty after the arrival of the white man. Oh, said Arana, liberty in this instance referred to the fact that 'they could not make war from tribe to tribe as they used to before'. Roberts then tried another approach. 'Among your papers here', Roberts began,

> is the original French basis of this book, which was edited by Senor Rey de Castro. I have looked through that and I find this passage omitted in the Spanish, 'the Indians care nothing for the preservation of their rubber trees, and rather desire their destruction. Eager to recover their lost liberty and their independence of former days, they think that the whites who have come into their dominions in quest of this valuable plant, will go away when it has disappeared. With this idea, they regard with favour the disappearance of the rubber trees, which have been the cause of their reduction to slavery. Without ambition or knowledge of the value of goods, they give their labour for a few worthless beads, for an old gun, an axe, or a cutlass.

Did Arana know that Rey de Castro had cut that passage out of the Spanish translation? 'No', he replied.

The point of the question, which Casement had insisted Roberts ask Arana, was to show that Rey de Castro had tampered with Robuchon's original French manuscript, a copy of which was found in the London offices of the Peruvian Amazon Company before it was translated into Spanish. By omitting passages such as the one above, which described the Indians wanting the white man to get out of their lands and to leave them alone, Rey de Castro was helping to portray Arana's company as bringing civilization and its material benefits to the region. But Arana did not rise to the bait, and the matter was dropped.

Throughout that day's questioning, Arana continued to maintain that he had known nothing about the conditions in the Putumayo as they had been described in *Truth*. When asked why Paredes could 'get at the stories of cruelty from the Indians', Arana replied that 'he was in the centre of Putumayo, and had a certain amount of authority in the matter'. When asked a similar question about Casement's discoveries, Arana retorted that it was 'necessary to have the experience of Sir Roger Casement, to have been in the Congo and lived there, and also to know the English language to be able to do this'.

Arana had a knack for sidestepping awkward questions. Roberts wanted to find out from him about the use of firearms in the Putumayo. He read from a letter written by Miguel Loayza, manager of El Encanto, in June 1909: 'It has not been possible to send the six single-barrel shot guns, as we have none here, but in order to deal with the Indians who run away we are now sending three double-barrelled guns.' When asked what he thought these guns were for, Arana simply answered, 'I do not understand what they were for; but what I can make out, they might have been for giving to the Indians – dividing among them – to give them guns in exchange for rubber'. Guns, Arana insisted throughout the day, were used to protect the employees from wild animals and to shoot game for the table. Shooting Indians, Arana added, was something he had learned about only since attending the select committee's hearings.

Questioned about the rights of the Indians in their relationship with the Company, Arana replied that the Indian 'only recognises his master, the man who pays him'; when asked whether such a system was not open to abuse, Arana, typically, evaded the issue, preferring to answer an imaginary question about employment contracts: 'With the whites', he said, 'it is a question of having a document signed or endorsed to do it; but the Indian cannot sign – he cannot sign his name – he cannot write.'

At that point, Douglas Hogg, Arana's counsel, turned to Roberts stating that Arana had heard that his wife was worse, and that though he could appear again on the following two days, he could not stay longer than that.

The *Manchester Guardian*'s reporter was distinctly unimpressed by Arana's performance. He commented sarcastically that Arana

left the witness-chair this afternoon on his own showing a much wronged man, accused of bribery, cruelty, or connivance in cruelty, and participation in a system of unspeakable savagery, while all the while his relations to the natives were those of Robinson Crusoe to his man Friday – of a paternal agent of civilisation towards a friendly and contented race.

The next day, Arana appeared as promised. He began by repeating his well-rehearsed theme that the problems in the Putumayo were the fault of the Colombians. They, Arana insisted, had originated the system of abuse. The people he employed, by contrast, were the best available.

When asked to explain two entries in the Company accounts – one called *Conquistar* and the other *Gastos de Conquistacion* ('To conquer or subject' and 'Capital Expenditures Incurred in Reducing Indians to Subjection') – Arana responded by saying that the first meant 'distributing goods and fitting out expeditions with a view to converting the Indians to the system of barter', while the second term referred simply to the costs involved in this 'pacific conquest'.

At one point Roberts asked Arana again about guns in the Putumayo, and why, in addition to a substantial sum spent on *Gastos de Conquistacion*, there was also a large sum spent on rifles. Arana repeated that the Winchesters ordered from London and New York were used solely for protection, stressing that 'there is no rubber collector in any region who does not carry with him one of these rifles.'

Roberts, finding it impossible to get a straight answer from Arana, changed topics abruptly in the hope of tripping up his witness. Asked about the incidence of flogging of Indians, Arana replied that he had known nothing of this until he had read about it in Hardenburg's and Casement's reports. Was Arana not aware that before these reports Saldaña Rocca had accused Arana's employees of flogging, asked Roberts. Arana replied that Saldaña Rocca's papers were considered rags and that, in any case, other papers had contradicted these accusations.

At this point, John Gordon Swift MacNeill, the firebrand Irish MP for South Donegal, sensing the frustration in the room, exclaimed: 'This witness never answers a question Yes or No, and the first thing I submit is to tell him to answer Yes or No, and make his explanation afterwards.' But MacNeill's outburst was as useless as the questioning that had preceded it: no one could get Arana to give a straight answer.

The questioning then turned to the subject of Walter Hardenburg. Willoughby Dickinson asked whether Arana would recognize Hardenburg if he ever saw him again. Arana, typically noncommittal, answered: 'Perhaps I might. I only saw him once, one night when he came to visit me'.

Now the critical question of Hardenburg's veracity was broached. Joseph King produced the circular Arana had written to the shareholders of the Company back in late December 1909, in which he had written, 'I produce to the board evidence of forgery on the part of Hardenburg . . .' This statement referred to a bill for £830 drawn on an Iquitos bank, which Hardenburg, as the bearer of the bill, presented and cashed in Manaus at the Bank of Brazil. The bill was sold on and made its way to the Rothschild Bank, but they protested that it had been tampered with and refused to accept it as a negotiable instrument. King then put it to Arana that the circular was an attempt to portray Hardenburg 'as a mere adventurer if not a criminal'. Arana sidestepped, and then King read out the passage from the circular in which Arana accused both Hardenburg and Whiffen of blackmail. Arana remained silent.

Roberts would have none of this. 'Answer the question, please, directly: Do you charge Hardenburg with having committed the forgery or not?' Arana now found his voice, and answered: 'That is entirely another thing.' Roberts asked again, 'Do I understand then that you do not charge Hardenburg with the act?' Arana sidestepped, again. 'I do not know who was the forger,' he protested, 'Hardenburg or someone else.' Joseph King tried once more to try to get Arana give a straight answer to a straight question. 'Then I will only ask you one more question on this subject. You do not now charge Hardenburg with forgery – do you or not?' 'No', said Arana finally, 'I do not accuse him now.'

At the end of the day's proceedings, Swift MacNeill took over the questioning of Arana. The subject was again Walter Hardenburg.

'When was your last interview with Hardenburg – was it not in April 1908?'

'The last was when I was in Iquitos in April, 1908.'

'Then did Hardenburg tell you what was going on in the Putumayo?'

'He spoke to me with great seriousness on the matter of my trying to get or making inquiries about his lost luggage.'

'And nothing more?'

'This was the object of the visit.'

'Did you say anything about blackmailing?'

'No.'

'Do you call him a forger now?'

'I have to repeat what I said before, that the suspicion falls on two persons, on the buyer or on the endorser.'

Then Swift MacNeill motioned to a man sitting in the audience to stand up.

'Turn around', said MacNeill to Arana, 'and see Hardenburg before you. Do not you know him?'

'Yes, I am very pleased to see him here, because we can then enter into other details.'

Walter Hardenburg had left England in February 1910 for Canada. After a period of two months in Toronto working for a local newspaper, he had headed west for Alberta, working in several jobs, including that of surveyor for the Canadian Pacific Railway.

While Hardenburg was in Canada, both John Harris and Travers Buxton had been writing to him, keeping him abreast of developments in the Putumayo and sending him copies of published documents which he otherwise would have been unable to obtain. Hardenburg knew, therefore, that Casement had gone out to the Putumayo with the Peruvian Amazon Company's commission, that he had reported to the Foreign Office with material backing up Hardenburg's allegations, and that the Commission's report did the same; he knew that Casement had returned to Iquitos a second time, and he knew that Dr Paredes, in his report, had also supported his allegations.

Roberts had thought of asking Hardenburg to appear as a witness, but when, in December, Thomas Fisher Unwin published Hardenburg's book, *The Putumayo: The Devil's Paradise*, the manuscript of which he had brought with him from Iquitos in August 1909, it seemed there was no need to bring him to London from so far away. After all, what could he add to what he had said in the book? No one, apart from Arana and his henchmen, had any doubt about Hardenburg. His book had been widely and favourably reviewed. John Harris, for one, praised Hardenburg, and claimed that had the two Americans reached their destination by the usual route, they would never have encountered Arana's empire, and the fate of the Indians would have been sealed. No one would ever have heard of the Putumayo.

Now the public could read for itself how he and Perkins had planned to cross the South American continent from the Pacific coast of Colombia and how, instead of paddling down the Putumayo to the Amazon, they unwittingly found themselves in the heart of Arana's empire; how they had witnessed the slaughter of David Serrano and other Colombians; how he and Perkins had become separated in the Putumayo, and eventually been reunited in Iquitos; how, while in Iquitos, he had come into the possession of Saldaña Rocca's documents and back issues of

La Felpa and *La Sancion*; and how, through this material, as well as the depositions and testimonials he had collected himself, he had learned of the horrible acts committed not only against the Colombians, which he had seen with his own eyes, but against the Indians, whom he had only glimpsed.

On his own account, then, Roberts had no reason to bother Hardenburg. But the Anti-Slavery and Aborigines' Protection Society had grown increasingly concerned that witnesses connected with the Peruvian Amazon Company – the likes of John Russell Gubbins, Sir John Lister-Kaye and Henry Read – kept telling the Committee that they had consistently refuted Hardenburg's allegations, siding with Arana against him. In their testimony, these men continued to refer to Hardenburg as a blackmailer and forger – allegations that the Society felt Hardenburg should answer in person. On 18 January 1913 Travers Buxton, the Society's secretary, wrote to Roberts:

> As the Directors have repeatedly stated that they still consider him to be a forger and blackmailer, it has occurred to us that it might be well to suggest to Mr Hardenburg . . . that he should consider coming over to this country in view of these persistent charges to clear his character.

Roberts agreed, and Hardenburg was contacted in Alberta. Hardenburg replied quickly that he was willing to come but could not afford to do so. Over the next couple of months, Buxton raised money for Hardenburg and finally, on 18 March 1913, with the finances secured, Hardenburg set off from Red Deer, where he was living, for London.

The *Mauretania* docked on 8 April in Liverpool. Hardenburg disembarked and was met by John Harris of the Anti-Slavery and Aborigines' Protection Society and Richard Mudie-Smith of the *Daily Chronicle*. Harris had told him that under no circumstances was he to say anything to the press, except to Mudie-Smith. Harris warned Hardenburg that 'the crowd behind Arana is composed of a very clever and unscrupulous lot of men, and they will take every advantage of anything you may say'. Arana had already been injured by the High Court of Justice's decision to remove him as the Company's liquidator.

Although Hardenburg did just as Harris told him, news of his arrival quickly spread. The *Manchester Guardian* reported that Hardenburg, 'whose clean shaven-face gives small clue to his age' (he would soon be twenty-seven years old), had arrived in England 'to confront those who have accused him of blackmail and forgery'.

Hardenburg's first stop was Bolton, where he had been invited, through the Anti-Slavery and Aborigines' Protection Society, to make a short speech at a public meeting to celebrate the hundredth anniversary of the birth of David Livingstone. This was the first time that Hardenburg had spoken in public about his part in the Putumayo story. 'Nearly four years ago', he began,

> I came to England with the terrible story of the Putumayo atrocities. That story, which I knew to be absolutely true, was generally regarded as incredible. To-day, upon returning here, I find that every allegation I made has been more than confirmed, and that the British public is taking every step within its power to put a stop to the horrible conditions which prevail on the Putumayo.

Hardenburg turned on those who were responsible for the atrocities, stating that instead of accepting responsibility they were confusing the issue by charging him with forgery and blackmail. He welcomed the opportunity of clearing his name in front of the select committee. In comparison to the crimes of the Putumayo, this was only a trifle. 'The great thing is to do everything we can to put an end to the horrible conditions which have in ten years reduced the numbers of the Indians in the Putumayo district from 40,000 to 10,000.'

The next day, 9 April, Hardenburg was in London. In Committee Room 11 he took a seat behind Arana, and listened to his questioning.

Hardenburg was scheduled to appear on Tuesday, 15 April. There was a sense of theatre in the committee room on the day of the confrontation between Arana and Hardenburg. Arana was described by a reporter from the *Daily Citizen* as a 'full-figured, swarthy product of his climes and his prosperity', while Hardenburg appeared as a western hero: 'Well-built, but on the small side, he is the essence of quick life and alertness, the sort of man to sum up a difficult situation at a glance, a man, too, of lightening decision and immediate action.' Hardenburg, the reporter added, looks exactly what he is, an engineer. There is about him, too, an air of courage – the courage that led him to face the Putumayo officials, to journey on to Iquitos, then to set out for London to tell his story to *Truth* and the Anti-Slavery and Aborigines' Protection Society, and now officially to retell it to the committee . . .

Hardenburg was taken through the events that led up to his first arrival in London. Once the background information had been covered, he was asked directly about the charge of blackmail. 'Have you ever been convicted, arrested, or charged in a Court either with forgery or blackmail?' asked Roberts. 'Never to my knowledge', was Hardenburg's answer.

Roberts then asked Hardenburg to clarify the episode of the banknote. Hardenburg explained that he had arrived in Manaus in June 1909 with a man he had met in Iquitos, in the rubber business, named Julio Muriedas. He had with him a bill drawn on an Iquitos bank for £830. Muriedas wanted the bill cashed in Manaus so that he could avoid the extortionate charges in Iquitos; but when they got to Manaus, Muriedas, suffering from fever, was unable to get to the bank. So Muriedas asked him to write 'Pay to the order of Senor W.E. Hardenburg' on the reverse side of the bill, and get it cashed. Hardenburg did this, and duly went to the bank, where he successfully cashed the bill and then handed the money over to Muriedas. When Muriedas recovered, the two men continued their trip down the Amazon to Pará, where they separated. Hardenburg caught the next ship for Liverpool. It was only in February of the following year that he learned that the bill had been forged.

Roberts produced the bill and showed it to Hardenburg. Yes, that was his handwriting on the reverse. Hardenburg then told the committee that, at the same time he had learned that the bill had been forged, he had also found out that Muriedas was in prison in Pará having been found guilty of forging another bill.

Hardenburg had come well prepared, and was able to provide ready answers to the Committee. He had already written a lengthy explanation of the tale about the bill to Robert Bennett, the editor of *Truth*, and a copy of this letter had been passed on to Roberts and the Committee. Hardenburg also presented to the Committee a sworn affidavit from Walter Perkins, who in late March 1913 was based in Lovington, New

Mexico. Perkins backed up everything Hardenburg had said about events in Iquitos and wrote eloquently about Hardenburg's good character.

Once the committee members were satisfied with their questioning, Raymond Asquith, the Peruvian Amazon Company's counsel, was given the opportunity to cross-examine the witness. The two men talked about the trip down the Putumayo, about the habits of the Putumayo Indians, and about the Colombian rubber concessions. Asquith seemed satisfied that Hardenburg had cleared his name. Hardenburg had accomplished what he set out to do by coming to London. When the hearing ended, and he was free to go, Hardenburg went to Queen Anne's Gate to thank the owner and staff of *Truth* for all they had done and for their support.

A week later, *Truth* published a spirited defence of Hardenburg and a denunciation of Arana and the Company's directors, whom they accused of hiding behind the untenable charges of blackmail and forgery. 'I think', the writer commented,

> no one who reads the evidence which he gave last week will doubt that he fully vindicated himself, and the impression which he made upon those who were present at the time was much stronger than what could be conveyed by the mere printed report of his evidence.

Flush with success, and with an untarnished reputation, Hardenburg made appearances at a number of public gatherings to talk about the Putumayo. These engagements culminated at the annual meeting of the Anti-Slavery and Aborigines' Protection Society, held on 23 April in the Westminster Palace Hotel. Hardenburg was the Society's guest of honour that day, and, in front of a distinguished audience, delivered an extremely well-received account of his Putumayo experiences, which ended with a call to support the Society's work in 'stripping off from the limbs of the slaves the corroding chains of a slavery of the most detestable kind known in modern times'.

Julio César Arana had by now left London, and would soon be returning to Manaus and Iquitos, never to visit England again. On 1 May 1913, Walter Hardenburg was aboard RMS *Majestic* of the White Star Line, on his way to New York. He, too, would never return to England.

By 30 April, when it had completed questioning its final witness, the select committee on the Putumayo had met on thirty-six occasions, thirty-one of which were in public, and had interviewed twenty-seven witnesses – a thorough cross-section of the principal characters in the affair.

The committee members spent a month discussing their findings and preparing a final report. Presented to parliament in early June, the report, which ran to more than 600 pages, contained the questions and answers of all the witnesses and the committee's conclusions and recommendations.

Arana was singled out as being responsible for the atrocities. Despite his claims of ignorance, the Committee was unconvinced, concluding not only that had he known what was going on, but that he had withheld this information from the British directors. The Committee agreed that the directors had only learned of the atrocities in September 1909, when the first reports were published in *Truth*.

The Peruvian Amazon Company, the Committee continued, could therefore not be held liable under British law: neither the Companies Act, which provided the legal framework in which companies with limited liability worked, nor the Slave Trade Acts, which provided the legislation to make the traffic in slaves illegal, applied in this case. However, the Committee censured the British directors for 'culpable negligence as to the labour conditions that prevailed under the company . . . they should not lightly have exposed to risk the good name of England'. 'We now know', the report stressed, 'what has been possible under the negligent ignorance of one section of the directors and under the callous indifference and guilty knowledge of another section of the board.'

Each of the directors came under the Committee's scrutiny, but Sir John Lister-Kaye probably came off the worst. He, the Committee said, knew nothing about the company he had agreed to join; nothing about the country where it operated; nor of the trade in which it was involved; nor the language often used at board meetings. In short, 'he deserves censure for taking a directorship under conditions so humiliating, and for allowing his name to be used as an inducement to attract investors into a company of whose business and proceeding he knew nothing at all'. For a man who shunned the public gaze, this was terrible. Lister-

Kaye's life was beginning to unravel; the shame of this exposure, together with his own mounting debts, finally led to his being declared personally bankrupt.

By singling out Lister-Kaye, the Committee was sending a clear and strong signal that the directors of an incorporated company had a responsibility to their shareholders (and therefore to the public) to know as much about the concern as they could. For directors to do otherwise, as Lister-Kaye had done – to sit on a board, ignorant of its operations while being rewarded for doing very little – was tantamount to being negligent in their duties. Unfortunately, the signal was not translated into legislation.

The report reiterated, as Casement and Paredes's reports had both clearly and starkly shown, that horrible atrocities had taken place, and that the British directors had been both lazy and unconcerned, and content to be hoodwinked by the Peruvian directors. It seemed incredible, the Committee pointed out, that the British directors had accepted the interpretation of the Spanish words, *conquistar, conquistadores* and *reducir* as referring to some peaceful and ordered labour system, rather than grasping their true meaning of the forcible subjection of the Indians. 'There appears to have been a tendency', the Committee concluded,

> to acquiesce in the view of the Peruvian directors that the use of force by the Company was legitimate. On the lowest ground a British trading company had no right to spend the money of its shareholders on the conquest of the Indians; the Company had taken no power to do so under its Memorandum and Articles of Association, and any money so spent was spent *ultra vires* [beyond its powers]. Apart from any financial question the Committee cannot but express their regret and surprise that any British directors should have thought fit to entertain such ideas.

Deception, which the Committee felt had been at the heart of the relationship between the British and the Peruvian directors, could also be seen in Carlos Rey de Castro's creative editing of Robuchon's travel journal – particularly the excising of Robuchon's passages relating to the Indians' lament for their lost freedom. Life in the Putumayo thus came across as (unrealistically) idyllic and peaceful. Furthermore, by having the journal published in Lima and publicized on its front page as

'Edicion Oficial', Arana, who used the publication as a prospectus for his company, had given it a false official status.

The Committee clearly understood that the knowledge of what was going on in the Putumayo had only come to light because of the 'public spirit of a chance traveller and of an English journal'. The truth, the report continued, had been established thanks to the initiative of the Foreign Office and 'the remarkable work of Sir Roger Casement'. Yet, in what was a very disturbing observation, the report pointed out that the committee members were convinced (after sifting through the mass of written documentation – most of it supplied to Roberts by Casement) that the Putumayo was not a 'single and local outbreak of crime', 'an isolated gang of exceptional criminals'. There were other examples, though they did not specify where. But the report did hint that the use of forced labour was not solely a South American phenomenon, but that as long as there was 'an increasing tendency for tropical regions to be developed by absentee and international capital through the use of coloured and native labour', abuses would continue. One would think, the Committee argued, that the 'economic waste of ill-treating, and perhaps exterminating, the native labour, by which alone such regions can be developed', was illogical. But, short-sighted or not, it did not prevent the abuses in the Putumayo; nor, by implication, would it do so elsewhere.

Some strengthening of the law was therefore necessary – but which law? The British Companies Acts were not the place to look, because they regulated the machinery of companies and already provided for redress through a civil action in case of 'gross and culpable negligence of an aggravated kind'. But this did not apply, apparently, to the British directors in the Putumayo. Criminal law, too, was unhelpful, since they had not committed a felony.

The Slave Trade Acts were then not of much use because, according to the report, 'the existing law as to slave-dealing and using persons as slaves in Foreign countries [as opposed to within the British Empire] needs to be re-stated, consolidated, and made clear.'

The best that the Committee could do was to state that, in cases where British directors could be accused of grave criminal or civil acts, the law as it stood could be applied. But it was not going to be easy to control a concern like the Peruvian Amazon Company, where 'a composite board of directors drawn from three nations, sitting in London, nominally professed to direct the operation of rubber production by wild Indians thousands of miles away in the depths of the Amazon forest'.

In the end, the Committee could not recommend any genuinely effective remedy. The best it could come up with was the suggestion that British companies 'employing coloured labour in foreign countries' should notify their intent to the Foreign Office and to the local British consul. But no sooner had they made this recommendation than they realized that it was probably doomed. In words that have eerie contemporary resonances, the report added:

> but any demand for detailed information which might be resented as inquisitorial, and still more any tax on the companies to provide supervision, would probably defeat their own purpose. The company would simply be registered elsewhere than in London.

Then, as now, governments were loath to regulate where it would discourage investment.

With that, the select committee's work was done, and it was now up to the House of Commons to take the matter further. Perhaps surprisingly, given the amount of publicity the Putumayo had received, there was hardly a murmur from parliament. The silence might, however, have been explained by the fact that the select committee did not produce recommendations strong enough for parliamentary action.

That was not, however, the view of the Anti-Slavery and Aborigines' Protection Society. It was not going to let the matter drop. In July, about a month after the publication of the report, the Society formed a sub-committee, chaired by Charles Roberts and composed largely of members of the original select committee, to extend its recommendations. It would meet at the House of Commons.

Over the coming months the sub-committee convened, and towards the end of November 1913 a petition was drafted for presentation to Herbert Asquith, the prime minister. It was signed by some of the most distinguished members of the political, religious and commercial community, including four lords who had achieved the highest political offices in the country.

The petition made three specific recommendations. The first, to extend and consolidate the Slave Trade Acts, was a recommendation that the select committee had already made, but the sub-committee wanted the Acts to specify the illegality of British companies, rather than individuals, engaged in slave-owning and slave-trading. The second recommendation concentrated on the British Anti-Slavery Treaties with Foreign Powers, and asked the government to revisit and revise these in light of the Putumayo revelations. The final recommendation returned to a point made by the select committee: that the Foreign Office should employ specially trained consuls who would visit the 'more inaccessible parts of the world' and report back on the conditions of indigenous labour, thereby making a great contribution to 'commerce, science and humanity' – a suggestion which had been made by Casement to Roberts nine months earlier.

But, again, the sentiments and ideas of the petition, though sanctioned by such distinguished men, fell largely on deaf ears. In March 1914, a bill was introduced into the House of Commons by William Chapple, the Liberal member for Stirlingshire, whose intent, to tighten and extend the Slave Trade Acts to other forms of coerced labour, was precisely what the select committee wanted. But the 'Slavery, Peonage and Forced Labour Bill' never got further than its first reading. Then, later in July 1914, Lord Lytton, who had taken over the sub-committee's chairmanship from Roberts when he had been given the position of under-secretary of state for India, presented another bill for consideration by parliament. This bill, fittingly entitled the Slavery Bill, like the Commons bill, sought quite radical changes to the Slave Trade Acts, but also included the issue of directorial responsibility. It read: 'any director of a British company which deals in slaves shall not be able to plead in defence ignorance of the acts of his agents if it was his business to know of them but for his wilful negligence'. Lytton's bill also wished to widen the term 'slave' to include 'anyone who is held to service against his free will under an agreement which he was induced to make by force, threats, or fraud'. Lytton fared no better than Chapple before him. The bill was read once, on 9 July, but went no further. The issue of directorial responsibility, which Lytton's bill so adventurously addressed, would remain dormant until it was revived after the Second World War, when the mass use of slave labour in German companies was revealed.

By the time of Lytton's bill, Europe was sliding into an abyss. Archduke Franz Ferdinand had been assassinated in Sarajevo less than two weeks before. This was the last time that the Putumayo atrocity appeared in the newspapers; it was shortly to disappear completely from public imagination and memory. On 4 August Britain declared war on Germany, and Europe would very soon have to deal with its own atrocities.

The Devil and Mr Casement

Julio César Arana was exposed, but not finished. On 9 July 1913 he issued a remarkable open letter from Manaus. He claimed that, after six years of suffering in silence 'a campaign of defamation' against his rubber business, he had been forced by the 'foolish attempt' to arrest him in Iquitos, and by the public pronouncements of the select committee in London, to defend himself. To this end he was having published in Barcelona pamphlets by himself and others aiming to show that his accusers were themselves suspect. These publications would show, he stated, that Saldaña Rocca, Hardenburg, Whiffen, the British government, the American government, Michell and Fuller all had their own motives and agendas, and were being influenced by Colombia 'to smirch the good name of Peru and to wound the honour of her sons'.

Casement's visits to the Putumayo and Iquitos, Arana continued, violated 'the most elementary principles of international good faith', and were

> subject to a plan made beforehand with the triple object of saving the reputation of an officer of the British Army, connected with magnates of his own country; to protect the interests of the review *Truth*, and to save the *amour-propre* of Mr Grey.

The letter concluded with the following remark:

> The least which is permissible to a man whose honour it has been attempted to wound, whom it has been found possible to damage severely in his finances and who has been dragged to the criminal's dock, is that

he shall not keep his silence, unmoved, aloof from all which makes up the reason of his existence and his right to be a conscious human being.

Arana's collection of pamphlets circulated widely. In time, they were joined by a number of other publications concerning the Putumayo, which appeared in Barcelona, London, New York and Lima, penned by Carlos Rey de Castro, Sidney Paternoster, Thomas Whiffen, Norman Thomson (a London-based expert on boundary issues between various South American republics, especially Peru and Colombia), Walter Hardenburg, and Carlos Valcárcel (the judge at the centre of the attempts to get the arrest warrants to stick in Iquitos). Even Frederick Bishop, who was Casement's interpreter and guide on his trip to the Putumayo, got in on the act, giving an exclusive interview recounting his side of the story in an English-speaking newspaper published in Valparaiso, Chile.

Most of the publications not only used the text to make their case, but carried supporting evidence from photographs: contrast, for example, the frontispiece of Hardenburg's book, which showed four naked, emaciated, shackled and chained Indian men, with Arana's, which showed a fully dressed, bountiful Huitoto woman on a shaded veranda, happily working at a sewing machine – the very picture of blissful domesticity.

In the war of words and pictures, however, Arana went one better than anyone else – a sign, perhaps, of his inventiveness and ambition. He had arranged for Silvino Santos, the photographer who had accompanied Arana and Rey de Castro on the consular visit to the Putumayo in the previous year, to spend three months in Paris at the studios of world-leading cinema producers Pathé and the Lumière Brothers, learning how to shoot and develop films. Arana's plan was to send Santos to the Putumayo to make a film about the Indians, showing how they lived and how they were benefiting from his presence in the area. Santos, who by now had married Arana's ward, spent two months filming in the Putumayo in the latter part of 1913. Back in Iquitos, Santos prepared the negatives, but had to send them to Lima to have positive copies made in anticipation of a wide showing, particularly in the United States. However, a German U-boat torpedoed the ship containing the negatives, and all but a tiny fragment of this, the first cinematographic record of the Putumayo people, was lost to the sea in 1914.

Roger Casement was back in England by 10 May. He had sailed to South
Africa to see his brother, unaware that Arana was to be in London. So
he had missed confronting Arana in the Palace of Westminster, and had
also missed meeting Hardenburg. He was now the only one of the three
main characters in the story left in London.

He was exhausted by the Putumayo, and assumed that Roberts was
too: 'I am sure you hate the name of Putumayo'. Casement had been
thinking of leaving the consular service, and was determined not to
return to his post in Rio de Janeiro. But what to do and where to go was
still in question. While he considered his future, news was appearing
in the Irish press of a terrible outbreak of typhus among the Irish-
speaking island communities of Connemara, in the west of Ireland.
Casement's first reaction was to refer to the tragedy, where poverty
and disease took their appalling toll, as the 'Irish Putumayo'. Writing
about it was one thing, but, like the Congo and the Putumayo, there
was no substitute for first-hand experience. On 7 June he travelled to
the area from Dublin via Galway, and remained there for two days. He
was shocked by the deprivation he saw. His reactions were summed up
in a note he wrote upon returning to Dublin: 'Very wet cold and tired
with to-day's glimpse of the Irish Putumayo . . . the white Indians of
Ireland are heavier on my heart than all the Indians of the rest of the
earth.'

What Casement had learned from his experience in the Congo, where
Europeans oppressed and exploited Africans, and from the Putumayo,
where Peruvians oppressed and exploited Indians, was that one people
or race could not be trusted with power over another. 'One thing is clear
to me', he wrote about the Connemara typhus outbreak: 'only Irishmen
and Irishwomen' could be relied on to 'clear it up'. One set of people,
the British, could not be trusted to govern another, the Irish, in an
enlightened and civilized way. People with power were all too likely to
abuse it. Those over whom they had power were seen as subhuman and
disposable, their suffering denied, their rights ignored.

Casement did not need such experiences to convert him to the Irish
cause. He had told Morel several years earlier that, as soon as he was done
with the Putumayo, he would put all his energies into freeing Ireland.
On 1 August 1913, Casement formally resigned from the Foreign Office.
From now on he would devote himself to the Irish cause.

He began writing strenuously about Irish affairs and about empire, appearing at rallies and giving speeches in which he articulated his vision of a united, independent and peaceful Ireland. In November he became deeply involved in the formation of the Irish Volunteers, a group organized to counter the unionist movement embodied in the creation of the Ulster Volunteers.

For the next several months, recruiting for and organizing the activities of the Irish Volunteers was Casement's main focus of activity and interest. They remained an unarmed force until the game changed in April 1914, when a shipment of over 20,000 German rifles and two million rounds of ammunition was landed to arm the Ulster Volunteers. These arms were brought in from Germany while the British authorities turned a blind eye. In response, Casement now threw himself into the business of arming the Irish Volunteers. This required money and help, and so, in July 1914, Casement travelled to the United States to meet with and drum up support from the powerful and vocal Irish nationalist communities along the country's eastern seaboard. By early October, the First World War was in its third month, and German troops had already swept through Belgium and were poised to launch a major attack in northeastern France. By this time Casement had thoroughly won over his Irish-American friends, the members of Clan na Gael. He had also, through the Clan, made close contact with representatives of the German government in the United States, who were being wooed by Clan members; they saw Germany, rather than Britain, as their natural ally.

In meetings held between Clan members and German representatives in New York, it was decided that Casement's next move would be to travel to Germany to convince the German imperial government that it should declare that, in the case of victory, it would support the Irish cause. On 15 October, Casement left from New York, bound for Germany via Norway. Two weeks later he was in Berlin.

Casement remained in Germany from the end of October 1914 until April 1916. During these long months, far away from Ireland and with difficult communications both to his homeland and to the United States, Casement travelled through Germany and its newly occupied territory, meeting high German officials and Irish prisoners-of-war. What he wanted from Germany was an ironclad declaration that it had no intention of invading and occupying Ireland, but would support its struggle for independence from Britain. He also sought Germany's support for the formation of an Irish Brigade, made up of Irish prisoners-of-war who, with the assistance of the German army and navy, would, at the appropriate time, be landed on Irish shores to spearhead a rebellion for the overthrow of British authority.

Though Casement had, at various times, received assurances from high-ranking officials, including Arthur Zimmermann, the under-secretary of state for foreign affairs, who were in agreement with his proposals, behind the scenes things were not going well. Plans were made to send Casement back to Ireland, together with the Irish Brigade, and to send a ship, separately, with arms. At the last moment, however, the German general staff was not prepared to release Irish prisoners-of-war as an Irish Brigade with back-up from German officers, and Casement left Germany without this support.

Just after midnight on Good Friday, 21 April 1916, the U-boat that Casement had boarded in Wilhelmshaven arrived in Tralee Bay, in County Kerry, on Ireland's western coast, after a long voyage by way of the Faeroe Islands. The arms ship, *Aud*, which was supposed to rendezvous with Casement, was nowhere to be seen. Unbeknown to him, the *Aud* had been intercepted by the Royal Navy on the same day, far to the southeast of the submarine's position, nearer Cork than Tralee.

Later that day Casement found himself looking at a policeman's revolver: he was under arrest. After his story that he was an author on a research trip found no credence, he was taken to the local town of Tralee. Casement's real identity was revealed during his short stay in custody. He was then quickly transferred to Dublin, and on from there to Holyhead, finally arriving in London on Easter Sunday, 23 April, where he was handed over to Special Branch.

He was now back in London for the first time in three years – still Sir Roger Casement, but now in circumstances so different from those when he had led the Putumayo mission as to be scarcely believable.

Events moved very quickly. For three days he was interrogated very closely by military intelligence, after which he was taken to the Tower of London and placed in military custody. On the day of his second interview, Casement learned from his interrogators that a rising against British rule had broken out in Dublin. During the interview Casement tried in vain to convince his inquisitors to get a message on his behalf to the rebel's leaders in Dublin to abort the rebellion. As it was, the rebel leaders went ahead with the rising despite knowing that Casement had been arrested, and that the *Aud* had been scuppered by its crew at the entrance to Cork Harbour, while under naval escort. With the arms at the bottom of the sea the rebellion had little chance of success, and was soon over.

It was all over, in fact. On 12 May, barely two weeks after the failure of the rising, most of the rebel leaders had been summarily executed on British military orders. On 15 May Casement was led from the Tower of London, placed under civil authority, and taken to Bow Street Magistrate's Court, where he was committed for trial at the Old Bailey, scheduled for 26 June, and taken to Brixton Prison.

While he was in Brixton Prison waiting for his trial to begin, Casement saw his remaining friends and relatives. Wednesday, 14 June was not a busy day, and Casement took the opportunity of the unusual calm to write to George Gavan Duffy, his solicitor, complaining about the previous day's meeting with his barrister.

While Casement was putting the finishing touches to the letter, the prison clerk approached the cell. He handed Casement a telegram. This was not the first telegram that he had received while in prison. Mostly they were from various parts of Britain and Ireland, and occasionally from the United States, from supporters and well-wishers. But this one was different. It was from Manaus, and from Julio César Arana. Casement began to read it.

> On my arrival here am informed you will be tried for High Treason. Want of time enables me to write you being obliged to wire you asking you to be fully confessing before the human tribunal your guilts only known by Divine Justice regarding your dealings in the Putumayo business ... Inventing deeds and influencing Barbadians to confirm unconsciously facts never happened, invented by Saldana and thief Hardenburg ... I hold some Barbadians declaration denying all you obliged them to declare pressing upon them as English Consul and frightening them in the King's name with prison if refusing to sign your own work and statements. You influenced the Judges in the Putumayo

affair who by your ill influence confirmed your own statements. You tried by all means to be a humanizer in order to obtain titles fortune, not caring for the consequences of your calumnies and defamation against Peru and myself doing me enormous damage. I pardon you, but it is necessary that you should be just and declare now fully and truly all the true facts that nobody knows better than yourself.

Casement's trial lasted four days, and ended with a guilty verdict. Despite the admiration he had received previously from people and governments throughout the world, most of the British public and the state were baying for his blood. Casement knew this and, in his final public utterance, in his impassioned, articulate and now famous speech from the dock, he railed against his accusers and spoke directly to the Irish people, his South American and African experiences layering every phrase.

> Self-government is our right, a thing born in us at birth; a thing no more to be doled out to us or withheld from us by another people, than the right to life itself – than the right to feel the sun or smell the flowers – or to love our kind. It is only from the convict these things are withheld for crime committed and proven – and Ireland that has wronged no man, that has injured no land, that has sought no dominion over others – Ireland is treated today among the nations of the world as if she was a convicted criminal. If it be treason to fight against such an unnatural fate as this, then I am proud to be a rebel – and shall cling to my rebellion with the last drop of my blood. If there be no right of rebellion against a state of things that no savage tribe would endure without resistance, then I am sure that it is better for men to fight and die without right than to live in such a state of right as this.

After the trial Casement was taken to Pentonville Prison and stripped of his honours. On 17 and 18 July, an appeal was heard but rejected. A whispering campaign, which had been gaining ground since May, now destroyed most of the support Casement had left. Only a few, such as George Bernard Shaw, remained steadfast. Rumour had it that Casement had led a secret dual life – a champion of human rights and a rebel, on the one hand, while, as private diaries found in his trunk at his

London flat revealed, he also inhabited another, hidden world. He was a man, it was rumoured, who had 'for years been addicted to the grossest sodomitical practices'.

Homosexuality was then a crime, and widely regarded as a perversion and a disgrace. He was finished. At 9 AM on 3 August 1916, Roger Casement was hanged, ostensibly for treason. The former hero was discredited and disgraced not only as a traitor, but also as a sodomite. The rumours that were circulated after his conviction no doubt contributed to the failure of his appeal. Casement himself probably never knew that his sex life had been exposed, and so could not defend himself (even if he had chosen to do so) against charges of perversions and unnaturalness. Now that homosexuality is generally legal and acceptable, it is easier to see how irrelevant Casement's sexual orientation was to this story. Of course, if it had come to light earlier in his career, the impact would have been enormous.

Casement's own life ended in tragedy, violently cut short by a rope. It seems incredible – picturing him tramping through the dense and steamy Amazonian jungle, his senses acute and permanently on guard, notebook and pencil always at hand, investigating the Putumayo atrocities – that this hero of international humanitarianism was executed for treason by the same state that had honoured him. Meanwhile, the perpetrators of the crimes he brought to light remained beyond the reach of the law; the British directors of the Company feigned ignorance and assumed no responsibility for what had happened; the state could find no way of punishing them within the laws of the time.

When news of Casement's execution reached him in New York, W.E.B. Du Bois, the great African-American man of letters, educator and tireless campaigner for universal human rights, wrote in the editorial of the September 1916 issue of *The Crisis*, the official magazine of the National Association for the Advancement of Colored People:

> Sir Roger Casement is dead. He has been put to death by the English Government on the charge of treason ... All the impressionable, vigorous years of [his] manhood ... were spent in witnessing acts of oppression and lawlessness and in efforts to offset those acts. He became

'obsessed' with a horror at the spectacle of the 'frightfulness' which
those in great places wreak upon those in small . . . Sir Roger Casement
– Patriot, Martyr.

Like Du Bois, Casement was a great humanitarian, but unlike most of
the others who fought against injustice, he risked his own life by actually
going to the scenes of 'oppression and lawlessness' and investigating
them with a rigour that was new at the time. As a servant of the British
state, in his capacity as a consular official, Casement brought to the
world's attention two of the worst atrocities of the early twentieth
century: the one, perpetrated in the African Congo; and the other in the
Putumayo region of South America.

Even after the Congo, Casement was shocked by what he had seen in
the Putumayo in 1910. He believed Arana's crime was proportionately
greater than Leopold's. Thirty thousand indigenous people – three-
quarters of the population in the area – had died for 4,000 tons of rubber,
which they had been violently forced to provide to a company registered
in London. Casement found it hard to capture the horror in words. He
tried phrases such as 'a carrion – a pestilence', 'syndicate of crime',
'reign of terror', 'piracy and terrorization', and 'not merely slavery but
extermination'; but he preferred a term which has now become all too
familiar: it was, he wrote, 'a crime against humanity'.

At the end of September, two months after Casement's execution, Sir
Edward Grey received a letter from George Lepper, Arana's London
lawyer, inquiring whether Casement had replied to the telegram. 'Mr
Arana', Lepper commented, 'is suffering from a keen sense of injustice
and it would be well to satisfy him upon the point.'

Arana continued to extract rubber from his Putumayo estates. The
Peruvian Amazon Company had been wound up by March 1914, and
Arana now traded under the name of his friend and business partner,
Cecilio Hernández. During the First World War the price of rubber
was maintained, and output returned to levels last seen during the
boom years of the previous decade. Arana did very well out of the
Putumayo in the war years, and continued to do so right through the
1920s. Arana's rubber, as before, went through Iquitos to Britain, his
main market.

Arana also entered national politics, and from 1921 to 1925 represented Loreto in Lima. During this time, the controversy between Peru and Colombia over its Amazonian border resurfaced, but under pressure from the United States the Salomón–Lozano Treaty was drawn up and signed, though not ratified, by both countries in 1922. Under the treaty's terms, Colombia agreed to cede lands between the Napo and the Putumayo rivers to Peru, and in return Peru agreed to cede lands from the Putumayo to the Caquetá rivers, and a parcel of land from the Putumayo south to the Amazon at the port of Leticia, to Colombia. The Putumayo River would become the border between the two countries, and Arana's property would end up being in Colombia.

Arana was vehemently opposed to the Treaty, and was directly involved in hindering its ratification. He campaigned vigorously from 1925, bombarding the Lima press and political leaders with pamphlets, telegrams and letters, most of them originating in Loreto. The argument against signing theTreaty came down to a matter of Peruvian pride. The patriotic front considered the government of President Augusto Leguía as too weak in its resolve against Colombia, and also too influenced by the American State Department's promise of generous loans should Peru sign. The protests against the Treaty delayed its ratification, but did not stop it. In December 1927 the Treaty came before the National Congress and passed with a large majority. Arana made a final stand when he published a last attack on the Treaty as it came up for consideration by the Congress, accusing the government of being unpatriotic in handing over territory to Colombia.

Arana stood to lose most from the Treaty, but he had at least ensured that his losses would be compensated. In 1921, the year in which he became a senator, the Peruvian government had granted Arana legal title to his properties in the Putumayo and, while the Treaty was being drafted, he made sure that under its terms he would receive recompense for his losses. Arana sought for compensation in the region of £2,000,000, but the Colombian government thought the figure preposterous – though they agreed that they and the Peruvians would both respect any land concessions made to private individuals. Arana took no further action in making a claim.

In August 1932 a patriotic junta in Iquitos, initiated by Arana and by Enrique Vigil, a wealthy Loretano landowner, and whose members included Arana's son and daughter, attempted to retake Leticia by force. Arana provided the rifles. Military responses by both Peru and Colombia led to a four-month war between the two, played out along the length of the Putumayo. A ceasefire, brokered by the United States and Brazil, was agreed on 25 May 1933, and the status quo of the Treaty was re-established.

Arana's hopes that his properties might remain in Peruvian territory were dashed. By then, however, in the midst of the world's severest depression, rubber prices fell to their lowest level since the beginning of the century, and it took Arana until 1939 to find a buyer for his Colombian claim.

One story has it that Arana was swindled; another that he simply made a bad mistake. In any case, he seems to have emerged from the deal penniless. He left Iquitos and the Amazon forever. He went to live in a small, dark house in Magdalena del Mar, a coastal suburb of Lima. A photograph of him from that time shows an elderly man slumped in a chair in front of a wooden hut – a far cry from his once glamorous life in London, Geneva and Biarritz.

In September 1952, Julio César Arana died aged eighty-eight, his passing virtually unnoticed by the public. His grave is in a cemetery reserved for the poor, marked by a simple tombstone made of cement.

EPILOGUE

A Crime Against Humanity

In February 1913, the United States Congress published *Slavery in Peru*. This 440-page volume was the result of a resolution passed by the House of Representatives in August 1912 to make publicly available the correspondence and reports that the State Department had received over the years about the Putumayo. The volume contained correspondence between London and Washington and reprinted all of the major investigations – Eberhardt's reports (now judiciously edited to exclude the comment about the genocide of the North American Indian), Paredes's report, Casement's Blue Book, and Stuart Fuller's report. The strong title seemed to promise further governmental involvement, or even intervention. However, in only a matter of weeks following publication, the State Department, in a message to Cecil Spring Rice, the newly installed British ambassador in Washington, effectively withdrew its concern for conditions in the Putumayo, clearly expecting Britain to do the same. 'In view of the vigorous policy', the note began,

> apparently animating the present administration in Peru, the remoteness
> of the district, and the attendant obstacles in the way of effective reform,
> I am of the opinion that any further action on the part of His Majesty's
> Government or of the American Government would appear inopportune,
> at least at the time being, inasmuch as it might be instrumental in stirring up
> public sentiment in Peru to such an extent as to hinder whatever real desire
> now exists there for bettering the conditions under which the Indians labor.

The State Department was as good as its word. In September 1913, the consulate in Iquitos was closed and Stuart Fuller was transferred to Durban, South Africa.

The British Consulate in Iquitos continued to function, but as far as the Putumayo was concerned, the Foreign Office followed the State Department's advice to leave the rest to Peru, and it took no further interest in the region. With Casement 'turned traitor', Ernest Rennie, the first minister at the British legation in Lima, advised that 'the intervention of His Majesty's Government in the further investigation of charges that were originally formulated by a man whose name is now the subject of universal reprobation' would be wholly unwelcome. He counselled that the Putumayo should no longer be mentioned in diplomatic encounters.

Casement would have been gratified to know that, a week after his execution, a group of Indians who had been working for the Atenas rubber station turned on their 'employers', who had force-marched them for three days to cut rubber without providing adequate food, and killed nine of them. The Indians wanted to 'clear the region of the whites'. Father Leo Sambrook, an Irish missionary and head of the four-man Franciscan mission at La Chorrera that had been sent to the area in November 1912 following the papal encyclical of the same year, reported to the British consul in Iquitos that there was a force of some 900 Indians, mostly Bora, intent on making the whites 'reap a little of what they have sown'. Though 'the shootings, tortures and all the villainy Casement exposed' seemed to have abated, the Indians, Sambrook observed, continued to be beaten, and the resentment they felt now exploded. He wondered why it had not happened before.

'Really they have had provocation enough, poor devils', remarked Sambrook, 'and I am afraid that if the whites come out on top, the natives will pay a fearful price for what they have done'. He was right. As soon as word got to Iquitos that some of Arana's employees had been killed, the authorities responded immediately by dispatching thirty troops to the area, some of them armed with machine-guns. One month later, Sambrook wrote that the uprising was over; the Atenas rubber station had been recaptured, the Indians' homes had been burnt to the ground, and the Peruvian troops were rounding up those rebels that remained alive.

The Huitoto, Andoke and Bora Indians did not encounter white men until the last decade of the nineteenth century; there was only one generation between their first encounter with the *caucheros* and the publication of the Blue Book that so shocked the civilized world. The whites' lust for latex had devastated the Indians in a dreadfully short time; there was nowhere for them to turn, nowhere for them to hide or escape to. Their homeland was virtually sealed off from the rest of the world – their only contact with it via the launches of the Peruvian Amazon Company.

Even after the demise of the Peruvian Amazon Company, Arana continued to export rubber from the Putumayo to Britain, and Britons as well as Arana continued to profit from the rubber trade. The slave labour of the Indians went on profiting their exploiters. From 1924 until 1930, during the years when he was trying to stall the ratification of the Salomón–Lozano Treaty, Arana, realizing the inevitability of losing his territory to Colombia, forcibly removed over 6,000 Huitoto, Andoke and Bora men, women and children from their homes around the Caraparaná and Igaraparaná rivers to the south bank of the Putumayo River, into what was to be Peruvian territory. Hardly any were left behind. Casement's words were vindicated: 'the whites . . . did not give a damn where the trees were, all they troubled about is where the Indians were'. The Indians were still at Arana's mercy.

Nothing and no one seemed to help the Indians. It took a papal intervention to establish the Franciscan mission in La Chorrera in 1912, but it lasted less than five years. The mission's work was limited by the Indians' fear of whites. It was only in 1933, when the Barcelona-based Capuchin missionaries settled in the area, that some of the Indians, who had been forcibly relocated to the south of the Putumayo River, were able to return to their homeland. The Capuchins had been invited into the area by the Colombian government to Christianize the Indians. A school was built, and the plots in which the Indians had formerly grown food were again cultivated.

The numbers of Huitoto, Andoke and Bora Indians had been severely depleted by Arana's brutal system. With the failure of armed resistance, and escape virtually impossible, the Indians were now taking matters into their own hands, using herbal abortifacients to limit the number of children they produced. According to Felix Ryan, one of Sambrook's colleagues, the Indians would sooner die out than live as slaves.

In the event, the Indians hung on, their numbers hardly changing over the decades. An estimate in 1940 put the number of Huitoto, Andoke and Bora living in their homelands within the area of the Putumayo and Caquetá rivers at 5,000. Recent estimates put the number of those speaking these indigenous languages at around 6,000.

Ironically, what really saved the Indians from extinction was that, on the other side of the world, one million tons of plantation rubber was being produced annually in British, Dutch and French colonies in Malaya, India, Indonesia and Indochina. A process of domestication of the rubber tree, begun in the 1890s using *Hevea brasiliensis* seeds stolen from Brazil, resulted in cheap, abundant and reliable plantation rubber. Wild rubber was no longer so important to the international market. Arana's thirty years of terror and exploitation had ended. That particular nightmare was over for the Indians, but a new one was around the corner.

Unfortunately, synthetic rubber, which came to surpass plantation rubber by 1960, is derived from petroleum. The Texaco Petroleum Company (now Chevron) 'invaded' the Upper Putumayo in 1963. The peaceful Indian village of Orito, Colombia, was transformed into a booming oil town. This time the outsiders did not require Indian labour: they helicoptered in their own personnel, but they took the Indians' land and their women and polluted their rivers. Although Texaco had moved on by the 1970s, their pollution remained, ruining the rivers as sources of food and water. The Indians are still victims of pollution, deforestation and the drugs trade. Caught in the crossfire between government troops, guerrilla groups, drug barons and loggers, they continue the struggle to maintain their lives and their culture.

Dramatis Personae

THE DEVIL – Julio César Arana

1864   born in Rioja, northern Peru, on 12 April

1887   marries childhood sweetheart, Eleanora Zumaeta

1889   establishes partnership with his brothers-in-law in the rubber trade in Iquitos

1903   creates J.C. Arana y Hermanos, concentrating on the rubber industry in the Putumayo region

1906   J.C. Arana y Hermanos becomes the largest rubber exporter in Peru

1908   Arana creates the Peruvian Amazon Company, registered in London with capital of £1,000,000, successor to J.C. Arana y Hermanos

1911   Peruvian Amazon Company goes into liquidation

1913   compulsory wind-up order for Peruvian Amazon Company

1921   Arana becomes Senator for Loreto in Lima

1927   Arana publishes a pamphlet vehemently criticizing his government for signing the Salomón–Lozano Treaty, giving Colombia jurisdiction over the entire Putumayo region

1932   Arana initiates an armed junta to take the Amazonian town of Leticia by force and return it to Peru, leading to four-month war between Peru and Colombia

1933   peace declared between Peru and Colombia; Salomón–Lozano Treaty comes into force, making the Putumayo River the border between the two countries

1939   Arana cuts all ties with the Putumayo

1952   Arana dies in Lima aged eighty-eight

MR CASEMENT – Roger Casement

1864   born in Dublin on 1 September
1883   travels to West Africa as purser on Liverpool-based ship
1884   decides to remain in Africa
1895   becomes British consul for Portuguese East Africa
1900   becomes British consul for Congo Free State and the French Congo
1904   Foreign Office publishes Casement's report on the administration of the Congo Free State
1905   Casement awarded the Companion of Saint Michael and Saint George for his Congo work
1906   appointed British consul in Santos, Brazil
1907   appointed British consul in Pará, Brazil
1909   appointed British consul-general in Rio de Janeiro
1910   arrives in Iquitos to investigate conditions in the Putumayo
1911   knighthood conferred for his work in Peru
1912   Blue Book published, containing Casement's report on the Putumayo
1913   resigns from Foreign Office
1914   travels to the United States and then Germany, where he remains until 1916
1916   arrested on west coast of Ireland on Good Friday and committed for trial on charge of high treason in London on 26 June
1916   hanged on 3 August, aged fifty-one

Acknowledgements

In researching and writing this book, I have benefited enormously from the generous support and assistance of many people and institutions. I would now like to thank them, each and every one.

In the United Kingdom: Cordelia Sealy, Eric Hirsch, Alan Knight, Steve Nugent, Rosario Flores, Tabitha Cadbury, Luciana Martins, Roger Sawyer, Lesley Wylie, Rob Burroughs, Rory Miller, Ruth Bloom, Ben Buchan, John Loadman, Stephen Hugh-Jones, Frank Dobson MP. In Ireland: Anthony McElligott, Séamas Ó Síocháin. In the United States: Vaughan Stanley, Larry Youngman, César Cornejo, Henry Lovejoy, Adam Hochschild, Michael Stanfield, Steve Topik, Michael Dove, David Hebb, Brad Barham, Zephyr Frank, Jan Jarrell, Robert Brandt, Marie Arana, Wade Davis, Miguel Pinedo-Vasquez, Miranda Mollendorf, Glenn Penny and Janet Browne. In Canada: Paul Lovejoy and Oliver Coomes. In France: Matthias Dörries, Arouna Ouedraogo, Jorge Gasché, Francis Ribemont. In Germany: Michael Kraus, Paul Hempel. In Panama: Fernando Santos-Granero. In Venezuela: Ariel Segal. In Colombia: Augusto Gómez, Jaime Arocha, Juan Alvaro Echeverri, Cindy Katherine Avendaño. In Peru: Alberto Chirif, Flica Barclay, Pepe Barletti. In Brazil: Márcio Souza, Selda Vale da Costa, Carlos Rojas, Aurelio Michiles, Andreas Valentin, William Cajueiro.

The staff of the libraries and archives I consulted were exemplary, and I would like to thank them for their support and valuable time. In the United Kingdom: University College London Library (particularly Interlending and Document Supply services); the National Archives, Kew; the Bodleian Library of Commonwealth and African Studies at Rhodes House, Oxford (particularly Lucy McCann); the British Library of Economics and Political Science, London; the British Library,

London; the Royal Botanic Gardens, Kew; the British Museum, London; the Liverpool Record Office; the World Museum Liverpool (especially Joanna Ostapkowicz); the Royal Anthropological Institute, London; the Pitt Rivers Museum, Oxford; the Public Record Office of Northern Ireland, Belfast. In Ireland: the National Library of Ireland; Birr Castle Archives, Birr (especially the Earl of Rosse). In the United States: the National Archives and Records Administration, College Park, Maryland; the Houghton Library, Harvard University; the New York Public Library; the National Anthropological Archives, Smithsonian Institution, Washington (especially Vyrtis Thomas). In France: Bibliothèque Nationale, Paris; Archives des Affaires Étrangères, Paris; Centre des Archives Diplomatiques de Nantes. In Germany: the Philipps-Universität Marburg. In Portugal: Arquivo Regional de Madeira, Funchal (especially Maria da Cunha Paredes); Serviço de Arquivo Histórico Diplomático, Ministerio dos Negócios Estrangeiros, Lisbon (especially Maria Isabel Fevereiro). In Colombia: Archivo General de la Nación, Bogotá. In Peru: Archivo Central Histórico, Ministerio de Relaciones Exteriores, Lima; Archivo Histórico de Límites, Ministerio de Relaciones Exteriores, Lima; Biblioteca Amazonica, Iquitos. In Brazil: Museu Amazônico, Manaus.

Early in the preparation for this book, I was very fortunate in making contact (initially through Larry Youngman) with Mary Bressi. With great kindness, she put me in touch with her mother-in-law, Deborah MacClosky, Walter Hardenburg's daughter, who generously invited me into her home, made me welcome as a member of the family, and shared her father's correspondence with me. I thank her so much. In France, I was equally thrilled when Jean-Pierre Remaud of the Conservation Départementale des Musées de la Vendée in La Roche-sur-Yon, introduced me to M. Georges Rondeau and his daughter, Mme Françoise Degois, who provided me with copies of Eugène Robuchon's correspondence and showed me their albums of the photographs he took while he was in Iquitos and in the Putumayo. I thank them for their generosity to me.

When, in 2005, I first began weighing up the possibilities of this book, my friend Tony McElligott put me in touch with Angus Mitchell. Angus had done a great deal of work on Roger Casement, focusing especially on his time in the Congo and the Putumayo. Out of this came a series of articles and books, all of which I fully acknowledge in the bibliography. Without this material, I would have found the research much more difficult. I thank Angus for that – but also for much more than that, since he has been a constant source of support, inspiration and friendship over the years.

Will Francis, my agent, deserves a special mention not only because he believed in this book from the very beginning and found a home for it at Verso, but also because he has read and reread several drafts, in the process making the book much better than it would otherwise have been. Thanks, too, to Anna Stein for her support and encouragement, and for getting this book to Farrar, Straus and Giroux.

Tom Penn, my editor at Verso, and Gena Hamshaw, my editor at Farrar, Straus and Giroux, guaranteed by their careful and creative reading of the manuscript that it could only become better. I hope they feel that their efforts were rewarded. Staff at both publishers have done brilliantly in getting this book into its final shape.

The Society of Authors generously supported the costs of a research trip to the United States and South America.

My final and biggest thanks goes to my partner, Dallas Sealy, who has lived through and contributed so very much to this book, all the while with wonderful love and support. No one can ask for more than that.

Abbreviations for Primary Material

ACH   Archivo Central Histórico, Ministerio de Relaciones Exteriores, Lima

AGN   Archivo General de la Nación, Bogotá

AHL   Archivo Histórico de Límites, Ministerio de Relaciones Exteriores, Lima

AR   Archives Robuchon, privately held

ASG   Archives de la Société de Géographie

BL   British Library, London

BLCASRH   Bodleian Library of Commonwealth and African Studies at Rhodes House, University of Oxford, Oxford

BLPES   British Library of Political and Economic Science, London School of Economics, London

BM   British Museum, London

BN   Bibliothèque Nationale, Paris

BodL   Bodleian Library, University of Oxford, Oxford

BPP   British Parliamentary Papers

CBCSP   *Correspondence Respecting the Treatment of British Colonial Subjects and Native Indians Employed in the Collection of Rubber in the Putumayo District*, British Parliamentary Papers, 1912–13 [Cd.6266] LXVIII.819

ETH   Ethnography

FDHAC   *Fuentes documentales para la historia de la amazonia colombiana. Volumen VI. Documentos relativos a las violaciones del territorio colombiano en el Putumayo. 1903–1910.* Universidad Nacional de Colombia. Augusto Javier Gómez López & Cindy Katherine Avendaño Castañeda, co-authors (in preparation).

HLHU	Houghton Library, Harvard University, Cambridge, Massachusetts
LRO	Liverpool Record Office, Liverpool
MCIHP	Maloney Collection of Irish Historical Papers
NARA	National Archives and Record Administration, College Park, Maryland
NLI	National Library of Ireland, Dublin
NYPL	New York Public Library, New York
PD	Parliamentary Debates (Official Report)
RBG	Royal Botanic Gardens, London (Kew)
RSRSC	*Report and Special Report from the Select Committee on Putumayo Together with the Proceedings of the Committee, Minutes of Evidence and Appendices*, British Parliamentary Papers, 1913 (148) xiv.l.
SP	*Slavery in Peru: Message from the President of the United States Transmitting Report of the Secretary of the Department of State, with Accompanying Papers, Concerning the Alleged Existence of Slavery in Peru*, United States House of Representatives, Document no. 1366 (62nd Congress, 3rd Session; Washington, DC, 1913)
TNA	The National Archives, London (Kew)
WHP	Walter Hardenburg Papers, privately held

Notes and Sources

In referring to the material I have used in researching this book, I have adopted the following system.

For manuscript sources, I have abbreviated the name of the depository (an archive or library) and continued the citation following the depository's own system. I have also abbreviated the title of government reports. A full list of these abbreviations can be found in the section titled 'Abbreviations for Primary Material' at pp. 251–2.

For published material, I have used shortened titles (often the first one or two words). The full bibliographical citation for each of these titles can be found in the section entitled 'Bibliography' at pp. 275–85.

Prologue

The parliamentary questions and answers are from PD.

For the history of *Truth*, I have relied on the following sources: Hirshfield, 'Truth'; Weber, 'Henry Labouchere'; and Hampton, 'Rethinking'. The quotation about the anxious moments felt by some as they opened their copy of *Truth* is from Joseph Hatton, the British novelist and journalist and contemporary of Henry Labouchere, as cited in Weber, 'Henry Labouchere', p. 41.

I have used a number of sources for the rubber regime of the Congo Free State. These include Harms, 'The End'; Louis, 'Roger Casement'; Grant, *A Civilised Savagery*; Hochschild, *King Leopold's*; and Stengers, 'King Leopold's'.

I have used a number of sources to reconstruct Casement's life and the contexts in which it evolved until his return from the Congo. These are Mitchell, *Casement*; Reid, *The Lives*; Inglis, *Roger Casement*; Daly,

Roger Casement; Ó Síocháin and O'Sullivan, *The Eyes*; Ó Síocháin, *Roger Casement*; Osborne, 'Wilfred G. Thesiger'; Burroughs, 'Britain's Travelling'; Louis, 'Roger Casement'; Cline, 'E.D. Morel'; Cline, *E.D. Morel*; Louis and Stengers, *E.D. Morel's*; Stengers, 'Leopold II'; Gann, 'The Berlin Conference'; Miers, 'Humanitarianism'; Hochschild, *King Leopold's*; Grant, *A Civilised*; and Mitchell, 'Roger Casement'.

The resolution passed by the House of Commons in 1903 is referred to in Ó Síocháin and O'Sullivan, *The Eyes*, p. 11. Casement's letter to Bigelow can be found in Ó Síocháin and O'Sullivan, *The Eyes*, p. 13.

Casement's dispatches to the Foreign Office from the Congo during the months from June to October 1903 are in TNA, FO 10/805, FO 10/806 and FO 403/338. The draft report is in TNA, FO 10/806; and the published version is in BPP, (1904), LXII.

1

Hardenburg and Perkins's experiences in the Putumayo are related in several places. In 1912, Hardenburg published a book, *The Putumayo*, telling the story. Hardenburg's unedited manuscript is in BLCASRH, Mss Brit. Emp., s.22, G325 and G329. I have used it rather than the book. There is very little in the published book about the pair getting from Buenaventura to the Putumayo. Perkins also wrote about his experiences mostly at the hands of the Peruvians in a correspondence he had with State Department officials. This material is in NARA, RG59, M862, Roll 860 (file 13,889). Perkins also provided the Anti-Slavery Society and Aborigines' Protection Society with a short description of the trip. This can be found in BLCASRH, Mss Brit. Emp., s.22, G338. The quotation about the purchase of half of Serrano's property is in a letter Perkins wrote to the State Department dated 22 May 1908, and is also in this file.

The full list of provisions Hardenburg and Perkins bought before setting out on the Putumayo is given by Hardenburg as

half a dozen felt hats, a dozen red shirts, seven machetes, ten pounds of assorted beads, two dozen small mirrors, nine butcher-knives, a dozen harmonicas. All these articles were for the Indians, while for our own use we got a shot-gun with plenty of powder, shot and percussion caps, a rifle, a machete, an *arroba* [25 pounds] of salt, another of rice, and a quantity of enameled iron crockery. In the afternoon we ordered the fabrication of two mosquito-bars, gloves and veils as a protection against the *moscos* [egg-laying gnats], also six pairs of trousers for presents to the Indian chiefs. In addition to this, we gave orders for the preparation of ten pounds of chocolate, half an *arroba* of cracked wheat and an equal quantity of *aco* – a specially prepared flour . . . composed of wheat, cinnamon, sugar and several other ingredients. The next afternoon we continued our purchases among which may be mentioned six dozen red handkerchiefs, an enormous quantity of fishhooks, several rolls of brightly-colored woolen yarn, some forty yards of muslin and a large assortment of needles and thread for the Indians, while for ourselves we bought a small stock of medicines, notably quinine and salts, several pairs of *alpargatas* [hemp sandals], a lot of rope and twine. The next day we finished our shopping by the purchase of a big ham, an outfit of knives, forks and spoons and most important of all a good lantern and a broiler.

Further information about the Colombian Pacific railway is in Rippy, 'Dawn', and Ortega, *Ferrocarriles*. The Madeira–Mamoré railway is the subject of Werner, 'All Aboard', and Gauld, *The Last*.

For background to the border problems between Colombia and Peru, and their partial solutions, including the modus vivendi, I have consulted the following sources: Ireland, *Boundaries*; Olarte Camacho, *Los convenios*; Thomson, *The Putumayo*; Bákula, *La política*; and Wagner de Reyna, *Historia diplomática*.

For information on the early rubber trade in the Putumayo, I have relied on Reyes, *Memorias*; Stanfield, *Red Rubber*; Dominguez and Gómez, *La economía extractiva*; and Santos-Granero and Barclay, *Tamed Frontiers*.

Hardenburg's letter to Miranda (and also one to his old boss in Buenaventura venting a similar outrage against the Peruvians) is in FDHAC (originals in AGN, Archivo diplomático y consular, Ministerio de relaciones exteriores, Sección República, Caja 600, 'Documentos relativos a las violaciones del territorio colombiano en el Putumayo, 1903–1910').

2

For the history of Iquitos, including the Jesuit period, I have used a number of sources, including Grohs, *Los indios*; Negro and Marzal, *Un reino*; García, *Historia*; Mörner, 'The Expulsion'; Reeve, 'Regional Interaction'; Santos-Granero and Barclay, *Tamed Frontiers*; Stanfield, *Red Rubber*; John, *A Liverpool*; Haring, *Boomtown*; and Romero, *Iquitos*.

The quote from Lucien Jerome, dated 20 January 1908, is in TNA, FO 369/161.

I have used a number of sources to tell the story of the early history of the rubber business, as well as that of bicycles, cars and tyres. These include Drabble, *Rubber*; Bardou et al., *Automobile Revolution*; Foreman-Peck, 'Multinational Companies'; Ribeill, 'From Pneumatics'; Herlihy, *Bicycle*; Ritchie, *King*; and Loadman, *Tears*.

For information about the rubber boom along the Amazon and down its many tributaries, I have consulted Drabble, *Rubber*; Weinstein, *The Amazon*; Barham and Coomes, 'Wild Rubber'; Burns, 'Manaus'; Frank and Musacchio 'Brazil'; Resor, 'Rubber'; Fifer, 'The Empire Builders'; Pennano, *La economía*; Bonilla, 'Estructura'; De la Flor Fernández, 'La economía'; Dominguez and Gómez, *La economía extractiva*; and Gómez, Lesmes and Rocha, *Caucherías*.

The description of tapping trees and preparing rubber in the Putumayo is taken from TNA, FO 371/1202.

3

The details of Perkins's enforced stay in El Encanto are recorded in a series of letters to the State Department held in NARA, RG59, M862, Roll 860 (file 13,889) and RG 59, 423.11P41.

I have relied on a number of sources to tell the story of Arana's life until 1908. They include Stanfield, *Red Rubber*; Lagos, *Arana*; Collier, *The River*; Karno, 'Julio César Arana'; Santos-Granero and Barclay, *Tamed Frontiers*; and De la Flor Fernández, 'La economía'. For conditions in the Ceará in the 1880s, I have benefited from Greenfield, *Realities*. Arana's own version of the events leading up to his controlling the entire rubber trade in the Putumayo can be found in his affidavit in TNA, J13/6373. The same statement was published in Spanish as Arana, *Las cuestiones*. The information about setting up the Peruvian Amazon Rubber Company and dropping the word 'rubber' from the name is taken from TNA, BT 31/18205/94839 and BT 31/18220/95023.

On the subject of debt peonage, I have relied on Knight, 'Debt'; and Dore, 'Debt'.

For information about Barbadians on the move in the early twentieth century, I have found the following sources very useful: Johnson, 'Barbadian'; Greenfield, 'Barbadians'; Thomas-Hope, 'The Establishment'; Roberts, 'Emigration'; and Newton, *The Silver Men*.

The argument about the change in Arana's labour system is made convincingly in Santos-Granero and Barclay, *Tamed*, pp. 48–9.

The events and ramifications of the 1907 bank panic are covered in Moen and Tallman, 'The Bank Panic'; Jeanne, 'Monetary Policy'; and Bruner, *The Panic*.

4

The description of Perkins meeting Arana on the Amazon is in a series of letters to the State Department held in NARA, RG59, M862, Roll 860 (file 13,889), and RG 59, 423.11P41. This source also includes the actual letter of the offer of sale. Perkins repeated the details in an affidavit he sent to the Anti-Slavery and Aborigines' Protection Society, which can be found in BLCASRH, Mss Brit. Emp., s.22, G338.

Hardenburg's dreams of seeing the Amazon are referred to in letters he wrote to his mother from Panama, Colombia and Iquitos. They are in WHP.

The story about Miguel Galvez is taken from Collier, *The River*.

I have used the English version of Saldaña Rocca's indictment that is printed in BLCASRH, Brit Emp s.22, G335. The Spanish original, which was printed in *La Sancion* in five instalments in October 1907, was also reproduced in the book by Olarte Camacho, *Las crueldades*. The translation of Saldaña Rocca's mission statement in the first issue of *La Sancion* is my own.

An almost full run of both *La Felpa* and *La Sancion* is in the Bodleian Library, University of Oxford. These were the issues that Walter Hardenburg brought with him from Iquitos. One issue of *La Felpa* and a few cartoons, all of which are missing from the Bodleian collection, can be found in AGN, Archivo diplomático y consular, Ministerio de relaciones exteriores, Sección República, Caja 600. When these collections are put together they make a full and complete run of *La Felpa*.

The depositions Hardenburg collected in Iquitos are in BLCASRH, Mss Brit. Emp., s.22, G823. How he collected these depositions in Iquitos is explained in RSRSC.

5

I have used a number of sources for the history of the British and Foreign Anti-Slavery Society and the Aborigines' Protection Society. These include Grant, *A Civilised*; Grant, 'Christian'; Louis, 'Roger Casement'; Porter, 'Sir Roger Casement'; Swaisland, 'The Aborigines'; and Nworah, 'The Aborigines'.

John Harris's recollection of first meeting Walter Hardenburg is in RSRSC.

The major source for the government's reactions and actions taken in response to the revelations in *Truth* is in TNA, FO 371/722.

Charles Eberhardt's dispatches to the State Department are in NARA, RG59 Microfilm M862, Rolls 481, 736, 757, 775, and 1207. One of these, Roll 757, entitled 'Indians of Peru', was subsequently published with the same title by the Smithsonian Institution in *Smithsonian Miscellaneous Collections* 52 (1910), pp. 181–94. The published version, however, omitted much of what Eberhardt had observed about the enslavement of the Indians. A good overview of the fear expressed in anthropology about the extinction of races is in Brantlinger, *Dark Vanishings*.

The report 'General Conditions in the Putumayo River District of Peru' is in NARA, RG59 Microfilm M862, Roll 775.

6

For biographical information and Whiffen's military record, I have used Cadbury, 'Imagining'; and TNA, WO 374/73501.

Whiffen's report to Ambrose Pogson is in TNA, FO 369/198. A subsequent dispatch to the French government, informing them of

Whiffen's conclusions regarding Robuchon's disappearance, is in TNA, FO 146/4102.

Whiffen's own account of his search for Robuchon was published as Whiffen, *The North-West Amazons.*

The details of Eugène Robuchon's life and of his two trips to the Putumayo, most of which have never been made public, are taken from material in AR; and BN, ASG/colis 11bis and BN, ASG/colis 37bis. Robuchon's copy of the journal he compiled during his first trip to the Putumayo is in BM, ETH/Doc 1347. A copy of a fragment of his second journal is in AGN, Archivo diplomático y consular, Ministerio de relaciones exteriores, Sección República, año 1911, Caja 743, carpeta 331, fol. 91–103 (I thank Juan Alvaro Echeverri for this reference).

Robuchon's artefacts make up a substantial part of the British Museum's Upper Amazon collection. Correspondence about this collection can be found in BM, Keeper's Letters, 1904 and 1905. Details about Jules Robuchon's photography, and therefore the background to Eugène Robuchon's own education in this field, can be found in Ribemont, *Jules Robuchon.*

The instructions for Robuchon's ill-fated final trip to the Putumayo are in the contract published in Robuchon, *En el Putumayo*, pp. xi–xiii.

Arana's letters to Hortensia and the photograph showing an Indian being flogged are in AR. Hardenburg's comment on the rumours surrounding Robuchon's death is in Hardenburg, *Putumayo*, p. 218, and Hispano's is in Hispano, *De París*, pp. 272–3.

Whiffen's report to the Foreign Office is in TNA, FO 371/722.

James Bryce's communication with the Foreign Office can be found in TNA, FO 115/1548.

7

This chapter is based mostly on documents in the following sources: TNA, FO 371/277, FO 371/967, TNA, FO 371/968, FO 115/1548; and BLCASRH, Mss Brit. Emp., s.22, G342.

, For the background to US policy towards Latin America, I have found the following sources most helpful: Veeser, 'Inventing'; Gilderhus, 'Monroe Doctrine'; Ricard, 'Roosevelt Corollary'; Scholes and Scholes, 'The United States'; Healy, *Drive*; and Gilderhus, *The Second Century*.

Sir Edward Grey's comment on the United States in Latin America comes from Salisbury, 'Great Britain', pp. 393–4.

Both the Foreign Office and the Colonial Office had files dating back to 1905 about the ill-treatment of Barbadians. It came about that in June of that year, two Barbadian women, Helen Sealy and Rebecca Harvey, wrote to the Governor of Barbados, Sir Gilbert Carter, in Bridgetown, about their respective sons, Stanley Sealy and Samuel Harvey. The two mothers had not heard from their sons since they had left the island for Peru earlier that year, but had heard from a returning Barbadian that conditions there were dangerous. The two mothers feared the worst: that Stanley, aged nineteen, and Samuel, aged twenty, were dead. Carter got in touch with Cazes in Iquitos, and he informed the Colonial Office that the source of the Barbadians' problems in the Putumayo was an employee of Arana called Ramon Sanchez. Cazes took the matter up with Arana, who, Cazes reported, not only listened to the complaints but promptly dismissed Sanchez. These files are in TNA, CO 28/264, CO 28/265, FO 177/326, FO 177/330, FO 177/327 and FO 177/331.

The Ecuador–Peru border dispute is discussed in detail in Zook, 'The Spanish Arbitration'; and Wood, *Aggression*.

Arana's letter to Cazes of 25 July 1910 is in TNA, FO 371/968.

8

Casement's letter to Edward Clarke is in Reid, *Lives*, p. 72.

The direct quotes in the chapter are from the following sources. Morel's description of meeting Casement for the first time is in Louis and Stengers, *E. D. Morel's*, pp. 158–62. Stephen Gwynn's description of Casement is in Gwynn, *Experiences*, p. 260. Herbert Ward also made a point of commenting on Casement's voice: Ward, *A Voice*, p. 237; his voice resembling a purr comes from Hambloch, *British Consul*, p. 71.

Casement's correspondence with Foreign Office personnel while he was working in Pará is in TNA, FO 128/324 and FO 169/123. His correspondence with Morel from Rio de Janeiro is in BLPES, Morel Papers, F8/23. Other correspondence with Morel used in this chapter is in BLPES, Morel Papers, F8/24.

Material for the section dealing with the selection of Casement as the Foreign Office investigator in the Putumayo comes from the following sources: TNA, FO 371/967 BLCASRH, Mss Brit. Emp., s.19, D3/1, BLCASRH, Mss Brit. Emp., s.22, G322; and Dudgeon, *Roger Casement*.

Casement's meeting with Arana on the *Clement* is reconstructed from a letter Casement wrote aboard RMS *Anselm* (for a copy of which I must thank Brendan Callaghan); LRO, BOO3/10; NLI, Collection List 103 (Casement to Francis Cowper, 18 March 1908); *A Provincia do Pará*, 22 February 1908; and RSRSC, Question 399.

Casement's despatch about the Peruvian assault on Colombian properties in the Putumayo is in TNA, FO 128/324. His recollection about Williamson visiting him in the Pará consulate is in RSRSC, Question 399.

I have reconstructed the voyage to Iquitos through the use of the following sources: Sawyer, *Roger Casement's*; Sawyer, *Casement*; Reid, *The Lives*; Mitchell, *Casement*; and, especially, Mitchell, *The Amazon Journal*.

Carlos Rey de Castro edited and translated Robuchon's journal of his first trip to the Putumayo for publication. Although Arana later stated that the publication was also available in a French and an English translation, there is no record that these were ever published. There was a copy of Robuchon's journal in the offices of the Peruvian Amazon Company in London, but this seems to have disappeared. However, Robuchon did send a copy of this journal to the keeper of the British Museum, Charles Read, in 1905, in the hope that he might find a publisher for it. Unfortunately Read did not think it was worthy of publication, but kept the copy. It can be found in the British Museum as BM, ETH/Doc 1347.

Casement kept notes of his conversation with Grey during their private meeting on 13 July. These are in NLI, MS 13,080 (6/iii).

The quotation from Casement's letter to Gertrude Bannister at the start of the chapter is from Reid, *Lives*, p. 75.

Casement's letter to Alice Stopford Green is in NLI, MS 10,464 (3)

9

This chapter draws on a wide range of archival material. The sources are: TNA, HO 161/3, FO 177/356, FO 371/968 and FO 371/1200; NLI, MS 13,087 (8).

The manuscript of Roger Casement's Putumayo journal, covering the period from 23 September to 6 December 1910, is in NLI, MS 13,087 but I have used the superbly annotated version in Mitchell, *Amazon Journal*. In addition to the journal itself, Mitchell's documentation takes the reader from 2 August 1909, when Casement was on his way to Pará, to 7 January 1911, a few days after he returned to London.

The quotation about India rubber comes from Mitchell, *Amazon Journal*, p. 85.

The Barbadian statements are printed in CBCSP. Casement's drafts and notes from the interviews he conducted are in NLI, MS 13,087 (27) and TNA, FO 371/1200.

10

Casement recorded his experiences in this trip to the Putumayo region in a number of places. His personal papers, which are in the National Library of Ireland, in Dublin, contain two significant collections: a scattered bunch of notes and parts of more sustained writings; and the journal covering the period from his arrival in La Chorrera on 23 September 1910 until his departure from Iquitos on 6 December 1910. This journal exists in two manuscript versions, one handwritten and the other typed. They are not identical, in the sense that the typed version takes certain liberties with the handwritten version. The journal has been published in two forms: an abridged version, published by Roger Sawyer, as one part of the book *Roger Casement's*; and Angus Mitchell's *Amazon Journal*, an accurate and total transcription, expertly annotated. Casement also wrote down his daily activities in two other places: the so-called Black Diaries, which are in the TNA, HO 161/3-5 (and have been published in various forms – see Singleton-Gates and Girodias, *The Black Diaries*; Dudgeon, *Roger Casement*; and Sawyer, *Roger Casement's*); and a green notebook, which is frequently referred to by Casement himself, but has, unfortunately, not yet surfaced.

This chapter draws on all of this manuscript material, namely: NLI, MS 13,087 and TNA, HO 161/3; plus FO 371/968, FO 371/1200; BLCASRH, Mss Brit. Emp., s.19, D3/1; Mitchell, *Amazon Journal*; and CBCSP. This latter official publication contains all of the Barbadian depositions

11

This chapter draws on much of the same material as the previous chapter, namely: NLI, MS 13,087 and TNA, HO 161/3; plus FO 177/286, FO 371/968, and FO 371/1200. All quotes from Casement's journal are taken from Mitchell, *Amazon Journal*.

A copy of Enrique Deschamps' letter and José Cavero's response, both of which were printed in *El Comercio*, can be found in TNA, FO 371/968.

Casement's admission that he went well beyond his instructions is contained in a letter to Charles Roberts, MP, which can be found in BLCASRH, Mss Brit. Emp., s.22, G344c. The letter from Arana to Cazes can be found in TNA, FO 371/968 (in English and Spanish), and a printed copy (in English) is in BLCASRH, Mss Brit. Emp., s.22, G335.

12

This chapter draws on material in the following sources: NLI, MS 13,087, TNA, FO 371/1200 and BLCASRH, Mss Brit. Emp., s.22, G335.

Many of the documents have been transcribed, annotated and published in Mitchell, *Sir Roger Casement's*.

Arana's letters to Casement are in BLCASRH, Mss Brit. Emp., s.22, G344a.

13

This chapter draws on material in the following sources: NLI, MS 13,087 (for letters to Roger Casement from the Peruvian Amazon Company's commission members); TNA, FO 371/1200, 1201 and 1202 (for all Foreign Office correspondence, including internal memos, and final report of the Commission as it was delivered to the Board of the Company); and BLCASRH, Mss Brit. Emp., s.22, G334a and G335 (for the minutes of the meetings of the Peruvian Amazon Company and for Roger Casement's notes during the time he was present.)

Many of the documents, with the exception of the internal Foreign Office memos, have been transcribed, annotated and published in Mitchell, *Sir Roger Casement's*.

The letter from Walter Fox to the Director of the Royal Botanic Gardens is in RBG, DC217, dated 13 November 1910. It is also printed in Schultes, 'Lacticiferous'.

Details on the financial situation of the Peruvian Amazon Company are drawn from RSRSC.

The newspaper interview with Arédomi and Omarino took place in William Rothenstein's London studio. It is discussed in correspondence between Casement and Rothenstein. Casement's letters to Rothenstein are in HLHU, BMS ENG 1148(234). Rothenstein's letters to Casement are in NLI, MS 13,073 (37).

14

The following sources have provided the material for this chapter: NLI, MS 13,073, MS 13,087 and MS 17,443; TNA, CO 28/279, FO 128/361, FO 369/400, FO 371/1200, 1201, 1202, 1203, 1450, and FO 369/400, HO 161/4 and HO 161/5; *New York Times*, 12 November 1948, p. 7; and BLCASRH, Mss Brit. Emp., s.22, G334a, G344c and G335.

Many of the documents in the sources above, especially letters written to and from Casement, have been transcribed, annotated and published in Mitchell, *Sir Roger Casement's*.

Casement's letters to Rothenstein are in HLHU, BMS ENG 1148(234). Rothenstein's letters to Casement are in NLI, MS 13,073 (37).

Herbert Dickey's recollections of his time with Casement appear in Dickey, *Misadventures*, in NLI, MS 17,443 and NYPL, MCIHP, 7IHP-116.

Judge Valcárcel's version of events is in Valcárcel, *El proceso*. A copy of Rómulo Paredes's typewritten version (1,350 pages) of the handwritten 3,000-page dossier of depositions and evidence that he had collected while visiting the rubber stations of the Peruvian Amazon

Company is in AHL, LEK 13-11. A copy of the full report Casement read in Iquitos is in AHL, LEK 13-13.

A copy of Paredes's report was forwarded to the Foreign Office in late March 1912. It was the same report that Casement had read, except that one section, Chapter 3, had been omitted. The Foreign Office copy is in TNA, FO 177/373. Another copy was sent to the State Department in Washington, again without Chapter 3. It is in NARA, Central Decimal File 823.5048. It was translated into English and was published in SP, pp. 144–72.

On 16 August 1912, *El Diario*, a Lima newspaper, published an interview with Paredes in which he amplified a number of points in his report (there is a copy of the article in TNA, FO 371/1453). It, too, was translated into English and published in SP, pp. 187–99. The manuscript original is in AHL, LEK 13-12.

Paredes's interview and his full report (including Chapter 3) are being republished by Centro Amazónico de Antropología y Aplicación Práctica, Lima, Peru, edited by Alberto Chirif.

15

This chapter draws on material in the following sources: NLI, MS 13,073 and 13,087; TNA, FO 115/1642 and 1698, FO 128/361, FO 371/1450, 1451 and 1452; NARA, M973, roll 176 and Central Decimal Files, 823.5048; BodL, MSS. Bryce, 48; BLCASRH, Mss Brit. Emp., s. 19, D2/3, D4/1, Mss Brit. Emp., s.22, G334a and G335; ACH, 5-17, Año 1912; and PD. Also of value were Karno, 'Julio César Arana'; and Karno, 'Augusto B. Leguía'.

The quotation from George Young is taken from Fisher, *James Bryce*, vol. 2, p. 24. The final quotation comes from a letter Casement wrote to his cousin, Gertrude Bannister, on 25 July 1912, and is kept in NLI, MS 13,074.

Paredes paraded his pro-Peruvian, anti-British sentiments in an interview which was published on 26 July 1912 in the *New York Herald*. He repeated these views in a longer piece in September, published in the magazine *American Review of Reviews*. (See bibliography under Paredes, 'Peruvian'.)

Further information about the papal encyclical can be found in Turvasi, *Giovanni*, and García Jordán, 'En el corazón'.

16

This chapter draws on material in the following sources: NLI, MS 13,073 and 13,087; TNA, FO 115/1642 and 1698, FO 128/361, FO 371/1450, 1451 and 1452; NARA, M973, roll 176 and Central Decimal Files, 823.5048; BodL, MSS. Bryce, 48; BLCASRH, Mss Brit. Emp., s. 19, D2/3, D4/1, Mss Brit. Emp., s.22, G334a and G335; ACH, 5-17, Año 1912; and PD.

The Blue Book was published as CBCSP.

Casement's report to Grey dated 24 November 1911 is in TNA, FO 128/361.

17

This chapter draws on material in the following sources: NLI, MS 13,073, 13,081 and 13,087; TNA, CO 28/278 and 279; FO 115/1642 and 1698, FO 128/361, FO 371/ 1452, 1453, 1454 and 1455, and FO 371/1732; NARA, M973, roll 176 and Central Decimal Files, 823.5048; BLCASRH, Mss Brit. Emp., s.22, G334a, G344b, G344c, and G335; ACH, 5-17, Año 1912. Also of use were Stanfield, *Red Rubber*; Martínez Riaza, 'Política regional'; and Quiroz, 'Redes'.

Consul Stuart Fuller's unpublished report is in NARA, Central Decimal Files, 823.5048, and was published in SP (pp. 9–70). Consul George Michell's unpublished report is in TNA, FO 369/495, and was published in BPP, 1913 [Cd.6678] li. 791.

Casement translated Alarco's interview in *El Comercio* for the Foreign Office; Charles de Graz, the British chargé d'affaires in Lima, translated the article in *La Prensa* referring to Saldaña Rocca and to Robuchon; and George Michell translated the newspaper article that reported the banquet in Iquitos.

18

I have used the respective issues of the *Manchester Guardian* and *The Times* to tell the story of Henson and the directors of the Peruvian Amazon Company. Henson recounted the event in his memoirs, *Retrospect*. For biographical information about Henson, I have relied on

Chadwick, *Hensley Henson*. The original letters to and from Henson are in BLCASRH, Mss Brit. Emp., s.19, D4/2a.

This chapter draws on material in TNA, FO 371/ 1452 and 1454 and in PD.

The cabinet minute authorizing the appointment of a select committee to inquire into the connection between the Peruvian Amazon Company and the Putumayo atrocities is in TNA, CAB 41/33. The description of Roberts was published in the 9 April 1913 issue of *Truth*.

19

This chapter draws on background material in TNA, FO 371/ 1452 and 1454.

The correspondence between Roberts and Casement is in two places. The National Library of Ireland has one set, which includes letters both ways – NLI, MS 13,073/36(i–iii). The other set, which include letters from Casement to Roberts only, is in BLCASRH, Mss Brit. Emp., s.22, G344c.

More on Casement's health problems during the hearings of the select committee can be found in Ó Síocháin, *Roger Casement*, pp. 346–8.

The verbatim proceedings of the select committee are to be found in RSRSC.

I have also used respective issues of the *Manchester Guardian* and *The Times*.

20

This chapter draws on material that can be found in TNA, FO 177/286, FO 371/1454, 1455, 1732 and 1733; FO 128/373; J13/6373; BLCASRH, Mss Brit. Emp., s.22, G344c; RSRSC; NARA, Central Decimal Files, 823.5048; and the *Anti-Slavery Reporter* (1914).

My discussion of the winding-up of the Peruvian Amazon Company is based on material in BLCASRH, Mss Brit. Emp., s.22, G322 and G345. These files also contain correspondence with Roberts. Buxton and Harris's correspondence with Hardenburg leading to his arrival in Liverpool can be found in BLCASRH, Mss Brit. Emp., s.19, D1/12, D2/4, and D3/8 and in Mss Brit. Emp., s.22, G343. Perkins's affidavit is in BLCASRH, Mss Brit. Emp., s.22, G338, and Hardenburg's letter to Bennett at the offices of *Truth* is in BLCASRH, Mss Brit. Emp., s.22, G323.

The proceedings of the select committee are to be found in RSRSC.

John Harris's review of Hardenburg's book appeared in the *Manchester Guardian*, 11 December 1912.

I have also used relevant issues of the newspapers and periodicals mentioned in the text. There is a scrapbook containing some of the principal articles in BLCASRH, Mss Brit. Emp., s.22, J28.

For information on the continuing struggle against slavery and its historical background in the twentieth century, I have relied on the following sources: Miers, *Slavery*; Bales, *Ending Slavery*; Bales, *New Slavery*; and Bales, *Understanding Global Slavery*.

The question of directorial responsibility at the Nuremberg trials after the Second World War is taken up in Ramasastry, 'Corporate Complicity', while McCartney and Arnold, 'A Vast Aggregate' looks at an earlier case.

21

The original and the English translation of Arana's open letter from Manaus are in TNA, FO 177/386. The pamphlets he referred to are listed in the Bibliography under the appropriate author's name – Arana, Larrabure y Correa, and Zumaeta.

The publications concerning the Putumayo mentioned in the chapter can be found in the Bibliography under the author's surname.

The story about Santos is told in Vale da Costa, *Eldorado*; Vale da Costa and Lobo, *No rastro*; and Souza, *Silvino Santos*. The nature of French cinematography, and especially the dominant role of Pathé, is told in Abel, *The Ciné* and Abel, *The Red Rooster*. Santos had better luck with his next Amazonian film, *Huitoto Indians of the Putumayo River*, once again financed by Arana and shown, for the first time, in Manaus in June 1916. Santos's reputation as a filmmaker, particularly on ethnographic subjects, led him to be invited in 1924 to accompany the American explorer Alexander Hamilton Rice and the German anthropologist Theodor Koch-Grünberg to the region near the frontier between Brazil and Venezuela. This story is covered in Martins, 'Illusions'.

Information about Casement's life after the Putumayo until his execution, and about the Irish political context, come from the following: Mitchell, 'Irish Putumayo'; Mitchell, 'John Bull's Other Empire'; Mitchell, *Casement*; Townshend *Easter 1916*; O'Síocháin, *Roger Casement*; Bowman, *Carson's Army*; Doerries, *Prelude*; Doerries, 'Hopeless Mission'; Roth, 'German Soldier' and Clayton, *Aud*.

In recent years the National Archives in Kew have released new documents concerning Casement's years in Germany and the time between his arrest and execution. These can be found in TNA, HO 144/1636; HO 144/1637; and KV 2/6-10.

The diaries in question are referred to in the notes accompanying Chapter 10 of this book.

Readers interested in pursuing the controversies surrounding Casement's afterlife will find the following sources helpful: Daly, *Roger Casement*; McCormack, *Roger Casement*; McDiarmid, *Irish Art*; Ó'Síocháin, *Roger Casement*; and Grant, 'Bones'.

Correspondence between Arthur Conan Doyle and Clement Shorter, the journalist and magazine editor, concerning the attempt to get Casement reprieved, together with the signed petitions, are in BL, Add. 63596. George Bernard Shaw's papers relating to Casement are in BL, Add. 50678.

W.E.B. Du Bois's obituary of Casement appeared in the September 1916 issue of *The Crisis*, pp. 215–16.

The phrase 'crime/crimes against humanity' is very widely used today, but it is probably just over a century old. One of the first uses of it, if not the first, can be traced back to a letter that George Washington Williams, a black American journalist, wrote to James Blaine, the US secretary of state, on 15 September 1890, concerning what he had seen in the Congo. The key sentence in Williams's letter is as follows: 'The State of Congo is in no sense deserving of your confidence or support. It is actively engaged in the slave trade and is guilty of many crimes against humanity.' This letter is reproduced in Bontinck, *Aux Origines*, pp. 448–9. A later appearance of the phrase was on 24 May 1915 in a joint communiqué from Britain, France and Russia, charging the Ottoman Empire with a 'crime against humanity' in their treatment of the Armenian people. That Casement should have used the same phrase in, at one end, a comment on the Congo, and, at the other, a comment on state-sponsored genocide, is very telling. Casement spoke of a 'crime against humanity' in his journal on 5 October 1910 while in the Putumayo (NLI, MS 13,087). It can also be found in Mitchell, *Amazon Journal*, p. 178. By this phrase he meant precisely what it has come to mean today: the systematic practice of inhumane acts – murder, enslavement, extermination, torture, and so on – committed against any civilian population.

There is a very large literature examining genocides and other crimes against humanity. I have found the following sources useful for thinking about this problem: Palmer, 'Colonial'; Stone, 'Historiography'; Dadrian, 'Patterns'; and Bartov, 'Defining Enemies'.

A copy of Arana's telegram to Casement, as well as the letter from George Lepper to Sir Edward Grey, are in TNA, FO 371/2798.

I have drawn on the following sources for Arana's life after his return to Peru in 1913: Stanfield, *Red Rubber*; De la Flor Fernández, 'La economía'; Karno, 'Julio César Arana'; Bákula, *La política*; Lagos, *Arana*; Ireland, *Boundaries*; García Jordán, 'En el corazón'; and Arana, *American Chica*.

Arana's attack on the legitimacy of the Salomón–Lozano Treaty was published as Arana, *El protocolo*.

Epilogue

Ernest Rennie's dispatch, dated 8 May 1916, is in TNA, FO 371/2739.

Leo Sambrook's and Felix Ryan's reports are in TNA, FO 371/2990. An account of the first year of the mission can be found in Gridilla, *Un año*.

The uprising may be the same as the one that is known in local oral culture as Yarocamena's Rebellion, though no one has been able to establish from the stories told about it precisely when it took place. However, the fact that Yarocamena's uprising began at Atenas suggests that it might be the same as the one reported by Sambrook. For the oral tradition of the uprising, see Yepez and Pineda Camacho, 'La rabia'.

The deportation of Indians to the Peruvian side of the Putumayo is recounted in San Román, *Perfiles*, and also in Pineda Camacho, *Holocausto*. Population figures for 1940 are from Steward, 'The Witotoan', pp. 750–1. Recent estimates are from www.ethnologue.com.

Forced labour is still a problem in Amazonia. See Sharma,

Contemporary Forms, for further information. A chilling reminder that debt peonage enforced by the rifle has not disappeared from Amazonia can be found in an article published in the *Guardian*, 3 January 2009, p. 25.

Rubber output figures come from Barker, *Rubber*. The story about the domestication of *Hevea brasiliensis* has been told in many places; the best account is Dean, *Brazil*. A biography of Henry Wickham, the man who smuggled the seeds out of Brazil, also tells the story (Jackson, *The Thief*).

Information about oil exploration and exploitation in the Upper Amazon is from Hvalkof, 'Outrage'. Other information can be found on websites, two examples of which are www.sacbee.com/static/live/news/projects/denial/cl_1.html and www.texacotoxico.org/eng/node/1. The legal case against Chevron is the subject of a recent documentary, *Crude* (USA, 2009), directed by Joe Berlinger.

Illustrations

As I mentioned in the final chapter of the book, towards the end of the Putumayo story as I have recounted it, a war of words and images broke out on both sides of the Atlantic. While we now take the use of images in cases of atrocities for granted, at the time of the Putumayo story, this was a novel practice. Thus we see Walter Hardenburg using a photograph of chained Indians to make his point, while Carlos Rey de Castro uses the photograph of a Europeanized, domesticated Indian to make his. Both of these photographs are reproduced in the book's inset of illustrations.

When images were first used in this way is not clear but it is most likely that the practice originated in the Congo atrocity where the photographs of mutilations were used to great effect by the Congo Reform Association in public lectures throughout Britain in the early years of the twentieth century. Grant, *A Civilised*, and Sliwinski, 'The Childhood', cover the use of photographs in publicizing the Congo atrocity.

The photographic record of the Putumayo atrocities is extensive. It began in 1903 with Eugène Robuchon and ended in 1916 with Silvino Santos. In the intervening years, Thomas Whiffen, Henry Gielgud, Roger Casement and Stuart Fuller contributed substantially to that record.

There is no doubt that what has survived from those years is but a portion of the total number of photographs taken. In addition, and for the most part, only a very few have been published.

I list below the major collections of Putumayo photographs known to me.

Eugène Robuchon: photographs at the Bibliothèque Nationale, Paris, but the bulk are in private hands in France.

Henry Gielgud: photographs in the World Museum Liverpool.

Thomas Whiffen: photographs in the Museum of Archaeology and Anthropology at the University of Cambridge. Copies of many of the images are widely scattered. There is one collection at the Royal Anthropological Society in London, another at the Bibliothèque Nationale in Paris and a third at the Philipps-Universität Marburg.

Roger Casement: photographs at the National Photographic Archive, Dublin. Copies of many of these are in the National Archives and Record Administration, College Park, Maryland.

Stuart Fuller: photographs at the National Archives and Record Administration, College Park, Maryland.

Silvino Santos: photographs in the Museu Amazônico, Manaus and in private collections in Brazil.

There is also a small set of postcards, many of them made from Robuchon's photographs, in the Pitt Rivers Museum, University of Oxford.

The best account of the Putumayo photographs is given in Flores Paz, 'The visual making'.

Bibliography

This bibliography contains full citations for all the published material referred to in the notes on chapters. Additionally, I include here published material I found particularly useful in working through the book's main themes.

Abel, Richard, *The Ciné Goes to Town: French Cinema 1896–1914*, Berkeley, CA, 1998.
———*The Red Rooster Scare: Making Cinema American, 1900–1910*, Berkeley, CA, 1999.
Alvaro Echeverri, Juan, 'The Colombo-Peruvian Border Conflict of 1932–1933 and the Magic of Nation and Border Common Sense', unpublished paper, 2007.
———'La suerte de Robuchon', unpublished paper, 2007.
Alzate Angel, Beatriz, *Viajeros y cronistas en la Amazonia colombiana: catálogo colectivo*, Bogotá, 1987.
d'Ans, André-Marcel, *L'Amazonie péruvienne: anthropolgie écologique, ethno-histoire, perspectives contemporaines*, Paris, 1982.
Anstey, Roger, 'The Congo Rubber Atrocities: A Case Study', *African Historical Studies* 4, 1971, pp. 59–76.
Arana, Julio C., *Las cuestiones del Putumayo*, Barcelona, 1913.
———*El protocolo Salomón-Lozano, o el pacto de límites con Colombia: al Congreso Nacional*, Lima, 1927.
Arana, Marie, *American Chica: Two Worlds, One Childhood*, New York, 2001.
Bákula, Juan Miguel, *La política internacional entre el Perú y Colombia*, Bogotá, 1988.
Bales, Kevin, *Ending Slavery: How We Free Today's Slaves*, Berkeley, CA, 2007.
———, *New Slavery*, Oxford, 2001.
———, *Understanding Global Slavery: A Reader*, Berkeley, CA, 2005.
Barclay Rey de Castro, Frederica, 'Olvido de una historia: reflexiones acerca de la historiografía andino-amazónica', *Revista de Indias* 61, 2001, pp. 493–511.
Bardou, Jean-Pierre, Jean-Jacques Chanaron, Patrick Fridenson, and James M. Laux, *The Automobile Revolution: The Impact of an Industry*, Chapel Hill, NC, 1982.
Barham, Bradford L. and Oliver T. Coomes, 'Wild Rubber: Industrial Organisation and the Microeconomics of Extraction During the Amazon Rubber Boom 1860–1920', *Journal of Latin American Studies* 26, 1994, pp. 37–72.
Barker, Preston W., *Rubber Statistics, 1900–1937*, Washington, 1938.

Bartov, Omer, 'Defining Enemies, Making Victims: Germans, Jews, and the Holocaust', *American Historical Review* 103, 1998, pp. 771–86.

Blanchard, Peter, 'The Recruitment of Workers in the Peruvian Sierra at the Turn of the Century: The Enganche System', *Inter-American Economic Affairs* 33, 1979, pp. 63–85.

Block, David, *Mission Culture on the Upper Amazon: Native Tradition, Jesuit Enterprise and Secular Policy in Moxos, 1660–1880*, Lincoln, NE, 1994.

Bonilla, Heraclio, 'El caucho y la economía del oriente peruano', *Historia y Cultura* 8, 1974, pp. 69–80.

——, 'Estructura y eslabonamientos de la explotación cauchera en Colombia, Perú, Bolivia y Brasil', *DATA: Revista del Instituto de Estudios Andinos y Amazónicos* 4, 1993, pp. 9–22.

Bonilla, Victor Daniel, *Servants of God or Masters of Men? The Story of a Capuchin Mission in Amazonia*, Harmondsworth, 1972.

Bontinck, François, *Aux Origines de l'État Indépendent du Congo*, Louvain, 1966.

Bowman, Timothy, *Carson's Army: The Ulster Volunteer Force, 1910–22*, Manchester, 2007.

Brantlinger, Patrick, *Dark Vanishings: Discourse on the Extinction of Primitive Races, 1800–1930*, Ithaca, NY, 2003.

Bruner, Robert F., *The Panic of 1907: Lessons Learned from the Market's Perfect Storm*, Hoboken, NJ, 2007.

Burns, E. Bradford, 'Manaus 1910: Portrait of a Boom Town', *Journal of Inter-American Studies* 7, 1965, pp. 400–21.

Burroughs, Robert M., 'Britain's Travelling Eyewitnesses: Narratives of the New Slaveries, 1884–1916', PhD thesis, Nottingham Trent University, 2006.

Cadbury, Tabitha, 'Imagining the Amazon: The Whiffen Collection at Cambridge', *Journal of Museum Ethnography* 16, 2004, pp. 85–100.

Carey, James C., *Peru and the United States, 1900–1962*, Notre Dame, IN, 1964.

Casa Aguilar, Justo, *Evangelio y colonización: una aproximación a la historia del Putumayo desde la época prehispánica a la colonización agropecuaria*, Bogotá, 1999.

Casement, Roger, 'The Putumayo Indians', *Contemporary Review* 102, 1912, pp. 317–28.

Chadwick, Owen, *Hensley Henson: A Study in the Friction between Church and State*, Oxford, 1983.

Chirif, Alberto, ed., *La defensa de los caucheros*, Iquitos, 2005.

——'Introducción', in Alberto Chirif, ed., *Carlos A. Valcárcel: El proceso del Putumayo y sus secretos ineditos*, Iquitos, 2004, pp. 15–77.

——'Presentación', in Alberto Chirif, ed., *La defensa de los caucheros*, pp. 51–72.

Clayton, Lawrence A., *Peru and the United States: The Condor and the Eagle*, Athens, GA, 1999.

Clayton, Xander, *Aud*, Privately published, 2007.

Cline, Catherine Ann, 'E.D. Morel and the Crusade Against the Foreign Office', *Journal of Modern History* 3, 1968, pp. 126–37.

——*E.D. Morel, 1873–1924: The Strategies of Protest*, Belfast, 1980.

Collier, Richard, *The River that God Forgot*, London, 1968.

Corp, Edward T., 'Sir William Tyrrell', The *Éminence Grise* of the British Foreign Office', *Historical Journal* 25, 1982, pp. 697–708.

Dadrian, Vahakn, 'Patterns of Twentieth-Century Genocides: The Armenian, Jewish, and Rwandan Cases', *Journal of Genocidal Research* 6, 2004, pp. 487–522.

Daly, Mary E., ed., *Roger Casement in Irish and World History*, Dublin, 2005.

Davies, Thomas M., *Indian Integration in Peru: A Half Century of Experience, 1900–1948*, Lincoln, NE, 1974.

Davis, Wade, *One River: Explorations and Discoveries in the Amazon Rain Forest*, New York, 1996.

Dean, Warren, *Brazil and the Struggle for Rubber: A Study in Environmental History*, Cambridge, 1987.

Deas, Malcolm, *Del poder y la gramática*, Bogotá, 1993.

De la Flor Fernández, Alejandro Juan, 'La economía de exportación en la Amazonía peruana 1898–1930: el caso de las gomas', Thesis, Pontificia Universidad Católica del Perú, Lima, 1989.

De la Pedraja, René, *Wars of Latin America, 1899–1941*, London, 2006.

De Osa, Verónica, *The Troubled Waters of the Amazon: The Plight of the Colombian Indians in Amazonia*, London, 1990.

Dickey, Herbert Spencer, *The Misadventures of a Tropical Medico*, London, 1929.

Doerries, Reinhard R., 'Hopeless Mission: Sir Roger Casement in Imperial Germany', *Journal of Intelligence History* 6, 2006, pp. 25–39.

———, *Prelude to the Easter Rising: Sir Roger Casement in Imperial Germany*, London, 2000.

Domínguez, Camilo and Augusto Gómez, *La economía extractiva en la Amazonia colombiana, 1850–1930*, Bogotá, 1990.

Dore, Elizabeth, 'Debt Peonage in Granada, Nicaragua, 1870–1930: Labor in a Noncapitalist Transition', *Hispanic American Historical Review* 83, 2003, pp. 521–59.

Drabble, John H., *Rubber in Malaya, 1876–1922: The Genesis of an Industry*, Kuala Lumpur, 1973.

Drinot, Paulo, 'Peru, 1884–1930: A Beggar Sitting on a Bench of Gold?', in Enrique Cárdenas, José Antonio Ocampo, and Rosemary Thorp, eds, *An Economic History of Twentieth-Century Latin America, Volume 1*, Basingstoke, 2000, pp. 152–87.

Dudgeon, Jeffrey, *Roger Casement: The Black Diaries*, Belfast, 2002.

Fifer, J. Valerie, 'The Empire Builders: A History of the Bolivian Rubber Boom and the Rise of the House of Suarez', *Journal of Latin American Studies* 2, 1970, pp. 113–46.

Fisher, H.A.L., *James Bryce*, London, 1927.

Flores Paz, Maria del Rosario, 'The Visual Making of a Regional Society: Photography and Amazonian History', PhD thesis, Birkbeck College, University of London, 2008.

Foreman-Peck, James, 'Multinational Companies and the International Transfer of Technology in the Motor Industry to 1939', in Lennart Jörberg and Nathan Rosenberg, eds, *Technical Change, Employment and Investment*, Lund, 1982, pp. 95–110.

Franco, Roberto, *Los carijonas de Chiribiquete*, Bogotá, 2002.

Frank, Zephyr and Aldo Musacchio, 'Brazil in the International Rubber Trade, 1870–1930', in Steven Topik, Carlos Marichal and Zephyr Frank, eds, *From Silver to Cocaine: Latin American Commodity Chains and the Building of the World Economy, 1500–2000*, Durham, NC, 2006, pp. 271–99.

Furneaux, Robin, *The Amazon: The Story of a Great River*, London, 1969.

Gann, Lewis H., 'The Berlin Conference and the Humanitarian Conscience', in Stig Förster, Wolfgang J. Mommsen and Ronald Robinson, eds, *Bismarck, Europe, and Africa: The Berlin Africa Conference, 1884–1885 and the Onset of Partition*, Oxford, 1988, pp. 321–31.

García, P. Lorenzo, *Historia de las misiones en la Amazonía ecuatoriana*, Quito, 1985.

García, Victor Manuel, 'Colombian and Peruvian Rubber Industry: A Regional Approach to the Putumayo Scandal 1850–1925', MA thesis, University of Texas at Austin, 2000.

García Calderon, V., *The White Llama*, London, 1938.

García Jordán, Pilar, ed., *La construcción de la Amazonía andina, siglos XIX–XX: procesos de ocupación y transformación de la Amazonía peruana y ecuatoriana entre 1820 y 1960*, Quito, 1995.

————'En el corazón de las tiembras . . . del Putumayo, 1890–1932: fronteras, caucho, mano de obra indígena y misiones católicas en la nacionalización de la Amazonía', *Revista de Indias* 61, 2001, pp. 591–617.

————ed., *Fronteras, colonización y mano de obra indígena Amazonía andina siglos XIX–XX: la construcción del espacio socio-económico amazónico en Ecuador, Perú y Bolivia, 1792–1948*, Lima, 1998.

————'El infierno verde. Caucho e indios, terror y muerte: reflexiones en torno al escándolo del Putumayo', *Anuario del IEHS* 8, 1993, pp. 73–85.

Gasché, Jürg, 'La ocupación territorial de los nativos Huitoto en el Perú y Colombia en los siglos 19 y 20', *Amazonía Indígena* 4/7, 1983, pp. 2–19.

Gauld, Charles A., *The Last Titan, Percival Farquhar: American Entrepreneur in Latin America*, Palo Alto, CA, 1964.

Gilderhus, Mark, 'The Monroe Doctrine: Meaning and Implications', *Presidential Studies Quarterly* 36, 2006, pp. 5–16.

————*The Second Century: US–Latin American Relations Since 1889*, Wilmington, DE, 2000.

Gómez, Augusto, 'Amazonía colombiana: formas de acceso y de control de la fuerza de trabajo indígena, 1870–1930', *DATA: Revista del Instituto de Estudios Andinos y Amazónicos* 4, 1993, pp. 99–122.

————, Ana Christina Lesmes and Claudia Rocha, *Caucherías y conflicto colombo-peruano: testimonios 1904–1934*, Bogotá, 1995.

Gómez Valderrama, Pedro, 'Los infiernos de Jerarca Brown', *Revista de la Universidad de los Andes* 10, 1960, pp. 3–27.

————*Los infiernos de Jerarca Brown y otros textos*, Bogotá, 1984.

Grant, Kevin, *A Civilised Savagery: Britain and the New Slaveries in Africa, 1884–1926*, London, 2005.

————'Bones of Contention: The Repatriation of the Remains of Roger Casement', *Journal of British Studies* 41, 2002, pp. 329–53.

————'Christian Critics of Empire: Missionaries, Lantern Lectures, and the Congo Reform Campaign in Britain', *Journal of Imperial and Commonwealth History* 29, 2001, pp. 27–58.

Gray, Andrew, 'Las atrocidades del Putumayo reexaminadas', in Alberto Chirif, ed., *La defensa de los caucheros*, Iquitos, 2005, pp. 15–50. English original, 'The Putumayo Atrocities Re-Examined', unpublished paper, 1990.

Greenfield, Gerald M., *The Realities of Images: Imperial Brazil and the Great Drought*, Philadelphia, PA, 2001.

Greenfield, Sidney M., 'Barbadians in the Brazilian Amazon', *Luso-Brazilian Review* 20, 1983, pp. 44–64.

Gridilla, Alberto, *Un año en el Putumayo*, Lima, 1943.

Grohs, Waltraud, *Los indios del Alto Amazonas del siglo XVI al siglo XVIII: poblaciones y migraciones en la antigua provincia de Maynas*, Bonn, 1974.

Guyot, Mireille, Le récit d'O'ioi', in Robert Jaulin, ed., *De l'ethnocide*, Paris, 1972, pp. 137–57

———, 'El relato de O'ioi', *Amazonia Indigena* 3/6, 1983, pp. 3–10,

———, 'Le travail du caoutchouc chez les Indiens Bora et Miraña Amazonie colombienne', in Georges Balandier et al. eds, *L'Autre et l'ailleurs: hommages à Roger Bastide*, Paris, 1976, pp. 380–92.

Gwynn, Stephen, *Experiences of a Literary Man*, London, 1926.

Hambloch, Ernest, *British Consul: Memories of Thirty Years' Service in Europe and Brazil*, London, 1938.

Hampton, Mark, 'Rethinking the "New Journalism", 1850s–1930s', *Journal of British Studies* 43, 2004, pp. 278–90.

Hardenburg, Walter E., 'Los Huitotos de la Chorrera en 1930', *Mirador Amazónico* 8, 1961, pp. 38–40.

———'The Indians of the Putumayo, Upper Amazon', *Man* 10, 1910, pp. 134–8.

———*The Putumayo: The Devil's Paradise*, London, 1912.

———'Story of the Putumayo Atrocities', *The New Review*, in seven consecutive instalments, July–December 1913 and January 1914.

———'Travel and Colonisation', *The Field* 114, 25 September 1909, p. 550.

———'The White Man's Burden', *New Review*, May 1913, pp. 495–501.

Haring, Rita, *Boomtown aan de Amazone: een Historisch-Sociologische Studie over de Peruaanse Amazoneregio en de Stad Iquitos, met Nadruk op de Periode 1880–1980*, Utrecht, 1986.

Harms, Robert, 'The End of Red Rubber: A Reassessment', *Journal of African History* 16, 1975, pp. 73–88.

Harris, John, *The Peruvian Rubber Crime*, London, 1912.

Harris, Peter James, 'From the Putumayo to Connemara: Roger Casement's Amazon Voyage of Discovery', *ABEI Journal* 4, 2002, pp. 131–8.

Healy, David Frank, *Drive to Hegemony: The United States in the Caribbean, 1898–1917*, Madison, WI, 1988.

Henson, Herbert Hensley, *Retrospect of an Unimportant Life*, vol. 1, Oxford, 1942.

Herlihy, David, *Bicycle: The History*, New Haven, CT, 2004.

Hirshfield, Claire, 'Truth', in Allin Sullivan, ed., *British Literary Magazines: The Victorian and Edwardian Age, 1837–1913*, London, 1984, pp. 423–32.

Hispano, Cornelio, *De París al Amazonas: las fieras del Putumayo*, Paris, 1914.

Hochschild, Adam, *King Leopold's Ghost: A Story of Greed, Terror, and Heroism in Colonial Africa*, New York, 1998.

Hvalkof, Søren, 'Outrage in Rubber and Oil: Extractivism, Indigenous Peoples, and Justice in the Upper Amazon', in Charles Zerner, ed., *People, Plants, and Justice: The Politics of Nature Conservancy*, New York, 2000, pp. 83–116.

Inglis, Brian, *Roger Casement*, London, 1973.

Ireland, Gordon, *Boundaries, Possessions, and Conflicts in South America*, Cambridge, MA, 1938.

Jackson, Joe, *The Thief at the End of the World: Rubber, Power, and the Seeds of Empire*, London, 2008.

Jarrell, Jan, '"A Tremendous Fascination": Medicine and Exploration in the South American Travel Narratives of Herbert Spencer Dickey, 1900–1925', unpublished paper, 2001.

Jeanne, Olivier, 'Monetary Policy in England 1893–1914: A Structural VAR Analysis', *Explorations in Economic History* 32, 1995, pp. 302–26.

John, Arthur H., *A Liverpool Merchant House*, London, 1959.

Johnson, Howard, 'Barbadian Migrants in the Putumayo District of the Amazon, 1904–11', in Mary Chamberlain, ed., *Caribbean Migration: Globalised Identities*, London, 1998, pp. 177–87.

Karno, Howard L., 'Augusto B. Leguía: The Oligarchy and the Modernization of Peru, 1870–1930', PhD thesis, University of California, Los Angeles, 1970.

————'Julio César Arana, Frontier Cacique in Peru', in Robert Kern, ed., *The Caciques: Oligarchical Politics and the System of Caciquismo in the Luso-Hispanic World*, Albuquerque, NM, 1973, pp. 89–98.

Kiernan, Ben, *Blood and Soil: A World History of Genocide and Extermination from Sparta to Darfur*, New Haven, CT, 2007.

Klarén, Peter F., 'The Origins of Modern Peru, 1880–1930', in Leslie Bethell, ed., *The Cambridge History of Latin America, Volume V c.1870 to 1930*, Cambridge, 1986, pp. 587–640.

Knight, Allan, 'Debt Bondage in Latin America', in Léonie J. Archer, ed., *Slavery and Other Forms of Unfree Labour*, London, 1988, pp. 102–17.

Lagos, Ovidio, *Arana, rey del caucho*, Buenos Aires, 2005.

Landaburu, Jon, and Roberto Pineda Camacho, *Tradiciones de la gente del hacha: mitología de los indios andoques del Amazonas*, Bogotá, 1984.

Larrabure y Correa, Carlos, *Perú y Colombia en el Putumayo*, Barcelona, 1913.

Lawrence, James Cooper, *The World's Struggle with Rubber 1905–1931*, New York, 1931.

Loadman, John, *Tears of the Tree: The Story of Rubber*, Oxford, 2005.

Louis, William Roger, 'Roger Casement and the Congo', *Journal of African History* 5, 1964, pp. 99–120.

————and Jean Stengers, eds, *E.D. Morel's History of the Congo Reform Movement*, Oxford, 1968.

McCartney, Sean, and A.J. Arnold, '"A Vast Aggregate of Avaricious and Flagitious Jobbing?" George Hudson and the Evolution of Early Notions of Directorial Responsibility', *Accounting, Business & Financial History* 11, 2001, pp. 117–43.

McConnell, Anita, 'La Condamine's Scientific Journey down the River Amazon, 1743–1744', *Annals of Science* 48, 1991, pp. 1–19.

McCormack, W.J., *Roger Casement in Death Or Haunting the Free State*, Dublin, 2002.

McDiarmid, Lucy, *The Irish Art of Controversy*, Ithaca, NY, 2005.

McEvoy, Carmen, *La utopía republicana: ideales y realidades en la formación de la cultura política peruana, 1871–1919*, Lima, 1997.

McKenna, Terence, *True Hallucinations: Being an Account of the Author's Extraordinary Adventures in the Devil's Paradise*, London, 1994.

Martínez Riaza, Ascensión, 'Política regional y gobierno de la Amazonía peruana', *Histórica* 23, 1999, pp. 393–462.

Martins, Luciana, 'Illusions of Power: Vision, Technology and the Geographical Exploration of the Amazon, 1924–1925', *Journal of Latin American Cultural Studies* 16, 2007, pp. 285–307.

Miers, Suzanne, 'Humanitarianism at Berlin: Myth or Reality?' in Stig Förster, Wolfgang J. Mommsen and Ronald Robinson, eds, *Bismarck, Europe, and Africa: The Berlin Africa Conference, 1884–1885 and the Onset of Partition*, Oxford, 1988, pp. 333–45.

——, *Slavery and Autislavery in the Twentieth Century*, Oxford, 2002.

——'Slavery and the Slave Trade as International Issues 1890–1939', *Slavery & Abolition* 19, 1998, pp. 16–37.

Miller, Rory, 'British Business in Peru: From the Pacific War to the Great Depression', in Nikolaus Böttcher and Bernd Hausberger, eds, *Dinero y negocios en la historia de América Latina*, Frankfurt am Main, 2000, pp. 379–412.

——, 'British Free-Standing Companies on the West Coast of South America', in Mira Wilkins and Harm Schröter, *The Free-Standing Company in the World Economy, 1830–1996*, Oxford, 1998, pp. 218–52.

Mitcham, Roderick Ellis, 'The Geographies of Global Humanitarianism: The Anti-Slavery Society and Aborigines' Protection Society, 1884–1933', PhD thesis, University of London, 2002.

Mitchell, Angus ed., *The Amazon Journal of Roger Casement*, London, 1997.

——'"An Irish Putumayo": Roger Casement's Humanitarian Relief Campaign among the Connemara Islanders 1913–14', *Irish Economic and Social History* 31, 2004, pp. 41–60.

——*Casement*, London, 2003.

——'John Bull's Other Empire: Roger Casement and the Press, 1898–1916', in Simon J. Potter, ed., *Newspapers and Empire in Ireland and Britain, c.1857–1921*, Dublin, 2004, pp. 217–33.

——'New Light on the "Heart of Darkness"', *History Today* 49, 1999, pp. 20–27.

——'Roger Casement in Africa: An Archaeology of Resistance to the Acts of Berlin and Brussels and the Origins of the Congo Reform Association, 1884–1904', PhD thesis, University of Limerick, 2004.

——*Sir Roger Casement's Heart of Darkness: The 1911 Documents*, Dublin, 2003.

Moen, Jon and Ellis Tallman, 'The Bank Panic of 1907: The Role of the Trust Companies', *Journal of Economic History* 52, 1992, pp. 611–30.

Mörner, Magnus, 'The Expulsion of the Jesuits from Spain and Spanish America in 1767 in Light of Eighteenth-Century Regalism', *The Americas* 23, 1996, pp. 156–64.

Morrison, Tony, Ann Brown, and Anne Rose, eds, *Lizzie: A Victorian Lady's Amazon Adventure*, London, 1985.

Mullen, Patrick, 'Roger Casement's Global English: From Human Rights to the Homoerotic', *Public Culture* 15, 2003, pp. 559–78.

Negro, Sandra and Manuel M. Marzal, eds, *Un reino en la frontera: las misiones jesuitas en la América colonial*, Lima, 1999.

Neilson, Keith, '"Control the Whirlwind": Sir Edward Grey as Foreign Secretary, 1906–16', in T.G. Otte, ed., *The Makers of British Foreign Policy: From Pitt to Thatcher*, Basingstoke, 2002, pp. 128–49.

Newton, Velma, *The Silver Men: West Indian Labour Migration to Panama, 1850–1914*, Kingston, 1984.

Nworah, Kenneth D., 'The Aborigines' Protection Society, 1889–1909: A Pressure-Group in Colonial Policy', *Canadian Journal of African Studies* 5, 1971, pp. 79–91.

O' Callaghan, Margaret, '"With the Eyes of Another Race, Of a People Once Hunted Themselves": Casement, Colonialism and a Remembered Past', in D. George Boyce and Alan O'Day, eds, *Ireland in Transition, 1867–1921*, London, 2004, pp. 159–75.

Olarte Camacho, Vicente, *Los convenios con el Perú*, Bogotá, 1911.

———*Las crueldades en el Putumayo en el Caquetá*, 1st edn, Bogotá, 1910.

Ortega Díaz, Alfredo, *Ferrocarriles colombianos*, Bogotá, 1920–49.

Orton, James, *The Andes and the Amazon; or, Across the Continent of South America*, New York, 1876.

Osborne, Emily Lynn, '"Rubber Fever", Commerce and French Colonial Rule in Upper Guinée, 1890–1913', *Journal of African History* 45, 2004, pp. 445–65.

Osborne, John B., 'Wilfred G. Thesiger, Sir Edward Grey, and the British Campaign to Reform the Congo, 1905–09', *Journal of Imperial and Commonwealth History* 27, 1999, pp. 59–80.

Ó Síocháin, Séamas, 'Roger Casement, Ethnography, and the Putumayo', *Eire* 29, 1994, pp. 29–41.

———*Roger Casement: Imperialist, Rebel, Revolutionary*, Dublin, 2008.

———and Michael O'Sullivan, *The Eyes of Another Race: Roger Casement's Congo Report and 1903 Diary*, Dublin, 2003.

Palmer, Alison, 'Colonial and Modern Genocide: Explanations and Categories', *Ethnic and Racial Studies* 21, 1998, pp. 89–115.

Paredes, Rómulo, 'Peruvian Rubber and International Politics', *American Review of Reviews* 46, September 1912, pp. 325–8.

Paternoster, G. Sidney, *The Lords of the Devil's Paradise*, London, 1913.

Pennano, Guido, *La economía del caucho*, Iquitos, 1988.

Philip, Kavita, 'Imperial Science Rescues a Tree: Global Botanic Networks, Local Knowledge and the Transcontinental Transplantation of Cinchona', *Environment and History* 1, 1995, pp. 173–200.

Pineda Camacho, Roberto, 'El Comercio infame: el Parlamento Británico y la Casa Cauchera Peruana Casa Arana', *Boletín de Historia y Antigüedades* 89, 2002, pp. 379–99.

———'Historia oral de una maloca sitiada en el Amazonas: aspectos de la rebelión de Yarocamena contra la Casa Arana', *Anuario Colombiano de Historia Social y de la Cultura* 16/17, 1988, pp. 163–82.

———*Holocausto en el Amazonas: una historia social de la Casa Arana*, Bogotá, 2000.

———'Novelistas y etnógrafos en el infierno de la Casa Arana', *Boletín de Historia y Antigüedades* 91, 2004, pp. 485–522.

———'Les orphelins de *La Vorágine*: mémoire, holocauste cauchero et reconstruction culturelle indigène dans le moyen Caquetá Amazonie colombienne', PhD Thesis, Université de la Sorbonne Nouvelle Paris III, 2006.

Porter, Andrew, 'Sir Roger Casement and the International Humanitarian Movement', *Journal of Imperial and Commonwealth History* 29, 2001, pp. 59–74.

Quiroz, Alfonso W., 'Redes de alta corrupción en el Perú: poder y venalidad desde el virrey Amat a Montesinos', *Revista de Indias* 66, 2006, pp. 237–48.

Ramasastry, Anita, 'Corporate Complicity: From Nuremberg to Rangoon. An Examination of Forced Labor Cases and Their Impact on the Liability of Multinational Companies', *Berkeley Journal of International Law* 20, 2002, pp. 91–159.

Reeve, Mary-Elizabeth 'Regional Interaction in the Western Amazon: The Early Colonial Encounter and the Jesuit Years: 1538–1767', *Ethnohistory* 41, 1993, pp. 106–38.

Reid, B.L., *The Lives of Roger Casement*, New Haven, CT, 1976.

Resor, Randolph R., 'Rubber in Brazil: Dominance and Collapse, 1876–1945', *Business History Review* 51, 1977, pp. 341–66.

Rey de Castro, Carlos, *Los escándalos del Putumayo: carta abierta dirigada a Mr Geo B. Michell consul de S.M.B.*, Barcelona, 1913.

———*Los escándalos del Putumayo: carta al director del Daily News & Leader, de Londres*, Barcelona, 1913.

———*Los pobladores del Putumayo*, Barcelona, 1914.

Reyes, Rafael, *Memorias, 1850–1885*, Bogotá, 1986.

Ribeill, George, 'From Pneumatics to Highway Logistics: André Michelin, Instigator of the "Automobile Revolution"', *History and Technology* 8, 1992, pp. 193–216.

Ribemont, Francis ed., *Jules Robuchon 1840–1922: imagier de la Vendée et du Poitou*, Bordeaux, 1999.

Ricard, Serge, 'The Roosevelt Corollary', *Presidential Studies Quarterly* 36, 2006, pp. 17–26.

Rippy, J. Fred, 'Dawn of the Railway Era in Colombia', *Hispanic American Historical Review* 22, 1943, pp. 650–63.

Ritchie, Andrew, *King of the Road*, London 1975.

Rivera, José Eustasio, *The Vortex*, transl. Earle K. James, Bogotá, 2001.

Roberts, G.W., 'Emigration from the Island of Barbados', *Social and Economic Studies* 4, 1955, pp. 245–88.

Robuchon, Eugenio, *En el Putumayo y sus afluentes*, Lima, 1907.

Romero, Fernando, *Iquitos y la fuerza naval de la Amazonía 1830–1933*, Lima, 1983.

Rosenberg, Emily S., *Financial Missionaries to the World: The Politics and Culture of Dollar Diplomacy, 1900–1930*, Cambridge, MA, 1999.

Rosenzweig, Alfredo, 'Judíos en la Amazonía peruana, 1870–1949', *Maj'Shavot* 12, 1967, pp. 19–30.

Roth, Andreas, '"The German Soldier is Not Tactful": Sir Roger Casement and the Irish Brigade in Germany during the First World War', *Irish Sword* 19, 1995, pp. 313–32.

Roux, Jean-Claude, *L'Amazonie péruvienne: un eldorado dévoré par la forêt 1821–1910*, Paris, 1994.

Ruiz, Jean L., 'Civilized People in Uncivilized Places: Rubber, Race, and Civilization during the Amazonian Rubber Boom', MA thesis, University of Saskatchewan, 2006.

Salisbury, Richard V., 'Great Britain, the United States, and the 1909–1910 Nicaraguan Crisis', *The Americas* 53, 1997, pp. 379–94.

San Ramón, Jesús Victor, *Perfiles históricos de la Amazonía peruana*, Lima, 1975.

Santos-Granero, Fernando and Frederica Barclay, *Tamed Frontiers: Economy, Society, and Civil Rights in Upper Amazonia*, Oxford, 2000.

Satre, Jowell Joseph, *Chocolate on Trial: Slavery, Politics, and the Ethics of Business*, Athens, OH, 2005.

Sawyer, Roger, *Casement: The Flawed Hero*, London, 1984.

——*Roger Casement's Diaries 1910: The Black and the White*, London, 1997.

Scholes, Walter V., and Marie V. Scholes, 'The United States and Ecuador, 1909–1913', *The Americas* 19, 1963, pp. 276–90.

Schultes, Richard Evans, 'Lacticiferous Plants of the Karaparaná-Igaraparaná Region of Colombia', *Acta Botanica Neerlandica* 15, 1966, pp. 178–89.

Segal, Ariel, *Jews of the Amazon: Self-Exile in Paradise*, Philadelphia, PA, 1999.

Serier, Jean-Baptiste, *Les Barons du caoutchouc*, Paris, 2000.

Sharma, Bhavna, *Contemporary Forms of Slavery in Peru*, London, 2006.

Simson, Alfred, *Travels in the Wilds of Ecuador, and the Exploration of the Putumayo River*, London, 1886.

Singleton-Gates, Peter and Maurice Girodais, *The Black Diaries: An Account of Roger Casement's Life and Times with a Collection of his Diaries and Public Writings*, Paris, 1959.

Sliwinski, Sharon, 'The Childhood of Human Rights: The Kodak on the Congo', *Journal of Visual Culture* 5, 2006, pp. 333–63.

Smith, Anthony, *Explorers of the Amazon*, London, 1990.

Souza, Márcio, *Silvino Santos: o cineasta do ciclo do borracha*, Rio de Janeiro, 1999.

Stanfield, Michael Edward, *Red Rubber, Bleeding Trees: Violence, Slavery and Empire in Northwest Amazonia, 1850–1933*, Albuquerque, NM, 1998.

Steiner, Zara, *The Foreign Office and Foreign Policy, 1898–1914*, Cambridge, 1969.

Stengers, Jean, 'King Leopold's Congo, 1886–1908', in Roland Oliver and G.N. Sanderson, eds, *The Cambridge History of Africa*, Cambridge, 1985, vol. 6, pp. 315–58.

——'Leopold II and the *Association Internationale du Congo*', in Wolfgang J. Mommsen and Ronald Robinson, eds., *Bismarck, Europe, and Africa: The Berlin Africa Conference, 1884–1885 and the Onset of Partition*, Oxford, 1988, pp. 229–44. Förster.

Steward, Julian H., 'The Witotoan Tribes', in Julian H. Steward, ed., *Handbook of South American Indians, Volume 3*, Washington, DC, 1948, pp. 749–62.

Stone, Dan, 'The Historiography of Genocide: Beyond "Uniqueness" and Ethnic Competition', *Rethinking History* 8, 2004, pp. 127–42.

Swaisland, Charles, 'The Aborigines' Protection Society, 1837–1909', *Slavery & Abolition* 21, 2000, pp. 265–80.

Taussig, Michael, 'Culture of Terror – Space of Death: Roger Casement's Putumayo Report and the Explanation of Torture', *Comparative Studies in Society and History* 26, 1984, pp. 467–97.

——*Shamanism, Colonialism, and the Wild Man*, Chicago, 1987.

Thomas-Hope, Elizabeth M., 'The Establishment of a Migration Tradition: British West Indian Movements to the Hispanic Caribbean in the Century after Emancipation', in Colin G. Clarke, ed., *Caribbean Social Relations*, Liverpool, 1978, pp. 66–81.

Thompson, Andrew S., 'The Language of Imperialism and the Meanings of Empire:

Imperial Discourse in British Politics, 1895–1914', *Journal of British Studies* 36, 1997, pp. 147–77.

Thomson, Norman, *The Putumayo Red Book*, London, 1914.

Townshend, Charles, *Easter 1916: The Irish Rebellion*, London 2005.

Triana, Miguel, *Por el sur de Colombia*, Bogotá, 1950.

Turner, John Kenneth, *Barbarous Mexico*, Chicago, 1911.

Turvasi, Francesco, *Giovanni Genocchi and the Indians of South America, 1911–1913*, Rome, 1988.

Ure, John, *Trespassers on the Amazon*, London, 1986.

Valcárcel, Carlos A., *El proceso del Putumayo y sus secretos inauditos*, Lima, 1915.

Vale da Costa, Selda, *Eldorado das ilusões. Cinema & sociedad: Manaus 1897/1935*, Manaus, 1996.

———and Narciso Júlio Freire Lobo, *No rastro de Silvino Santos*, Manaus, 1987.

Veeser, Cyrus, 'Inventing Dollar Diplomacy: The Gilded-Age Origins of the Roosevelt Corollary to the Monroe Doctrine', *Diplomatic History* 27, 2003, pp. 301–26.

Wagner De Reyna, Alberto, *Historia diplomática del Perú, 1900–1945*, Lima, 1964.

Ward, Herbert, *A Voice from the Congo*, London, 1910.

Weber, Gary, 'Henry Labouchere, *Truth* and the New Journalism of Late Victorian Britain', *Victorian Periodicals Review* 26, 1993, pp. 36–43.

Weinstein, Barbara, *The Amazon Rubber Boom, 1850–1920*, Palo Alto, CA, 1983.

Weisbord, Robert G., 'The King, the Cardinal and the Pope: Leopold II's Genocide in the Congo and the Vatican', *Journal of Genocide Research* 5, 2003, pp. 35–45.

Werner, Louis, 'All Aboard to Nowhere: The Mad Mary', *Américas* 42, 1990, pp. 6–17.

Whiffen, Thomas, 'A Short Account of the Indians of the Issa-Japura District South America', *Folklore* 24, 1993, pp. 41–62.

———*The North-West Amazons: Notes of Some Months Spent Among Cannibal Tribes*, London, 1915.

Wolf, Howard and Ralph Wolf, *Rubber: A Story of Glory and Greed*, New York, 1936.

Wood, Bryce, *Aggression and History: The Case of Ecuador and Peru* Ann Arbor, MI, 1978.

Woodroffe, Joseph F., *The Rubber Industry of the Amazon and How Its Supremacy Can Be Maintained*, London, 1915.

———*The Upper Reaches of the Amazon*, London, 1914.

Wylie, Lesley L., 'Colonial Tropes and Post-Colonial Tricks: Rewriting the Tropics in the *Novella de la Selva*', PhD thesis, University of Cambridge, 2007.

Yepez, Benjamín and Roberto Pineda Camacho, 'La rabia de Yarocamena', *Tolima* 2, 1985, pp. 29–59.

Yungjohann, John C., *White Gold: The Diary of a Rubber Cutter in the Amazon 1906–1916*, Oracle, AZ, 1989.

Zook, David H., Jr., 'The Spanish Arbitration of the Ecuador–Peru dispute', *The Americas* 20, 1964, pp. 359–75.

Zumaeta, Pablo, *Las cuestiones del Putumayo*, Barcelona, 1913.

Index

Towns listed without accompanying countries
are located in Putumayo disputed regions.